CW00515837

GREAT FAMILY
DAYS OUT 2008

GREAT FAMILY
DAYS OUT 2008

THE NATIONAL TRUST

First published in the United Kingdom in 2008 by
National Trust Books
10 Southcombe Street
London W14 0RA
An imprint of Anova Books Company Ltd

ISBN-13: 9781905400584

A CIP catalogue record for this book is available from the British Library.

15 14 13 12 10 09 08
10 9 8 7 6 5 4 3 2 1

Reproduction by Rival Colour Ltd, London
Printed and bound by CT Printing Ltd, China
Designed by Lee-May Lim and Mark Holt

This book can be ordered direct from the publisher at the website www.anovabooks.com, or try your
local bookshop or National Trust shop.

The publisher and the National Trust are committed to respecting the intellectual property rights of
others. We have therefore taken all reasonable efforts to ensure that the reproduction of all content on
these pages is done with the full consent of copyright owners. If you are aware of any unintentional
omissions please contact National Trust or the publisher directly so that any necessary corrections may
be made for future editions.

All photographs by NTPL except National Trust/Harriet Clarke:119, Sara Thomas:125, John Willis:128,
129 bottom, National Trust/ NaturePL/Niall Benvie:89, Chris Packham:112, National Trust Photo
Library/Matthew Antrobus:front cover top right, 28, 37, 57 bottom, 73, 81, 106, 153, 171, 172, 185,
189, 191, 197, Bill Batten:93, 183, Andrew Butler:front cover bottom, 32, 33 top & bottom, 45,47, 67,
68, 80, 109, 120, 141, 142 left, 173, 192, Michael Caldwell:86, 198, Joe Cornish:17 right, 21 top, 23
top right, 24 top & bottom, 30, 60, 151, 152, 164, 165, 166, 174, 178, 182, 186, 187, 205, 208, 213,
214, 218, Stuart Cox:77, Derek Croucher:50, 58, 64, 70, 75, 207, Will Curwen:184, Andreas von
Einsiedel:39, 49, 53, 71, 79, 95, 104, 121, 123, 124, 136, 137 top & bottom, 138, 139 bottom, 154,
157, 160 right, 179, 180, 195 bottom, 202, 203, 211, Geoffrey Frosh:66, 132, 149 top, David
Garner:56, Chris Gascoigne:34, Dennis Gilbert:140, Andrew Halam:131, John Hammond:170, 194, Jerry
Harpur:48, 54, 217, Paul Harris:146, Andrea Jones:44, 55 top & bottom, David Levenson:front cover top
left & top centre,spine bottom, 1,2,10,12,15,16 left,17 left, 18, 23 bottom, 35 left, 36, 94, 98, 101, 122,
142 right, 175, 190, 193, 199, 221, Nadia Mackenzie:27, 99 top, 114 left, 159, Marianne Majerus:115,
Leo Mason:20, 21 bottom, 100, Nick Meers:23 top left, 57 top, 130, 134, 135, 150, 201, Andrew
Montgomery:19, 103, Robert Morris:127, Peter Muhly:206, David Noton:29, 38, 52, 129 top, 162,
NTPL:200, Richard Pink:46, Magnus Rew:40, Stephen Robson:43, 85, 91, 148, 161, David Sellman:88,
Ian Shaw:back cover left, centre & right, spine top, 16 right, 25, 31, 35 right, 42, 72, 90, 96, 97, 107,
110, 111 top, 113, 116, 126, 139 top,155, 168, 196, 204, 209, 212 left & right, Rob Talbot:149 bottom,
Rupert Truman:105, 114 right, 133, 158, 160 left, 169, 195 top, Charlie Waite:111 bottom, Paul
Wakefield:62, 102, 176, Ian West:78, 83, J.Whitaker:65, 166, Andy Williams:76, 82, Mike Williams:87, 99
bottom, 108, 144, 156, 181, 210, Jennie Woodcock:22, 26, 41, 74, 92, 118, George Wright:51

**Information correct at time of going to press. Please check with the property before making a
long journey.**

Contents

The properties by region

Places to visit

90 Kedleston Hall
91 Mr Straw's House
92 Shugborough Estate
93 Snowshill Manor
94 Sudbury Hall & the National
    Trust Museum of Childhood
95 The Workhouse

Wales
131 Aberdulais Falls
132 Bodnant Garden
133 Chirk Castle
134 Dinefwr Park & Castle

135 Dolaucothi Gold Mines
136 Erdigg
137 Llanerchaeron
138 Penrhyn Castle
139 Plas Newydd
140 Powis Castle & Garden

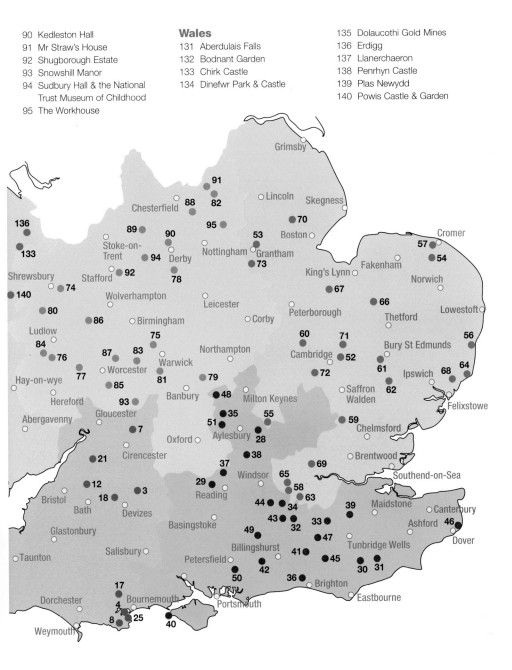

North East & North West

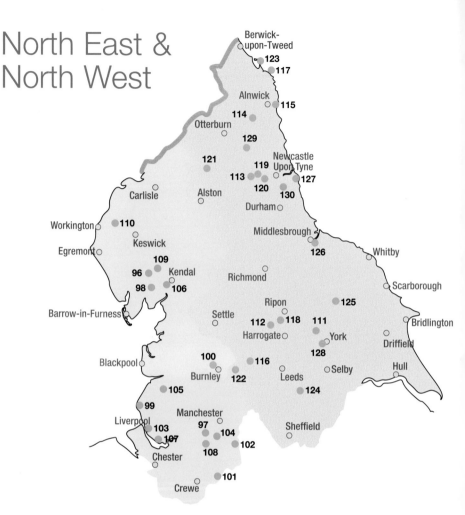

Northern Ireland

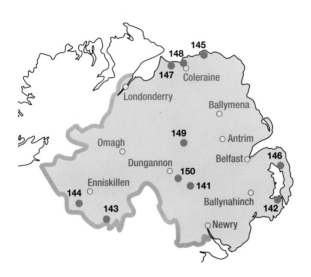

Northern Ireland

Introduction

Great Family Days Out is for anyone who would like to find a fun and educational place to visit.

At each of our specially selected properties – historic houses, castles, gardens or beautiful stretches of coast and countryside – the whole family will find all kinds of things of interest to see and do.

There are so many places in the care of the National Trust that have so much to offer to families, but, as we can't cram them all into this book, we've chosen some of our particular favourites. The wonderful thing is you never know what interest you might awaken in your children – or yourself – with a visit to a National Trust property. From rare birds, insects, farm animals, statues, dolls' houses, mazes and mills to mines, children's lives in past times and life 'below stairs' … the list is endless. Or you may all simply enjoy having an invigorating day out in the open air, making the most of the glorious countryside that the National Trust protects and cares for. There's something for the whole family in every region. More ideas for great days out in your local area can be found on our website: www.nationaltrust.org.uk.

For more information about joining the National Trust, please see p.222, visit our website (you can join online), ring 0870 458 4000 (or 0844 800 1895 from March 2008), or email enquiries@thenationaltrust.org.uk.

How to use this book

Properties are arranged by region – please look at 'Places to Visit' on p.6 or have a look at the maps on p.6–9 for a place near you.

What to see
As well as pointing out fabulous views and features, this section includes quirky things at each property that children might find interesting, such as secret priests' holes and gruesome creatures carved into the woodwork.

What to do
This gives suggestions for things children and families can do at each property – from running down grassy slopes to trying on replica clothes. This section also includes details of activities especially designed for children. These take place usually, but not exclusively, in the school holidays and can range from butter-making in the Tudor kitchen at Buckland Abbey to pond dipping at Wicken Fen. There is sometimes a very small extra charge for these activities. Please check our website (www.nationaltrust.org.uk) and contact individual properties for up-to-date details of activities.

Special events
Entries under this heading include larger, one-off events such as a teddy bears' picnic at Castle Ward or Apple Days at Newton's house. There will often be a charge for these and any one event can attract thousands of families. Events are mainly held in the summer holidays but many properties run Halloween and Christmas events and Easter-egg trails. Events will, of course, change every year and those included for each entry are a taster only. Please check the website and contact individual properties for up-to-date details of activities.

By the way...
This section includes extra useful information such as baby-changing facilities or children's menus. It also provides some details of accessibility. Please note that the guide's information was correct at the time of going to press, but please check with the property concerned before your trip.

Things to know before visiting

Learning and discovery
The National Trust is committed to learning and providing experiences that are inspiring, stimulating and fun. We provide a range of family-focused activities, such as children's guides, tracker packs, special trails and objects that can be handled. Please ring ahead of your visit to find out what each property has to offer. Also have a look at www.nationaltrust.org.uk/learning for details of activities and events.

Admission prices
Admission prices vary, so check the National Trust Handbook or website for the latest details, or ring 0870 458 4000 (or 0844 800 1895

from March 2008). Under 5s are admitted free unless other conditions apply, and children aged 5–16 usually pay half the adult entry price. A family ticket usually allows two adults and up to three children to visit all sections of a property (e.g. house, garden, museum, etc.) for a set price. Costs may vary. Buying National Trust family membership may be good value if you plan to visit several Trust properties over the year. It includes free entry to most Trust properties during normal opening times and free parking in Trust car parks (see p.222 for details).

Busy properties
Properties can be extremely popular at Bank Holidays and summer weekends. At some, timed tickets may be in operation to ensure a smooth flow of visitors and avoid overcrowding.

Shopping and eating
The National Trust runs restaurants, shops and tearooms to help fund our work. Many properties have shops offering a wide range of related merchandise, often including pocket-money toys for children. Our restaurants and tearooms offer a welcoming atmosphere, value for money and traditional home cooking, with many properties featuring menus with an historical theme, often cooked with local and seasonal produce as well as children's menus.

Picnics
Many properties welcome picnickers and some provide designated areas. If you are planning a picnic at a Trust property, please phone in advance to check. Fires and barbecues are not usually allowed.

Facilities for young families
Many properties provide baby-feeding and changing areas, sometimes in purpose-designed parent and baby rooms. Restaurants have highchairs, children's menus, colouring sheets and, in some cases, play areas. Staff are very happy to advise you about what is on offer. In historic buildings, visitors with small babies are welcome to use front slings, which are often available on loan; hip-carrying infant seats or reins for toddlers can also be borrowed at some properties. There are usually arrangements for storing prams or pushchairs at the entrance, as it is not always possible to take these into fragile areas. Some houses can admit baby back-carriers at all times, while in others, it will depend how busy the property may be. We understand that the restrictions on back-carriers, prams and pushchairs may be awkward for those with older and/or heavier children, and as access arrangements vary at each property, we suggest that you telephone in advance for details of any restrictions. We have tried to include some details of access arrangements for each place to visit.

And before you go
To avoid disappointment, we recommend phoning ahead to check that a property is going to be open, or an activity is definitely on, or is not booked up – events can get very busy in the holidays or on summer weekends. And remember that events are always being organised, especially in the summer holidays, the Christmas and Easter seasons and other school breaks. Go to the website and check the property you want to visit – there's a special section for 'events', or give the place a call to see what they have planned.

Symbols

Playground or play area.

Picnic area.

Animals. This means children can see wild, farm or domestic animals while on a visit. For instance, this symbol is shown for Wimpole Home Farm. It is also included if there are significant numbers of animals such as squirrels, deer or sheep in parkland around houses, or on other parts of a property.

Quiz sheet, trail sheet or children's guide. Many properties have fun quiz sheets, trails or guidebooks especially written for children. These cost from just 25p to £2–3 at ticket points or in National Trust shops at individual properties. Some are free. They are generally written in a child-friendly style and will greatly enhance a child's experience of a property.

Café or restaurant.

Children's menu. Highchairs in restaurant. Toys in restaurant. These three symbols relate to practical provision for families in the café or restaurant. Where toys are indicated, these range from Trusty colouring sheets through to robust table-top toys. Bottle warming can be arranged on request. The National Trust is constantly aiming to improve in this area and most properties now offer children's menus and high chairs.

Wheelchair access. This symbol indicates that a reasonable amount of the property can be enjoyed from a wheelchair without undue difficulty. Outside, wheelchair-friendly areas are likely to be suitable for pushchairs too; for instance, where boardwalks or paths are smooth and flat.

Shop.

Dogs on leads in park and garden. Except for guide dogs and hearing dogs, dogs are not allowed into Trust houses, restaurants and gardens. This symbol means dogs are allowed on a lead in parkland. In countryside areas it is advisable to keep your dog on a lead because of the potential danger to animals and other wildlife. Signs at the property will advise whether this is necessary.

No dogs. A few properties do not allow dogs at all.

Baby-changing and feeding facilities. This symbol indicates that there are facilities for baby changing and feeding, often in a purpose-designed parent and baby room.

Front-carrying baby slings for loan. Baby back-carriers cannot usually be admitted to houses because of the danger of accidental damage. This symbol indicates whether front slings are available for loan as a substitute. Babies carried in front slings are obviously very welcome.

OUTDOOR HIGHLIGHTS

Get on your bike!

Cycling is fun! All the family can explore the countryside and keep fit, and you'll find that as part of the Trust's green travel policy, lots of properties will welcome people who arrive on two wheels with free entry. So get on your bike and take a look at our top 10 places to cycle:

1. Saltram, Devon (see p.53)
2. Blickling Hall, Norfolk (see p.98)
3. Ickworth House, Suffolk (see p.104)
4. Crom Estate, Co. Fermanagh (see p.206)
5. Carding Mill Valley & the Shropshire Hills, Shropshire (see p.142)
6. Beningbrough Hall & Gardens, Yorkshire (see p.166)
7. Baddesley Clinton, West Midlands (see p.119)
8. Dolaucothi Gold Mines, Carmarthenshire (see p.193)
9. Clumber Park, Nottinghamshire (see p.126)
10. South Downs Way, West Sussex (see Devil's Dyke, p.84)

Wonderful walks

There are hundreds of fantastic coast, countryside and parkland properties to explore, whether you want a gentle stroll or a more energetic hike. Here are our top 10 family walks. For other walks, look at the end of each regional section of this book or on the National Trust website at www.nationaltrust.org.uk

1. Sherborne Park Estate, Gloucestershire (see p.60)
2. Ashridge Estate, Buckinghamshire (see p.64 and p.86)
3. East Head, West Sussex (see p.88)
4. Flatford Bridge Cottage & Dedham Vale, Suffolk (see p.116)
5. Calke Abbey & Park, Derbyshire (see p.123 and p.144)
6. Brockhampton Estate, Herefordshire (see p.146)
7. Arnside Knott, Lancashire (see p.162)
8. Formby, Merseyside (see p.164)
9. Wallington, Northumberland (see p.184 and p.188)
10. Crom Estate, Co. Fermanagh (see p.206 and p.218)

Playground adventures

Swing, climb and slide away on the National Trust's spectacular adventure playgrounds, here's 10 to get you going.

1. Belton House, Lincolnshire (see p.96)
2. Lanhydrock, Cornwall (see p.48)
3. Fell Foot Park, Cumbria (see p.151)
4. Tatton Park, Cheshire (see p.161)
5. Cragside, Northumberland (see p.168)
6. Castle Ward, Co. Down (see p.204)
7. Wimpole Home Farm, Cambridgeshire (see p.110)
8. Lyme Park, Cheshire (see p.153)
9. Chirk Castle, Wrexham(see p.190)
10. Penrhyn Castle, Gwynedd (see p.197)

A-mazing mazes

If you want a bit of exercise with some puzzling thrown in, then come along to one of our mazes. There are all kinds at the Trust's properties, from simple grassy decorative mazes to more complex ones with tall hedges and intricate designs.

1. Charlecote Park, Warwickshire (see p.125)
2. East Riddlesden Hall, Yorkshire (see p.171)
3. Glendurgan Garden, Cornwall (see p.43)
4. Greys Court,Oxfordshire (see p.84)
5. Kedleston Hall, Derbyshire (see p.131)
6. Peckover House & Garden, Cambridgeshire (see p.115)
7. Speke Hall, Liverpool (see p.158)
8. Cragside, Northumberland (see p.168)
9. Belton House, Lincolnshire (see p.96)
10. Trerice, Cornwall (see p.57)

MILLS, MINES & MACHINERY

Come, step inside and take a look at Britain's fascinating industrial heritage. The National Trust cares for a broad range of industrial sites and buildings, together with the machinery inside them. They're a captivating way to learn more about Britain's industrial past, and a real eye-opener for all members of the family. Often there's a chance to try things 'hands-on' and see industrial machinery in action.

Textile mills
Quarry Bank Mill in Cheshire has working machinery, and reveals a unique insight into the lives of Victorian pauper child workers.
Wellbrook Beetling Mill in Country Tyrone is another example of a textile mill, and still produces calico, which is on sale in the shop.

Wind power
Wind power today is seen as a modern and cutting-edge source of renewable energy. But, just to show that there's nothing new under the sun, why not come and visit some of the many windmills in Britain? There's **Pitstone Windmill** in Buckinghamshire, which is an example of one of the earliest forms of windmill, or there's **Bembridge Windmill** on the Isle of Wight – one of the Island's famous landmarks, or there's the wonderfully named **Horsey Windpump**, in Norfolk.

Water power

Visit **Cragside** in Northumberland, the home of eccentric 19th-century inventor and engineer, William Armstrong. He used water to power his lifts, lighting and central heating, not to mention his loos! Or why not get 'hands-on' at the medieval **Winchester City Mill** in Hampshire, where you can have a go at hand-milling the flour. If you fancy seeing some machinery still at work today, there's **Patterson's Spade Mill** in Templepatrick, Northern Ireland, the last surviving water-driven spade mill in Ireland – and you can still place your own spade order today. Or call in at **Finch Foundry** in Devon, another mill where you can often see demonstrations of machinery in action. In fact, you can pretty much guarantee that where there's some windswept countryside or a rolling river, a mill was built to take advantage of all that free power. So here's a list of a few other mills which you may like to go and see: Houghton Mill in Cambridgeshire, Nether Alderley Mill in Cheshire, Stainsby Mill near Hardwick Hall in Derbyshire, Bourne Mill in Essex, and Dunster Working Watermill and Stembridge Tower Mill in Somerset.

Mines
Mining has played a crucial part in Britain's heritage, and you can see powerful reminders at **Aberdulais Falls** in Wales – complete with water wheel and hydroelectrics – and the **Dolaucathi Gold Mines** in Carmarthenshire. Not much gold there now, but you can always dream! **Cornish Mines and Engines** (awarded World Heritage Site status in 2006) are partly restored to working condition, and are a dramatic reminder of Cornwall's important mining history. You can see a giant 27m (90ft) beam engine and then visit the fascinating Industrial Discovery Centre to learn more. In Cumbria, the **Force Crag Mine** in

Borrowdale was the last working mineral mine in the Lake District, and the buildings and machinery have been restored. (It's very remote, so telephone to check when it's open.)

Coastal defences

While no man is an island, so they say, Britain is. That means that coastal defences have always been important. The same building and mechanical innovations that brought mills and mining, also provided better military protection. On the Isle of Wight you can marvel at the original cannon at the **Needles Old Battery and New Battery** and explore the fascinating military history, or in East Anglia admire the Martello Tower at **Orford Ness**, built against a potential Napoleonic invasion. Orford Ness has a long military history through both World Wars, so if that's your interest you'll enjoy the many military buildings and exhibitions here. Fortifications and defences go back a long way to pre-industrial times – take a brisk Northumbrian walk along **Hadrian's Wall** and visit **Houstead's Fort** to see how the Romans did it.

Visit the National Trust website at **www.nationaltrust.org.uk** to find more information about the many other industrial and commercial buildings owned by the National Trust.

COUNTRYSIDE CAPERS

South West

Devon and Cornwall have some amazing stretches of coastal countryside, so its time to breathe in the sea air and head off on an exhilarating coastal walk. For family-friendly woodland strolls, try **Heddon Valley** a varied walk with stepping stones and bridges along the river, or **Plym Bridge Woods**, which is great for walks and cycle rides. Don't forget **Dartmoor National Park**, with great walking in **Whiddon Deer Park** and **Fingle Bridge**. Dorset, the Cotswolds and Gloucestershire have **Melbury Down**, a rich chalkland with lovely views, and **Haresfield Beacon**, **Sherbourne Park** (see p.60–61 for a fantastic walk there), **Minchinhampton** and **Rodborough Commons** all are worth a look. A highlight for families is **Leigh Woods** in Bristol, especially if you have a pushchair to deal with. **Dyrham Park** also offers family parkland.

South & South East

It's surprising that the the South East, one of England's most densely populated areas, actually has quite a bit of open space. The **White Cliffs of Dover** need no introduction, but there's also **Box Hill**, **Leith Hill** and, back in Kent, 4.8km (3 miles) of the scenic **Royal Military Canal**. **The Witley Centre** is a fascinating place to find out more on the countryside and its management. Sussex offers walks over open downland at **Crowlink** and **Devil's Dyke**. Around the Thames and Solent rivers, there are countryside finds like **Coombe Hill**, and the famous horse cut into the chalk escarpment at **White Horse Hill**, in Oxfordshire. (While you're there, visit **Uffington Castle** and nearby **Dragon Hill** – no dragons, we're sorry to say.)

East of England

The East of England has both open countryside and some fascinating historical sites. **Whipsnade Tree Cathedral** in Bedfordshire is unique, or take a walk on **Dunstable Downs**, **Wicken Fen** or in leafy **Hatfield Forest**. In Hertfordshire there are miles of footpaths across the **Ashridge Estate** and Suffolk's 'Constable country' has lovely pathways over **Dedham Vale** (see our walk through Counstable country featured on p.116–117).

Central

In the Midlands there's the peaceful **Carding Mill Valley** and the former railway walk at the **Leek & Manifold Valley Light Railway**. (No trains now, but the surfaced track leads through dramatic limestone scenery.) While you're in the area, enjoy the family events at **Dudmaston**, **Attingham Park** and, in particular, **Shugborough**, a working historic farm that always has a lot going on.

If you're off to the East Midlands, the **Peak District National Park** is the place to wander – and the National Trust owns over 12 per cent of it. Especially beautiful parts are **Dovedale**, the **Longshaw Estate** and the stunning drive (or walk) through **Winnats Pass**. For the brave and hardy, take in the impressive views from the windswept plateau of **Kinder Scout** (not for youngsters).

North West

You're spoilt for choice in north-west England, with the Lake District, Cumbria, Cheshire and Merseyside to pick from. Pop over to **Helsby Hill** or **Alderley Edge**, just a stone's throw from Liverpool and Manchester. Make a Lakeland holiday of it, and explore the dunes at **Sandscale Haws**. Or move inland to **Arnside Knott** and **Holme Park Fell**, both wonderfully unspoilt areas with a wide variety of wild flowers and butterflies. Walk through ancient forests at **White Moss Common** or be stunned by the dramatic waterfall at **Aira Force**. Consider a dip in **Tarn Hows**, a gorgeous lake with a pushchair-friendly circular walk, or take a cruise across **Coniston Water** in the Trust's steam yacht Gondola.

North East

Yorkshire and the North East have amazing stretches of moorland and coastline in Britain. Explore miles of beautiful coastline along the the **Cleveland Way National Trail** and call in at **Robin Hood Bay** to see the education and exhibition centre there. For the landlubbers among you, move inland to **Wallington** or **Cragside**; both are properties with extensive grounds and loads of interest for younger folks.

Wales

Wales has just oodles of mountain scenery and lush green valleys. How about the family-friendly beaches at **Broadhaven**, Porthdinllaen and Llanbedrog, or even a chance to see dolphins at **Mwnt**? Then there are lovely summer meadow walks at **Lanlay Meadows** and freshwater lily ponds at **Bosherton** while the **Dommelynllyn Estate** has one of Wales's most impressive waterfalls, **Rhaedr Ddu**.

Northern Ireland

Northern Ireland is famed worldwide for its outstanding natural beauty, from the coastal paths at the foot of Ulster's highest mountain, **Slieve Donard**, to the gorse-covered Sperrin Mountains in the North. Don't forget the extraordinary **Giant's Causeway**, with extensive walks along the North Antrim Cliffs.

That was just a few countryside highlights. Visit the National Trust website at **www.nationaltrust.org.uk** to find more information on all the other countryside areas that you can explore.

BACK TO NATURE

The National Trust protects many areas that are official Nature
Reserves, National Nature Reserves or Sites of Special Scientific
Interest (SSSIs). These areas need special protection because many of
the species and creatures in them are endangered by development and
pollution. Visiting our nature reserves can give your family a wonderful
understanding of how and why humans and nature need to coexist.
And besides, these beautiful areas are such wonderful places to enjoy
at any time of year – take your binoculars, put on your walking shoes
or wellies and get back to nature.

As old as the hills (or fens)

Many nature reserves are the last remnants of lands that have been
nearly lost to development and the spread of human habitation.
Ulverscroft in Leicestershire is part of an ancient forest with a beautiful
bluebell season. **Wicken Fen** in Cambridgeshire is an ancient area of
fenland with wild ponies, rare butterflies and, if you're lucky, a sighting
of an otter or two. **Crom Estate** in Northern Ireland is an area with
tranquil islands, woodland and rare pine martens – one of the Trust's
most important reserves. There are little pockets of ancient woodland
all over, like **Curbridge** in Hampshire, often within the parklands of the
many historic houses owned by the Trust. Visiting these magical places
reminds us of what we've lost and need to preserve.

Coastal beauty

Murlough National Nature Reserve was Ireland's first national nature
reserve, and offers some lovely boarded walkways to the dunes.
Orford Ness in Suffolk is a National Nature Reserve on the wild and
remote extremity of eastern England. This fascinating saltmarsh area
also has an interesting military history to explore, having once been an
important radar site. At **Blakeney Point** in Norfolk, you can enjoy an

undeveloped coastal area that's noted for its colonies of breeding terns and migrant birds. You can also get a close-up look at seals, both common and grey. **Studland Beach & Nature Reserve** in Dorset is noted for its sandy beaches, but you may also sight seabirds diving into the waves, deer in the dunes and even lizards and snakes. You can take a peek at rare birds from the bird hides at **Little Sea** or learn more from the visitor centre. Quite a few nature reserves have bird hides, like those at **Malham Tarn Estate** in North Yorkshire. If sea birds, including puffins, take your fancy, you can get close to them at **Farne Islands** in Northumberland and enjoy a bracing boat trip there and back. But make sure you wear a hat – the terns are not fussy about who they poo on!

Nearer than you think

Not all nature reserves are in areas of wild or remote countryside – far from it. Many are an oasis of unspoilt natural habitat near to cities and other urban places. **Leigh Woods** near Bristol is a National Nature Reserve that has access for buggies and wheelchairs, and **Hatfield Forest** is a rare surviving example of a medieval hunting forest in Essex, not that far from London. Some nature reserves are small, but no less exciting or important. How about **Boarstall Duck Decoy** in Buckinghamshire, a rare survival of a 17th-century decoy beside a lake (complete with trained dog to get the ducks).

Rare treasures

Today there are only around 160,000 red squirrels in Britain – not that many in the grand scheme of things. The National Trust has four sites that are a particular haven for these busy little bushy-tailed creatures – **Brownsea Island** in Dorset, **Formby** in Merseyside (hopefully our walk on p.164–165 will give you a change to spot some), **Wallington** in Northumberland (for our walk there see p.188–189) and the **Isle of Wight**. Look out for our guided walks and special events when we celebrate red squirrel week each year in September. The natural places that the Trust cares for are also home to many other interesting little bugs and birds – from ant-lions to natterjack toads. And the plants and flowers you'll find range from miniature orchids to imposing skunk cabbages. Our walk through the parkland of **Calke Abbey Estate** in Derbyshire is great for bird watching, or try the **Brockhampton Estate** in Herefordshire for spotting insects (see p.144–147). Come outside and enjoy our special places.

Many of our nature reserves and other wildlife areas have visitor centres where you can find out much more about what you're seeing (and hearing) in nature. Look at our website **www.nationaltrust.org.uk** to find out what natural wonders are near to you.

COASTING ALONG

The National Trust owns over 700 miles of coastline, ranging from windswept cliffs to sumptuous sandy beaches. We'll let this selection entice you – visit our website for full details on all our wonderful coastal sites.

Beaches and clifftops

If it's a traditional day at the beach you're after, **Studland Beach & Nature Reserve** in Dorset has 4.8km (3 miles) of sandy beaches, and safe shallow water to swim in. While you're there, take a walk along the Jurassic Coast, to the impressive chalk cliffs of **Old Harry Rocks**. In Wales, the 8km (5 miles) of superb beach at **Rhossili Bay**, at the tip of the Gower Peninsula, is the place to head for if you've got young children. While you're there, take a breezy cliff walk, or look out for the wooden ribs of the shipwrecked *Helvetia* at low tide. The **Lleyn Peninsula**, **Pembrokeshire** and **Cardigan Bay** are also wonderful Welsh coastal sites, offering dramatic cliffs, beaches and a chance to see rare birds and other wildlife.

Cornwall has some of the most stunning coastal scenery in the UK, with secluded coves, craggy cliffs and sandy beaches. **Crackington Haven** is a perfect family beach, with surfer's waves and rock pools as well as plenty of sand at low tide. It's not itself a National Trust site, but the cliff walks either side are – one of these, High Cliff, is the highest cliff in Cornwall.

Walks

Boscastle, on Cornwall's north coast, is a dramatic starting point for a coastal walk (a bit of a tough one, so maybe best for older children). **Fowey** and **Kynance Cove** and **Lizard Point** are excellent places for a day's outing with some walking and views attached. Cornwall offers a great many gorgeous cliff walks (but remember to keep dogs on the lead). Irish coast-lovers also have a wealth of choices. Marvel at the **Giant's Causeway**, and then take a giant walk down 22.5km (14 miles) of the **North Antrim** cliff path (or just a little walk down a bit of it). **Portstewart Strand** – a magnificent 3km (2 mile) strand from Portstewart to the Bann estuary – is also a great place to watch birds feeding and stretch your legs. Or how about a wobbly walk across a rope bridge 24m (80ft) above the chasm to **Carrick-a-Rede**, a rocky island in **Country Antrim**?

Wildlife

The north Norfolk Coast is a bird-watcher's paradise. Enjoy the boat trip out to **Blakeney Point**, where you can get close to basking seals. Walk across the marches at **Morston and Stiffkey**, or drink in the view of the sea from **Sheringham Park**, which also has some great walks and an old steam railway. Visit **Brancaster** a large area of coastal wildlife – with a trip to **Scolt Head Island** if the tides permit. Why not head off on a boat trip and explore an island? Islands are fantastic places for sighting wildlife because they are so far away from it all. Go to the **Farne Islands** in Northumberland and see puffins, seals and dive-bombing terns. Jump on a boat to **Brownsea Island** in Dorset and see red squirrels, peacocks and deer, and while you're there young smugglers and explorers can follow the beckoning trails. If you're in Devon, take a trip over to **Lundy Island**, to see a large variety of migratory seabirds, grass and heathland habitats. Remember, if you're planning a trip, make sure you ring up first to see if the boats are running – it sometimes depends on the tides or weather.

Lighthouses

There are hundreds of National Trust-owned buildings on the coast, including, Roman forts, radar stations and coastguard cottages. The lighthouses are particularly intriguing and make an interesting visit. How about a visit to the world's first electric lighthouse, **Souter Lighthouse** in Tyne & Wear? You can take a cliff-top walk to it, and climb up to look at the fantastic views over Marsden Bay. If you are on the opposite end of the country, take a visit to the distinctive **South Foreland** lighthouse on the White Cliffs of Dover. If lighthouses grab you, here's a few more you can try: There's **Longstone Lighthouse**, **Orford Ness**, **Beachy Head** and the **Gribbin**, for starters. You can also see lighthouses on the **Lizard Peninsular** and on **Lundy Island**. One of the oldest lighthouses is the 14th-century **St Catherine's Oratory** on the Isle of Wight, a tower that was used as a lighthouse in medieval times.

So get out to the coast and feel the wind in your hair, it's an exhilarating way for all the family to get some exercise and enjoy the beauty of the natural environment. Visit our website at www.nationaltrust.org.uk to find more information on all the other coastal sites that you can explore, and to download maps of coastal walks.

EASTER EGGSTRAVAGANZA

A La Ronde, Devon

Baddesley Clinton, West Midlands

Basildon Park, Berkshire

Blickling Hall, Gardens & Park, Norfolk

Calke Abbey, Derbyshire

Canons Ashby House, Northamptonshire

Castle Drogo, Devon

Chirk Castle, Wrexham

Coughton Court, Warwickshire

Croft Castle & Parkland, Herefordshire

Dunster Castle, Somerset

East Riddlesden Hall, West Yorkshire

Greys Court, Oxfordshire

Ham House & Garden, Surrey

Hardwick Hall, Derbyshire

Hatfield Forest, Hertfordshire

Ickworth House, Park & Gardens, Suffolk

Lacock Abbey, Fox Talbot Museum & Village, Wiltshire

Lanhydrock, Cornwall

Melford Hall, Suffolk

Newark Park, Gloucestershire

Osterley Park & House, Middesex

Oxburgh Hall, Garden & Estate, Norfolk

Powis Castle & Garden, Powys

Quarry Bank Mill & Styal Estate, Cheshire

River Wey & Godalming Navigations & Dapdune Wharf, Surrey

Saltram, Devon

Shugborough Estate, Staffordshire

Snowshill Manor, Gloucestershire

Speke Hall & Garden, Liverpool

Springhill, Co. Londonderry

Standen, West Sussex

Sutton Hoo, Suffolk

Tatton Park, Cheshire

Trelissick Garden, Cornwall

Trerice, Cornwall

Wallington, Northumberland

As the chill of winter begins to fade and the first signs of spring emerge, thoughts turn to Easter and the Easter holidays. The National Trust has plenty to help keep both children and adults occupied, with around 200 properties offering Easter activities every year.

Our excellent Easter-egg trails are hugely popular, so come along with the whole family, and why not make a tradition of it? Follow clues, solve puzzles and claim a chocolate surprise at the end. Our properties are stunning locations for egg hunts and include unusual places to visit.

You'll find that some of our properties are offering more than just Easter trails. How about joining in with a craft activity, running in an egg race, or having your face painted Easter-style? Whatever you decide to join in with, we're sure you'll find lots to choose from, so check out the National Trust website (www.nationaltrust.org.uk) around Easter time and you'll find details of events going on near you. See left for a list of properties where you're bound to find something going on (not exclusive).

We're delighted to be working with Cadbury to provide this years' Easter trails. For more details and to find your nearest trails go to www.eastereggtrail.com.

HALLOWEEN HORRORS

Halloween is the time to pluck up your courage and come and investigate the spookier side of the Trust's properties. And they're beckoning you to take part in some truly horrifying happenings. Be prepared to be scared (just a little).

Terrifying tales and tours
Come and take a terrifying tour around some of the houses, and listen to their spooky tales. Or creep around one of the castles and listen to the stories of their ghostly residents.

Fanciful fancy dress
If you fancy dressing up, there are plenty of properties where you can do so. Some properties offer free entry to children in fancy dress and others hold fancy-dress competitions, so come along and make sure you look grotesque. Check our website for details nearer the time.

Haunted hunts
There are spooky clues, ghostly questions and horrible answers on the National Trust's Halloween trails. They take you into the darkest corners, but join in and you'll find out whether there is a trick or treat waiting for you at the end!

Ghoulish games and crazy crafts
There will be pumpkin-carving, mask-making, pumpkin skittles and apple-bobbing. These are just a taster of the crazy crafts and ghoulish games that are going on – so come along and join in. And if all that fear is making you hungry, pop into one of the restaurants and take a look at some of the terrifying menus.

Animal magic
Come along and watch one of the magicians, and see what tricks they have up their sleeves. And this is your chance to meet some magical creatures – there's owl handling at some properties and scary bat hunts too.

Each year there is an exciting programme of ghoulish activities, so check the National Trust website for what's going on near you. At **Rufford Old Hall** in Lancashire, for example, usually there are crafts in the Education Room, a pumpkin hunt around the grounds and a children's 'things that go bump in the night' Halloween trail. Follow our ghoulish trail and collect a prize on completion. Or perhaps you are brave enough to meet the ghosts that haunt **Lodge Park**? You might even see the witch who was walled up in the cellar. Have a go at our spooky trail, and win a prize. Take a spooky tour of the **Dolaucothi Gold Mines** and follow the children's Halloween trail – prepare to be scared! If you would prefer Halloween events that are more fun than frightening, try the family trail at **Prior Park**. It looks at the magic and mystery surrounding the autumn – there is a goodie bag for all those who complete the trail and Halloween-inspired treats for sale from the tea hut. See right for a list of properties that also usually offer activities.

Basildon Park, Berkshire

Blickling Hall, Gardens & Park, Norfolk

Charlecote Park, Warwickshire

Chedworth Roman Villa, Gloucestershire

Croft Castle and Parkland, Herefordshire

Dudmaston, Shropshire

Dunster Castle, Somerset

East Riddlesden Hall, West Yorkshire

Florence Court, Co. Fermanagh

Hardwick Hall, Derbyshire

Hatfield Forest, Hertfordshire

Ickworth House, Park and Gardens, Suffolk

Nostell Priory and Parkland, West Yorkshire

Powis Castle & Garden, Powys

Saltram, Devon

Speke Hall, Garden & Estate, Liverpool

Sutton Hoo, Suffolk

Tatton Park, Cheshire

Arlington Court & the National Trust's Carriage Collection

Historic house Garden Park Countryside Farm Museum Lake Wood

South West

Arlington, nr Barnstaple,
Devon, EX31 4LP
01271 850296

OPENING TIMES
House & Carriage Collection
16 Mar 08–2 Nov 08
11am–5pm Mon, Tue, Wed,
Thu, Fri, Sun
**House & Carriage Collection
(guided tours only)**
2 Mar 08–9 Mar 08 12am–4pm
Sun
**Shop/tearoom/garden/
bat-cam**
2 Mar 08–9 Mar 08 12am–4pm
Sun
16 Mar 08–29 Jun 08
10:30am–5pm Mon, Tue, Wed,
Thu, Fri, Sun
30 Jun 08–31 Aug 08
10:30am–5pm Mon–Sun
1 Sep 08–2 Nov 08
10:30am–5pm Mon, Tue, Wed,
Thu, Fri, Sun
7 Nov 08–21 Dec 08
11am–4pm Fri, Sat, Sun

Notes
Whole property open Sat of BH
weekends. Other Sats in July
and Aug only gardens, bat-
cam, shop and tearoom open.
Light refreshments only 2
Nov–16 Dec. Grounds open
dawn–dusk, 1 Nov–March 08.

Most people bring back a few things when they go on holiday
abroad, but one-time owner Rosalie Chichester just didn't know
when to stop – the house is packed with fascinating objects.

Animal antics
Rosalie's three peacocks, Spangles, Sapphire and Speckles, were
allowed to wander about inside the house. And the ponies and sheep
you'll see are descendants of animals she introduced to the estate.

What to see
● Cabinets full of model ships, seashells, silver spoons, snuff boxes,
  paperweights and stuffed birds.
● In the nursery, a clockwork tortoise and a Victorian trapeze artist in a
  glass case (that's a model, not stuffed).
● Over 50 horse-drawn carriages and chariots – and one designed to
  be pulled by a dog.

What to do
● Grab the reins and drive the 'please touch' carriage – the metal
  horse won't go far, though.
● Take a carriage ride in the 12-hectare (30-acre) grounds.
● Use the bat-cam to see bats roosting in the roof (May–Aug).

Special events
Look out for our Experience Carriage Driving Day and take the reins
yourself in a one-horse-power vehicle. There are also events and craft
workshops for younger members of the family at other times, so get in
touch to find out more.

By the way...
● There's a children's play area, baby-changing facilities and you can
  borrow a baby sling or a hip-carrying seat as pushchairs cannot be
  taken into the house. Don't worry though – we provide rain covers
  and padlocks for them. Children's menu in the Old Kitchen tearoom.
  For those with mobility problems, there are many steps to the
  entrance, so ask us about the alternative entrance (near the
  tearoom). We have wheelchairs for loan.

Avebury

Stone circle Countryside Museum

Avebury's prehistoric stone circle is one of the biggest in Europe and is thought to date back over 4,000 years. Ranking alongside the Taj Mahal and the Pyramids as a World Heritage Site, it is not to be missed. Soak up the ambience of this ancient space, then explore interactive displays and fascinating finds in the museum galleries.

Megalithic mystery

For centuries it was thought many of the missing stones had been demolished or stolen, but the technological magic of geophysics recently discovered at least 15 more, buried in the ground. It's thought they may have been pushed over and hidden in the 13th or 14th centuries, when people thought they were dangerous pagan symbols.

What to see
- The massive standing stones, arranged in circles.
- The Barber Surgeon's stone – where the remains of a medieval man with some scissors in his pocket were discovered in 1938.
- The huge ditch around the stones, dug by picks made from antlers, and shovels made from the shoulder blades of oxen.
- Archeological finds and audio-visual displays, which tell the story of the stones.

What to do
- Discover more about 'Marmalade Millionaire' Alexander Keiller's megalithic discovery. One of his great passions was archaeology – he used his fortune to buy and excavate the site at Avebury and re-erected many of the stones in the 1930s.
- Visit the Stables Gallery, which depicts life in Neolithic times, while the barn is home to five species of bats, the interactive 'story of the stones' and also a vintage car (a 1914 Sizare Berwick) that belonged to Alexander Keiller himself.

Special events
Trails, living-history craft workshops, art exhibitions and more. Special interest talks and tours also offered.

By the way...
- There's a picnic area by the barn as well as a restaurant.
- The museum is accessible, but only parts of the circle are. There's a Braille and large-print guide, as well as items that can be handled. Please book if possible.

nr Marlborough,
Wiltshire, SN8 1RF
01672 539250

OPENING TIMES
Stone circle
All year Mon–Sun
Museum/galleries
1 Feb 08–31 Mar 08
10am–5pm Mon–Sun
1 Apr 08–31 Oct 08
10am–5pm Mon–Sun
1 Nov 08–31 Jan 08
10am–4pm Mon–Sun
Circle restaurant
1 Feb 08–31 Mar 08
10am–5pm Mon–Sun
1 Apr 08–31 Oct 08
10am–5:30pm Mon–Sun
1 Nov 08–31 Jan 08
11am–3:30pm Mon–Sun
Shop
1 Feb 08–28 Feb 08
11am–4pm Mon–Sun
1 Mar 08–31 Mar 08
11am–5pm Mon–Sun
1 Apr 08–30 Sep 08
10am–6pm Mon–Sun
1 Oct 08–31 Oct 08
10am–5pm Mon–Sun

Notes
Closes dusk if earlier. Closed 24–26 Dec. Barn gallery may close in very cold weather.

South West

Brownsea Island

Countryside Coastline Nature reserve Harbour

Poole, Dorset, BH13 7EE
01202 707744

OPENING TIMES
15 Mar 08–18 Jul 08
10am–5pm Mon–Sun
19 Jul 08–31 Aug 08
10am–6pm Mon–Sun
1 Sep 08–27 Jan 08
10am–5pm Mon–Sun
28 Sep 08–26 Oct 08
10am–4pm Mon–Sun

Notes
Shop and Villano Café close
30 mins before island. The
island is open during the winter
to booked groups only. Part of
the island is leased to Dorset
Wildlife Trust (tel. 01202
709445 for information).
Brownsea Castle is not open
to the public.

Brownsea Island is an unspoilt natural haven with a colourful history. It has been a coastguard station, a Victorian pottery and even a daffodil farm, and was once the perfect haunt for smugglers who used to hide their booty in the castle. Now it's one of the last places where you can see red squirrels as well as many different kinds of seabirds. There are many walks on its 500 acres (200 hectacres), some suitable for even the youngest would-be smuggler. Explore this relaxing car-free place, and admire the spectacular view across Poole harbour towards Studland and the Purbeck Hills.

Wartime disguises
During World War II, Brownsea Island was used as a decoy to protect the nearby towns of Poole and Bournemouth from Nazi bombing. Fires were lit on the island to confuse the pilots into thinking they had already reached their target. Today the many bomb craters on the island have become important habitats for rare wildlife.

What to see
- A variety of wildlife, including red squirrels and deer.
- Cormorants, oyster-catchers, terns, shelduck and other seabirds, nose-diving into the sea.
- Proud peacocks strutting their stuff alongside free-ranging chickens.
- Excellent views from the cliffs; to the south-east you can see the chalk formations Old Harry Rocks – supposedly where the devil laid down for a moment (Old Harry's wife, a smaller rock, collapsed some time ago).
- The stretch of water between Brownsea and Furzey, known as 'Blood Alley' because it is so shallow.
- A fascinating collection of restored 19th-century carts, wagons and machinery from Brownsea Island, near the visitor centre.

What to do
- Take the boat to Brownsea from Poole Quay and Sandbacks (every half-hour). Services available from Bournemouth and Swanage (see local information for fares and timetables).
- Follow the Smugglers' Trail to the treasure chest, with letter clues along the way. Ideal for 6–10 year olds, it takes around an hour, with a smuggler's certificate and sticker at the end. For a longer walk, take the Historical Trail, with a walk round the island and a look at the ruins of the old pottery.
- Watch the birds on the lagoon from the public hide (designed with full wheelchair access). Take a picnic, or pick up a lunch box from the café.
- Go for a guided walk in the Dorset Wildlife Trust nature reserve (£2 adults).

Special events
There are many fun family events held throughout the year, including daily summer and half-term holiday activities like storytelling, pottery

demonstrations and special picnics or walks. The island is also home to the Brownsea Open Air Theatre, which puts on a Shakespeare play every summer.

By the way...

- If you have small children, we can provide a free loan of one of our all-terrain baby buggies to help you get around. We also have a larger buggy for older explorers with restricted mobility. The rough terrain means that certain parts of the island are not very accessible, although there are tractor trailer trails for disabled visitors Mon–Fri (please contact us to book). The castle isn't open to the public, and part of the island is a nature reserve with an additional charge. Sorry, no dogs allowed on the island because of the wildlife. There's a café near the landing quay, as well as a sweet shop that also sells ice cream and cold drinks.

Buckland Abbey

Historic house Garden Countryside

South West

Yelverton, Devon, PL20 6EY
01822 853607

OPENING TIMES
Estate/garden/restaurant/
shop
16 Feb 08–9 Mar 08
12:30pm–5pm Sat, Sun
15 Mar 08–2 Nov 08
10:30am–5:30pm Mon, Tue,
Wed, Fri, Sat, Sun
8 Nov 08–21 Dec 08
12am–4pm Fri, Sat, Sun
13 Feb 08–31 Jan 08
12am–4pm Fri, Sat, Sun
Abbey
16 Feb 08–9 Mar 08 2pm–5pm
Sat, Sun
15 Mar 08–2 Nov 08
10:30am–5:30pm Mon, Tue,
Wed, Fri, Sat, Sun
8 Nov 08–21 Dec 08
12am–4pm Fri, Sat, Sun
13 Feb 08–31 Jan 08
12am–4pm Fri, Sat, Sun

Notes
Admission by timed ticket at
busy times. Last admission 45
mins before closing

Set in a beautifully secluded valley near the Tavy river, the ruins of the 13th-century abbey church point to Buckland's origins as a medieval monastery. Later the Abbey was converted to a house by seafarer Sir Richard Grenville. But it's most famous as home to Grenville's arch-rival, Sir Francis Drake. In fact it's rumoured that Drake still haunts the 700-year-old building, along with his 'hell hounds'. There is fascinating memorabilia about him as well as interesting grounds to explore, including an Elizabethan garden.

Winning ways

Sir Francis Drake, famous for leading the defeat against the Spanish Armada in 1588, once owned Buckland Abbey. See the elaborately ceilinged Great Hall, which is much as it was in his day, and the place where he planned his tactics for his famous sea battles.

What to see

- The hand-crafted plasterwork ceiling in Drake's Chambers. A replacement for the original, which burnt down – believe it or not, this new one is made of yak-hair plaster.
- The 'magic' drum in the Treasures Gallery. It's said that if ever England is in danger you should beat the drum and Drake will rise from the dead.
- The traditional craft workshops in the ox sheds, where you can see crafts like wood turning.
- The original monastery's chancel arch on the abbey's tower.

What to do

- Discover how to find your way on the oceans with replica Tudor navigational instruments.
- Have a go at butter-making or old-fashioned tub laundry.
- Pick up a map at reception, and follow any of four woodland walks.

Special events

There are many special events suitable for all. Regular events include an Elizabethan weekend, with dancing workshops, live music and cooking in the kitchen. Also a re-creation of a medieval encampment, complete with craft demonstrations. There are often children's activity days with games, puzzles and hands-on activities. Get in touch to find out what's on, as booking is sometimes necessary.

By the way...

- There is picnic space in the car park and also the quarry orchard.
- The normal visitor route has many steps, and the grounds are only partly accessible. Alternative routes and wheelchairs are available. There are Braille guides and touchable objects.
- Children should be accompanied by an adult for family events (and vice versa).
- Dogs are welcome in the car park only, and only on leads. There are dog posts in the shade so your dog can wait in comfort.

Castle Drogo

Castle Garden Park Countryside

Drewsteignton, nr Exeter, Devon, EX6 6PB. 01647 433306

OPENING TIMES
Castle and tearoom
1 Mar 08–9 Mar 08 11am–4pm Sat, Sun; 15 Mar 08–23 Mar 08 11am–5pm Mon, Wed–Sun; 24 Mar 08–20 Apr 08 11am–5pm Mon–Sun; 21 Apr 08–25 May 08 11am–5pm Mon, Wed–Sun; 26 May 08–1 Jun 08 11am–5pm Mon–Sun; 2 Jun 08–20 Jul 08 11am–5pm Mon, Wed–Sun; 21 Jul 08–31 Aug 08 11am–5pm Mon–Sun; 1 Sep 08–25 Oct 08 11am–5pm Mon, Wed–Sun; 26 Oct 08–2 Nov 08 11am–4pm Mon–Sun; 29 Nov 08–14 Dec 08 12am–4pm Sat, Sun; 18 Dec 08–22 Dec 08 12am–4pm Mon, Thu–Sun
Garden/shop/visitor centre
1 Mar 08–9 Mar 08 10:30am–4:30pm Sat, Sun; 15 Mar 08–23 Mar 08 10:30am–5:30pm Mon, Wed–Sun; 24 Mar 08–20 Apr 08 10:30am–5:30pm Mon–Sun; 21 Apr 08–25 May 08 10:30am–5:30pm Mon, Wed–Sun; 26 May 08–1 Jun 08 10:30am–5:30pm Mon–Sun; 2 Jun 08–20 Jul 08 10:30am–5:30pm Mon, Wed–Sun; 21 Jul 08–31 Aug 08 10:30am–5:30pm Mon–Sun; 1 Sep 08–25 Oct 08 10:30am–5:30pm Mon, Wed–Sun; 26 Oct–2 Nov 10:30am–4:30pm Mon–Sun; 8 Nov 08–14 Dec 08 10:30am–4:30pm Sat, Sun; 18 Dec–22 Dec 08 11am–4:30pm Mon, Thu–Sun

Notes
Last admission 30 mins before close. To book Christmas lunch in tearooms tel. (01647) 434131.

Situated high on a rocky outcrop above the dramatic Teign Gorge, it looks like a real medieval castle but it's actually an early 20th-century confection designed by the famous architect Edwin Lutyens. Inside it's a modern, comfortable home with a large garden where young visitors can let off steam.

Supermarket man

The first owner, Julius Drewe, became a millionaire at age 33 through his chain of grocery shops. He really wanted to have famous ancestors so he 'discovered' that he was descended from a Norman baron called Drogo de Teign – hence the name of the castle. Spot the fake castle features like arrow slits and portcullis.

What to see

● Family-events programme running from March to December, with trails, re-enactments, themed weekends and something to do daily during school holidays.
● See how many lions you can see – it was the family emblem.
● Look in the Bunty House in the garden and see if you can find the castle cats, Boots and Fluffy.

What to do

● Walk down the servants' staircase – they had their own, so that the family wouldn't have to bump into them.
● Find the telephone and the lift, which were 'mod-cons' at the time.
● Have fun following one of the three free family trails in the house.

Special events

Easter-egg trail, family trail every day of the school holidays, week of Halloween activities, woodland sculpture workshops and Drogo Christmas with Father Christmas.

By the way...

● There's a children's play area and we can lend you hip-carrying infant seats. There are baby-changing facilities and a picnic area, and there's a children's quiz/trail. Wheelchairs are available and there is a ramped entrance, but no access upstairs.

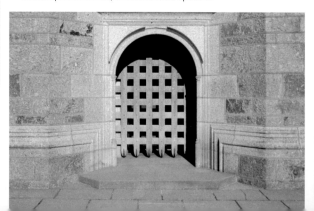

Chedworth Roman Villa

Museum Roman villa

A stately home with a difference – it's over 1700 years old. Here are the remains of one of the largest Romano-British villas in the country, nestled in a beautiful wooded valley in the heart of the Cotswolds. Unlike some Roman sites, a lot has been uncovered here, and you can really get a sense of how the villa would have been in Roman times.

Hypo heat
Did you know that the Romans had fancy underfloor heating to keep their tootsies warm? You can still see evidence of hypocausts at Chedworth – that's special flooring that was held up by columns to let the hot air through.

What to see
- Mosaics, bath-houses and latrines (Roman loos).
- The remains of a water shrine.
- About 1.6km (over a mile) of ancient walls.

What to do
- Follow the site trail and imagine life as a rather posh Roman. Our audio-visual show brings the archaeology to life.

Special events
There are archeological events throughout the year, and we also have special holiday activities and weekend days – like re-creations of life as a gladiator (including battles) and spooky Halloween days.

By the way...
- Most of the site has steps although the entrance is ramped and we have a wheelchair. We have lots of living-history events with re-enactors to talk to and artefacts to handle.

South West

Yanworth, nr Cheltenham, Gloucestershire, GL54 3LJ
01242 890256

OPENING TIMES
1 Mar 08–16 Mar 08
11am–4pm Tue, Wed, Thu, Fri, Sat, Sun
18 Mar 08–2 Nov 08
10am–5pm Tue, Wed, Thu, Fri, Sat, Sun
4 Nov 08–16 Nov 08
10am–4pm Tue, Wed, Thu, Fri, Sat, Sun

Notes
Open BH Mons. See noticeboard for shop/tea tent opening times

Corfe Castle

Ruins Visitor centre Medieval garden

South West

The Square, Corfe Castle,
Wareham, Dorset, BH20 5EZ
01929 481294

OPENING TIMES
1 Mar 08–31 Mar 08
10am–5pm Mon–Sun
1 Apr 08–30 Sep 08
10am–6pm Mon–Sun
1 Oct 08–31 Oct 08
10am–5pm Mon–Sun
1 Nov 08–31 Jan 08
10am–4pm Mon–Sun

Notes
Shop and tearoom close
5.30pm April–Sept. Closed 25,
26 Dec. High winds may cause
closure of parts of grounds

A storybook ruined castle – the inspiration for Kirrin Castle in Enid
Blyton's *Famous Five* books. Corfe Castle was built in the 11th
century by William the Conqueror and has a history full of violence
and murder. After years as an important stronghold, the castle was
destroyed by Parliamentarians in the later 1600s.

Wicked old John
In the 13th century King John went to great lengths to improve the
building. He built a fine hall and chapel, and buildings for his domestic
staff. But he also ordered 22 knights to be locked in the grisly
dungeons and starved to death – he wasn't exactly one for modern
prison methods.

What to see
- Spooky ruins and even some medieval loos.
- Murder holes in the gatehouse – solders would fling stones, boiling
  oil and other nasties through them at their enemies below.

What to do
- Pop into the visitor centre to find out what Lady Bankes thought
  about those medieval loos, and which English king was the first to
  wear a dressing gown. While you're there, play with all the
  interactive displays and exhibitions.
- Have a Famous Five picnic in the castle, Enid Blyton's inspiration for
  Kirrin Castle.
- Follow the trail in the family guide book. Imagine living here hundreds
  of years ago – how would you have stormed the castle?
- Roll down the castle slopes – but be careful!

Special events
- Family fun days with treasure trails in the grounds and storytelling.
- Open-air cinema in the castle grounds.
- Children's theatre shows and lots more. We have many free holiday
  activities that you don't need to book for.

By the way...
- Find out if the Swanage Steam Railway is open when you plan your visit – they operate a steam-train service to the nearby station.
- Pushchairs and back-carriers are fine. Children must be accompanied in the castle as there are steep slopes and drops to be aware of.
- There is a fragrant medieval herb garden outside the visitor centre and a magnetic 'build a castle' display inside it.
- Please keep dogs on a lead.

Cornish Mines & Engines

Discovery centre Mine

South West

Pool, nr Redruth,
Cornwall, TR15 3NP
01209 315027

OPENING TIMES
Centre/shop
19 Mar 08–2 Nov 08
11am–5pm Mon, Wed, Thu,
Fri, Sun

Notes
Nov to end Jan 09 by
arrangement only; please tel. for
details or to arrange group visits
at any time of year.

Today Cornwall's landscape is dotted with disused mine shafts and
engine houses, a dramatic reminder of the time when this part of
England was the centre for tin, copper and china clay mining. This
site gives you a chance to find out what it must have been like in the
19th century, when the great steam-powered beam engines were
used for pumping water up from depths of over 500m (1640ft), and
for winding men up and down into the mines.

Knock knock, who's there?
Maybe working down below by candlelight with tapping picks and
shovels brought on that feeling of being watched. Cornish legends
abound with tales of pixies and sprites, including the 'knockers' –
invisible elfin creatures who supposedly lived in the mines. Fearing bad
luck if they upset these rather pesky spirits, miners would leave them a
portion of their own meal before going on with their work.

What to see
- The massive 75cm (30in) working beam engine, which extends up
  three floors of the mine building, with huge piston rods and wheels.
- The even larger 225cm (90in) engine used to pump water from the
  mine's murky depths (not working now).

What to do
- Visit the Industrial Discovery Centre, which provides an overview of
  Cornwall's mining heritage, and has a fascinating film.
- Follow the children's quiz/trail to make the visit more fun for younger
  visitors as well as going to many events held at the property.

By the way...
- There's a lift which takes disabled visitors up and down the engine
  house. The lower part of the engine house is accessible by ramp.
- Many of the original artifacts are available to touch, and there are
  guides who will be happy to assist.
- Not open between November and March, except by arrangement.
- Nearby working Levant Mine and Beam Engine (Trewellard,
  Pendeen, nr St Just, Cornwall TR19 7SX, 01736 786156) is also
  National Trust-owned.

Cotehele

Historic house Garden Countryside Quay

This magical house is hidden away in the Tamar valley, reached by a network of narrow lanes. There are no electric lights, so a tour through the dimly lit rooms can be an exciting experience. There are some lovely walks through the woods, in the gardens and down to the quay. The unique atmosphere of Cotehele and the friendly stewards and staff make it worth putting aside a whole day for your visit.

What to see
- A whale's jawbones in the Tudor Great Hall.
- Lots of medieval armour.
- A water-mill, a medieval dovecote, and a Victorian summer house.
- Woodpeckers and other wildlife in the woods.

What to do
- Take the walk to the quay, down fairly steep wooded slopes, which is quite charming. The trees are enormous and mossy so you feel you are enclosed in a magic world.
- See the quay where the restored sailing barge *Shamrock* is moored on the lapping, tidal waters of the Tamar. It's hard to imagine this was once a hubbub of trading activity.
- Take a trip on the little boat to Calstock quay (one-hour round trip, subject to tides, May to September).

By the way...
- Wear sensible shoes, there are some steep slopes.

St Dominick, nr Saltash,
Cornwall, PL12 6TA
01579 351346

OPENING TIMES
House
15 Mar 08–2 Nov 08
11am–4:30pm Mon, Tue, Wed, Thu, Sat, Sun
Hall of House with garland
24 Nov 08–23 Dec 08
11am–4pm Mon–Sun
Garden
All year 10am–dusk Mon–Sun
Restaurant/shop/plants/ gallery
17 Feb 08–14 Mar 08
11am–4pm Mon–Sun
15 Mar 08–2 Nov 08
11am–5pm Mon–Sun
3 Nov 08–23 Dec 08
11am–4:30pm Mon–Sun
Edgcumbe Arms
17 Feb 08–2 Nov 08
11am–5pm Mon–Sun

Notes
Open Good Fri. Barn Restaurant closed Fridays 21 March–31 Oct. Edgcumbe Arms closes at dusk if earlier than 5pm. Limited opening in Nov/Dec, tel. for details.

Dunster Castle

Castle Garden Park

Dunster, nr Minehead,
Somerset, TA24 6SL
01643 821314

OPENING TIMES
Castle
15 Mar 08–23 Jul 08
11am–4:30pm Mon, Tue, Wed,
Fri, Sat, Sun
25 Jul 08–3 Sep 08 11am–5pm
Mon, Tue, Wed, Fri, Sat, Sun
3 Sep–31 Oct 11am–4pm Mon,
Tue, Wed, Fri, Sat, Sun
Garden/park
1 Jan 08–14 Mar 08
11am–4pm Mon–Sun
15 Mar 08–2 Nov 08
10am–5pm Mon–Sun
3 Nov 08–31 Dec 08
11am–4pm Mon–Sun
Shop*
4 Feb 08–14 Mar 08
11am–4pm Mon–Sun
15 Mar 08–24 Jul 08
10:30am–5pm Mon–Sun
25 Jul 08–4 Sep 08
10:30am–5:30pm Mon–Sun
5 Sep 08–2 Nov 08
10:30am–5pm Mon–Sun
3 Nov 08–31 Dec 08
11am–4pm Mon–Sun

Notes
Open Good Fri. Castle closed
for private function 6 and 27
June, 11 July, 1 and 15 Aug
and 12 Sept. Gardens and
shop open as normal. Garden,
park and shop closed 25/26
Dec. Shop closed Jan.
*Shop short-term relocation,
please call to confirm opening
times.

This fantasy castle with its fairy-tale turrets and towers is largely a 19th-century re-creation. Enjoy exploring the zig-zagging paths of the gardens and tiptoeing around the spooky crypt.

Tall tale
In the 1870s workmen found at 2.3m (7ft) skeleton in what was known as an 'oubliette' – a tiny cell in which a prisoner was locked up and left to rot. No one knows the identity of the mysterious skeleton.

What to see
- It's worth cricking your neck to catch a glimpse of the intricate plasterwork in the ceiling of the dining room which dates from 1681.
- Watch out in some of Dunster Castle's rooms for spooks, as they are reputedly haunted by a man in military uniform, a lady in grey and a disembodied foot!

What to do
- Children can poke their heads into the secret compartment (probably a priest's hole) in King Charles' bedroom. It may have connected with a escape passage to the village. Elderly people have memories of playing in the passage as children.
- Take a picnic and sit under the stunning 300-year-old oak tree after wearing everyone out with activity sheets and quizzes.

Special events
Dunster hosts some great events, including Easter-egg trails, Civil War living history, pirates days and Halloween fun. Contact us for more details.

Dyrham Park

Historic house Garden Park

There's a welcoming atmosphere at Dyrham Park on a Sunday afternoon, with lots of relaxed families picnicking on the grass in front of the house. Search for the furry maple and other oddly named trees, and head down to the fascinating 19th-century 'below stairs' rooms.

Double Dutch
Look out for all things Dutch in the house, such as blue-and-white Delft china and lots of tulips. The reason? The house was built c.1700 for William Blathwayt, Secretary at War to Dutchman, King William III.

What to see
- A clever trick painting by the Dutch artist Samuel van Hoogstraeten. It really confuses everyone!
- The fascinating Victorian 'below stairs' rooms. You'll get a good idea of how hard servants worked when you see the huge kitchen ranges and other equipment.
- Peacocks and fallow deer in the park and some wonderful sounding trees – the 'strangle tree', the 'lanky lime' and the 'furry maple'.

What to do
- Imagine you're Sarah Saunders, the housekeeper here in 1710. She had to write down every single item in the house for an inventory. What a task!
- Go for a park walk and hoard your precious findings in a paper bag.

Special events
Dyrham occasionally runs family events. Check for details.

By the way...
- Treat your kids to a children's book illustrated by Ben Blathwayt, a descendant of the first owner – it's on sale in the shop. Have a picnic at Old Lodge and play on the tractor.

Dyrham, nr Bath,
Gloucestershire, SN14 8ER
0117 937 2501

OPENING TIMES
House
14 Mar 08–2 Nov 08
11am–5pm Mon, Tue, Fri,
Sat, Sun
Garden/shop/tearoom
14 Mar 08–29 Jun 08
11am–5pm Mon, Tue, Fri,
Sat, Sun
30 Jun 08–31 Aug 08
11am–5pm Mon–Sun
1 Sep 08–2 Nov 08 11am–5pm
Mon, Tue, Fri, Sat, Sun
8 Nov 08–14 Dec 08
11am–4pm Sat, Sun
7 Feb 08–8 Mar 08 11am–4pm
Sat, Sun
Park
All year* 11am–5:30pm
Mon–Sun

Notes
Open BH Mons and Good Fri:
11–5. Last admission 1hr
before closing. *Except 25 Dec.

41

Finch Foundry

Museum River

Sticklepath, Okehampton,
Devon, EX20 2NW
01837 840046

OPENING TIMES
15 Mar–2 Nov 08 11am–5pm
Mon, Wed, Thu, Fri, Sat, Sun

The Finch brothers set up this water-powered 'edge-tool' works here in 1814 to make mining and agricultural tools. At one time 400 tools a day were produced here. Three water wheels drove the huge tilt hammer and grindstone, which you can still see working today.

It's a dog's life
Workers had to lie flat across the stone wheel to reach it with their tools for sharpening. In winter that was a rather chilly experience, so dogs were especially trained to sit on the men's legs to keep them warm!

What to see
- Three water wheels driving the huge tilt hammer and grinding stone (when working).
- An exhibition about all the different tools made here – from the Devon potato chopper to the swan-neck hoe.

What to do
- Watch the hourly demonstrations of water power by staff or volunteers.
- Take the 'four village trail' walk that starts at the foundry.
- Explore the foundry building, garden and riverside walk.
- Try out the quiz and trail, created especially for younger members of the family.

Special events
Recent events include a vintage car rally, Jazz on the Lawn and the famous St. Clement's Day – the blacksmiths' saint's day – where blacksmiths' from around the country meet in competition.

By the way...
- Dogs are welcome except in the tearoom and shop and in the foundry during demonstrations.
- There's loads to touch, smell and hear – the crashing water, smell of the coke fire and metalwork objects.
- The shop has a level entrance but the foundry does have a few steps to contend with.

Glendurgan Garden

Garden Coastline Maze

This sheltered and warm sub-tropical garden was created in the 1820s, and developed by the Fox family over many years. It runs right down to the charming little village of Durgan and its sandy beach with a wealth of interesting rockpools. Everyone in the family will love the laurel maze, which looks like a serpent laid out on the grass and dates from 1833. There are also many rare and exotic plants, as well as carpets of wild flowers in the spring.

Shipping news

Alfred Fox, who started this wonderful garden, worked in the shipping industry. And his choice for the garden's location is no accident – nearby Fal estuary is a deep-water harbour that was the first port of call for ships coming back from the Americas, the Far East and Africa. Guess how the Fox family managed to import all those exotic plants and seeds!

What to see

- Giant rhubarb and the enormous tulip tree – called canoe wood by Native Americans, who could make a canoe out of a single trunk.
- If you're lucky, you might spot one of the rough-legged buzzards flying overhead.
- The reconstructed cob and thatch schoolroom.
- Holy Bank – planted with trees and plants mentioned in the Bible, including a yew, a tree of heaven and a crown of thorns.

What to do

- Get lost in the laurel maze, but don't panic – mums and dads (and older children) will be able to see over the 1m (3ft) high hedges.
- Swing on one of the six ropes around the enormous Giant's Stride – that's a maypole with attitude.
- Catch the ferry from Durgan beach to Helford village.

By the way...

- Only the splendid garden is open to the public – the house is privately occupied.
- The grounds are not very accessible to disabled people, due to steep paths, but the viewing path is, and so are the shop and café.

Mawnan Smith, nr Falmouth, Cornwall, TR11 5JZ
01326 250906

OPENING TIMES
9 Feb 08–3 Aug 08
10:30am–5:30pm Tue, Wed, Thu, Fri, Sat
4 Aug 08–25 Aug 08
10:30am–5:30pm Mon, Tue, Wed, Thu, Fri, Sat
26 Aug 08–1 Nov 08
10:30am–5:30pm Tue, Wed, Thu, Fri, Sat

Notes
Open BH Mondays. Closed Good Friday. Last admission 1hr before closing.

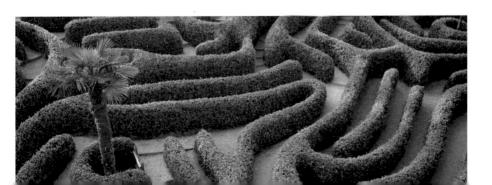

Greenway

Garden Boathouse Conservation Workshop

South West

Greenway Road, Galmpton,
nr Brixham, Devon, TQ5 0ES
01803 661903

OPENING TIMES
1 Mar 08–25 Oct 08
10:30am–5pm Wed, Thu, Fri,
Sat, Sun

Notes
Barn Gallery: open as garden,
showing modern contemporary
art by local artists

Famed as Agatha Christie's holiday home, Greenway is sited high on a promontory above the River Dart. The house is currently undergoing extensive refurbishment (opening 2009); however the glorious woodland garden has an equally rich history, with the earliest part formed on terraces levelled by Spanish Armada prisoners. This beautiful place is ideal for all the family to explore with its atmosphere of wildness and timelessness – a true 'secret garden'. At the boathouse you can imagine Sir Walter Raleigh smoking his pipe or at the conservators workshop you can see the cleaning and restoring of the beautiful and extraordinary contents of the house.

Murder most foul
The boathouse is well known to millions of Agatha Christie's readers as the place where Marlene Tucker was strangled in *Dead Man's Folly* – a strange fictional identity for such a real and timeless place.

What to see
- The newly restored early Victorian vinery, in the south walled garden.
- The 'Mother and Child' statue reclining on a field of Cyclamen and narcissi.
- The boathouse with its salt-water bathing room beneath and bats in its roof.
- The 18th-century bastion known as The Battery – sticking out into the river it is a great place to watch for herons.
- The conservators workshop to see 'conservation in action' and maybe get involved yourself.

What to do
- Arrive by boat, or on foot, for a great day out that helps the environment.
- Go to the visitor reception where you'll find trails, tracker packs and leaflets for all ages.
- Explore the many nooks and crannies and enticing 'secret places' in the garden.

Special events
There are a number of special events suitable for all ages, many combined with a river cruise. Watch out particularly for Easter-egg trails, bat walks and open-air theatre.

By the way...
- Picnics can be enjoyed anywhere in the garden but please take your litter home.
- Some paths can be steep or difficult so please ask for details of the accessible route for wheelchairs and buggies.
- We have large-print guides, Braille guides, hearing loops and even brilliant volunteers who can lend a hand if you wish.
- Dogs on leads on main drive and café courtyard – not in the garden.

Killerton

Historic house Garden Park Countryside Museum Visitor centre

Killerton was built in 1778 for Acland family. After a fire in the 1920s the inside was re-designed, and it's now furnished in the style of a country house from between the two World Wars. The hillside garden is spectacular, and the huge park and woods encompasses the two villages of Broadclyst and Budlake. Perhaps the most fascinating feature is the Paulise de Bush collection of costumes – over 9000 outfits.

Mind the dragon
Near Killerton House there's an Iron Age hill fort known as Dolbury Hill. There's meant to be a lot of treasure buried in it that's guarded by the Killerton dragon. Supposedly the dragon flies across the valley to the mound every night – we think that might be a bit of a shaggy dragon story...

What to see
- The Victorian laundry, with mangles and irons.
- The bear house, a funny little summer house that was once home to a pet Canadian black bear.
- Lots of costumes from the 18th–20th century on display.

What to do
- Try and find the ice house in the garden.
- Visit the discovery centre to try various activities (limited opening, check we're open before you come), and try the quiz and trail.
- Play with Victorian toys.

Special events
We have all sorts of special days, often on Sundays. Bat-watching evenings, autumn walks and a day when our portraits 'came to life' and talked about themselves were just a few recent ones. Booking is sometimes necessary for evening events.

By the way...
- Dogs are only allowed in the park, on leads, but there is shady parking in the overflow car park.
- There is lots of room to picnic in the park, and children's menus in both the restaurant and tearoom.
- See the collection of touchable objects in the discovery centre.
- There are quite a few steps to negotiate, but we can provide a ramp if you ask.

Broadclyst, Exeter, Devon, EX5 3LE. 01392 881345

OPENING TIMES
House
1 Mar 08–9 Mar 08 2pm–4pm Sat, Sun
12 Mar 08–31 Jul 08 11am–5pm Mon, Wed, Thu, Fri, Sat, Sun
1 Aug 08–31 Aug 08 11am–5pm Mon–Sun
1 Sep 08–29 Sep 08 11am–5pm Mon, Wed, Thu, Fri, Sat, Sun
1 Oct 08–2 Nov 08 11am–5pm Wed–Sun
6 Dec 08–23 Dec 08 2pm–4pm Mon–Sun
Park/garden
All year 10:30am–7pm Mon–Sun
Restaurant
As house 12am–5pm
Tearoom
1 Feb 08–29 Feb 08 11am–4pm Wed–Sun
1 Mar 08–2 Nov 08 11am–5:30pm Mon–Sun
5 Nov 08–30 Nov 08 11am–5pm Wed–Sun
Closes 4:30pm on Tues.

Notes
House open Mon 20 Oct (in half-term week). Shop/plant sales close 5pm when house closed, 3pm on Christmas Eve. In winter shop and tearoom may not open in bad weather. Restaurant open as house 12 March–2 Nov and on selected dates in Dec for Christmas lunches (booking essential).

Kingston Lacy

Historic house Garden Park Countryside

Wimborne Minster,
Dorset, BH21 4EA
01202 883402

OPENING TIMES
House
15 Mar 08–2 Nov 08
11am–4pm Wed, Thu, Fri, Sat,
Sun
Garden/park
3 Feb 08–9 Mar 08
10:30am–5:30pm Sat, Sun
15 Mar 08–2 Nov 08
10:30am–6pm Mon–Sun
7 Nov 08–21 Dec 08
10:30am–4pm Fri, Sat, Sun
Shop/restaurant
2 Feb 08–9 Mar 08
10:30am–5:30pm Sat, Sun
15 Mar 08–2 Nov 08
10:30am–5:30pm Mon–Sun
7 Nov 08–21 Dec 08
10:30am–4pm Fri, Sat, Sun

Notes
Admission by timed ticket to
house may operate on BH Suns
and Mons. Open BH Mons.
Last admission 4pm. Special
snowdrop days in Jan/Feb.

Part of The National Trust's largest lowland estate, Kingston Lacy
House sits in 300 acres of parkland and gardens. The wider estate is
criss-crossed by 100km (72 miles) of footpaths and bridleways (map
available from visitor reception) and stretches from the River Stour in
the south to beyond Badbury Rings in the north. Badbury Rings is
an Iron Age hill fort, a possible site for Mount Badon in Arthurian
legends, and home to a host of wild flowers including 15 varieties
of orchid.

Edwardian splendour
A beautiful country house, set in a wide parkland with a woodland
perimeter, Edwardian garden and Victorian fernery. The house is
presented at its Edwardian hey-day and appears as if the family has
gone out to tea, and the housekeeper has let you in for a look around.
The lawns and pastures are open access and lead through the gardens
and into the shelter-belt walks and play areas.

What to see
- In the house there are keys to Corfe Castle, a leather-hung Spanish
  room, a marble staircase and carvings, tented rooms and the
  Egyptian collection.
- In the garden visit cedar walk, the obelisk and sarcophagus, a
  fernery, lime walk and Japanese gardens.
- In the park see North Devon cattle, a shepherd's hut, cedar avenue,
  woodland walks and play areas.

What to do
- Follow the Trusty Tree Trail and learn their story, or the Garden Trail
  and see what Henrietta (Granny Bankes) did on Lady's Walk. Use
  the Family House Guide to discover how William John Bankes
  changed his English country house into an amazing Italian palace.

Special events
Drop-in events and children's' craft days throughout the year.
Edwardian sports day in August followed by the House vs Village
croquet match. Open-air concerts in July, open-air theatre in August.
For more information, see the estate events leaflet or get in touch.

By the way...
- Dogs on leads are welcome in the parkland but not in the formal
  gardens or the restaurant. Allow around 1½ hours to see the house.

Lacock Abbey, Fox Talbot Museum & Village

Historic house Park Village Museum

'Say cheese'! This phrase probably wouldn't be so familiar if William Fox Talbot hadn't taken the first negative photo here in 1835. Find out more about the history of photography in the museum and visit Talbot's home, Lacock Abbey.

A true story
In the 16th century Olive Sharington jumped off the tower at Lacock Abbey because she couldn't marry the man she loved. Her skirt acted like a parachute and she floated safely down, landing on top of her loved one and knocking him out! PS Her father relented...

What to see
- In the museum, see the tiny print of the Abbey's oriel window, a copy of the first negative photograph. Picturesque medieval half-timbered houses in the village. Not surprisingly, Lacock has starred in TV and film productions such as *Emma*, the *Harry Potter* films and, most recently, the *Cranford Chronicles*.

What to do
- Explore the Abbey with help from the children's quiz.
- Enjoy a picnic in the paddock opposite visitor reception where there's a small play area in the adjacent playing field.

Special events
Young visitors have recently enjoyed live historical re-enactment days, woodland trails, circus activities, an Easter-egg hunt, Artrageous events, family learning weekends and a production of 'Robin Hood'.

Lacock, nr Chippenham,
Wiltshire, SN15 2LG
01249 730459

OPENING TIMES
Museum
23 Feb 08–2 Nov 08
11am–5:30pm Mon–Sun
8 Nov 08–21 Dec 08
11am–4pm Sat, Sun
3 Jan 08–15 Feb 08
11am–4pm Sat, Sun
Grounds/cloisters
1 Mar 08–2 Nov 08
11am–5:30pm Mon–Sun
Abbey
15 Mar 08–2 Nov 08
13pm–5:30pm Mon, Wed, Thu,
Fri, Sat, Sun
Shop
23 Feb 08–14 Mar 08
11am–4pm Mon–Sun
15 Mar 08–2 Nov 08
10am–5:30pm Mon–Sun
3 Nov 08–15 Feb 08
11am–4pm Mon–Sun

Notes
Museum, Abbey & Grounds closed Good Fri, but High Street shop open. Museum (only) open winter weekends (11am–4pm), but closed 22 Dec–2 Jan 09 incl. High Street shop closed 25, 26 Dec and 1 Jan 09. Admission by timed ticket to the Abbey may operate on BH weekends.

Lanhydrock

Historic house Garden Park Countryside

Bodmin, Cornwall, PL30 5AD
01208 265950

OPENING TIMES
House
15 Mar 08–30 Sep 08
11am–5:30pm Tue, Wed, Thu,
Fri, Sat, Sun
1 Oct 08–4 Nov 08 11am–5pm
Tue, Wed, Thu, Fri, Sat, Sun
Garden
All year 10am–6pm Mon–Sun
Plant centre
1 Mar 08–14 Mar 08
11am–4pm Mon–Sun
15 Mar 08–30 Sep 08
11am–5:30pm Mon–Sun
1 Oct 08–2 Nov 08 11am–5pm
Mon–Sun
Shop and refreshments
2 Feb 08–3 Feb 08 11am–4pm
Sat, Sun
9 Feb 08–14 Mar 08
11am–4pm Mon–Sun
15 Mar 08–30 Sep 08
11am–5:30pm Mon–Sun
1 Oct 08–2 Nov 08 11am–5pm
Mon–Sun
3 Nov 08–24 Dec 08
11am–4pm Mon–Sun

Notes
Open BH Mons. Refreshments:
open 10:30 17 March–4 Nov.
Shop and restaurant are inside
the tariff area.

Lanhydrock is a magnificent Victorian country house, with servants' quarters, gardens and loads of period 'Upstairs/Downstairs' atmosphere. It is set in over 360 hectares (900 acres) of woods and parklands, and there are many different footpaths and trails. An earlier house burnt down in 1881, although a 17th-century wing with a 29m (32yd) long gallery remains. The present 19th-century building featured the latest in mod cons – central heating.

Picture this
Lanhydrock and its grounds starred in the film of *Twelfth Night* with Helena Bonham-Carter. It was dressed up a bit for the film – there was a temporary grotto built from sea scallop shells, and flowers, leaves and vines were strewn about inside to make it look dreamy and romantic.

What to see
- Mythical beasts and Old Testament characters carved into the Long Gallery ceiling.
- Lots of Victorian toys in the nursery.
- A moose head and a great big fishy pike.

What to do
- Visit over 50 rooms, packed with portraits and trophies, and an authentic kitchen complete with spits and ranges.

- Find out about our dormouse monitoring programme.
- Go mad in the adventure playground with wobbly bridge, scramble nets and animal sculptures.
- Pianists may play the piano in the Long Gallery Special Events.
- Join in many family and holiday activities, including pond dipping, kite making, tractor rides and other events. Get in touch to find out when they're on.

Special events
Easter-egg trails, children's holiday activities, estate walks, Halloween and Christmas family events, and family fun day in the summer.

By the way...
- In spring you can tiptoe through the bluebell woods. Pick up a leaflet on walks in the grounds.
- There are some stairs, but we have wheelchairs and alternative routes for those who need them.
- It's quite a walk from the car park to the house, though we have a drop-off point.

Lydford Gorge

Countryside River Waterfall

The Stables, Lydford Gorge,
Lydford, nr Okehampton,
Devon, EX20 4BH
01822 820320

OPENING TIMES
Gorge/shop/tearoom
15 Feb 08–14 Mar 08
11am–3:30pm Fri, Sat, Sun
15 Mar 08–5 Oct 08
10am–5pm Mon–Sun
6 Oct 08–2 Nov 08 10am–4pm
Mon–Sun
Gorge/shop
3 Nov 08–28 Dec 08
11am–3:30pm Fri, Sat, Sun
Tearoom
3 Nov 08–28 Dec 08
11am–3:30pm Sat, Sun
**Gorge (waterfall entrance
only)**
29 Dec 08–31 Jan 08
11am–3:30pm Mon–Sun

Notes
Please tel. for details of winter
opening times.

This is the deepest gorge in south-west England, stretching some 2.5km (1½ miles) from the spiralling whirlpool known as the Devil's Cauldron to a 30m (90ft) cascade called the White Lady Waterfall at the other end. Older children will love the exciting paths, though you will definitely want to hold on to toddlers and younger children in some sections. This is one of the few venues that is made more spectacular after a few weeks of British rain.

Into the ravine
During the 17th century Lydford Gorge was infamous for being the hide-out of a large family of outlaws, the Gubbins, who terrorised the neighbourhood and stole sheep from the farms of Dartmoor. In the 19th century, when wealthy people couldn't go on the 'Grand Tour' of Europe because of the Napoleonic War, Lydford proved a good substitute tourist adventure, and has been an attraction ever since.

What to see
- Variety of wildlife: from glamourous butterflies, dragonflies and dazzling damselflies to creepy bugs and beetles hiding under the fallen trees and logs.
- Watch out for woodland and river birds, including the dipper bobbing by the river.
- Check out the 'what to look for' board at the entrance. You can't miss the thunderous White Lady Waterfall, which cascades 30m (90ft). And you'll definitely hear the thundering Devil's Cauldron.

What to do
- Take a short circular walk to the waterfall and Cauldron or a 4.8km (3 mile) circular walk of the whole gorge.
- Walk out over the bubbling Devil's Cauldron.
- Watch the wildlife.

Special events
There's a lot going on at Lydford for all the family. Past events include sculpture-making days, autumnal woodland walks, fungi forays and special storytelling and trails for children, with some very spooky items hidden along the way. Some events are free with admission.

By the way...
- The walking is an adventure trail, so it's not ideal for anyone with a heart complaint or other health issues, or for very young children. Dogs are welcome, if kept on a lead. Get more information on the walks from visitor reception at either entrance. There's a small shop, tearoom and a good picnic spot at the waterfall entrance.

Overbeck's

Historic house Garden Coastline Museum

Visit this elegant Edwardian house and gardens to see the weird and wonderful artefacts collected by scientist and inventor Otto Overbeck. Explore 3 hectares (7 acres) of beautiful exotic gardens and admire the stunning view over the Salcombe estuary, or join the kids in following tracker packs and trails. The staff are friendly, and so is Fred the ghost, who you might find if you look carefully.

Don't try this one at home
One of Otto's more ambitious inventions was 'the popular rejuvenator', meant to make people look young again by giving them an electric shock. Check it out in the Staircase Hall – but we don't recommend you plug it in, however much you'd like to recapture your youth!

What to see
- Shark's teeth, a crocodile skull, bird's eggs and even hyena droppings in Overbeck's strange natural-history collection
- Ship-building tools and model boats, including one of the Phoenix, built at Salcombe in 1836
- Dolls, dolls' houses and tin soldiers.
- Real orange trees, a Japanese banana plant in the conservatory and a Japanese banana plant in the exotic gardens.

What to do
- Follow clues to the secret children's room crammed with old toys.
- Go on a ghost hunt for Fred the friendly ghost.
- Ask to hear the polyphon – a gigantic old-fashioned musical jukebox (a bit bigger than a CD player).
- Create a miniature Overbeck's with our magnetic dolls' house.
- Explore the gardens for exotic fruits on our Hungry Explorers Trail.
- Any one for a game of croquet? On Fridays, come and play our special animal croquet and see how many animals you collect.

Special events
Watch out for special events celebrating 60 years of Overbeck's being open to the public.

Sharpitor, Salcombe,
Devon, TQ8 8LW
01548 842893

OPENING TIMES
Garden
1 Feb 08–8 Feb 08 10am–5pm
Mon, Tue, Wed, Thu, Fri, Sun
9 Feb 08–24 Feb 08
10am–5pm Mon–Sun
25 Feb 08–30 Jun 08
10am–5pm Mon, Tue, Wed,
Thu, Fri, Sun
1 Jul 08–31 Aug 08 10am–5pm
Mon–Sun
1 Sep 08–2 Nov 08 10am–5pm
Mon, Tue, Wed, Thu, Fri, Sun
3 Nov 08–31 Jan 08
10am–5pm Mon, Tue, Wed,
Thu, Fri
House & shop
15 Mar 08–30 Jun 08
11am–5pm Mon, Tue, Wed,
Thu, Fri, Sun
1 Jul 08–31 Aug 08 11am–5pm
Mon–Sun
1 Sep 08–2 Nov 08 11am–5pm
Mon, Tue, Wed, Thu, Fri, Sun
Tearoom
9 Feb–24 Feb 08 11am–4pm
Sat, Sun
15 Mar 08–30 Jun 08
11am–4:15pm Mon, Tue, Wed,
Thu, Fri, Sun

Notes
Open Sats of BH weekends.
Closed Christmas Day, Boxing Day and New Year's Day.
Garden closes dusk, if earlier.

St Michael's Mount

Castle Garden Coastline

South West

Marazion, nr Penzance,
Cornwall, TR17 OHS
01736 710507/01736 710265

OPENING TIMES
1 Jul 08–31 Aug 08
10:30am–5pm Mon, Tue, Wed,
Thu, Fri, Sun
1 Sep 08–2 Nov 08
10:30am–5pm Mon, Tue, Wed,
Thu, Fri, Sun
16 Mar 08–30 Jun 08
10:30am–5pm Mon, Tue, Wed,
Thu, Fri, Sun

Notes
Last admission 45 mins before
castle closing time. Sufficient
time should be allowed for
travel from the mainland. Castle
open during winter months for
guided tours. Private garden
open weekdays in May and
June; Thu and Fri July–Oct.
Special garden tours some
evenings – see local information
or website.

What could be more mysterious and romantic than a medieval church and castle perched on a rocky island? At low tide you can walk over the historic causeway, or you can take a boat trip when the tide is up. The oldest buildings date from the 12th-century Benedictine priory, and the more recent castle is still lived in by the Aubyn Family who acquired the island after the Civil War.

Now that's sleep-walking
Legend has it that the mount was built by the Giant Cormoran, who had a nasty habit of stealing people's sheep for his tea. Jack, a local lad, decided to catch him out. He dug a big hole in the path from the castle, then blew on his horn to wake Cormoran up. The sleepy giant stumbled right into the pit.

What to see
- Interesting rooms from many different eras, and lots of winding corridors, nooks and crannies.
- The door to the dungeon – in the church where they found a skeleton 2.3m (7ft) tall – maybe it's sleepy old Cormoran.

What to do
- Make a wish on the wishing stone by the church steps.
- Clamber up the cobbled paths, including the garden trail – some are quite steep, so wear your walking shoes.
- Try the quiz book (best for older children).

Special events
Please see the website for details.

By the way...
- Baby-changing facilities and children's menu in the Sail Loft Restaurant. Please note: the site is steep in parts and with cobbled and uneven surfaces.

Saltram

Historic house Garden Park

Saltram stands high above the River Plym in a rolling and wooded landscaped park. With its magnificent white exterior and grand design you could be forgiven for thinking it's the biggest wedding cake in the world. Inside it's full of opulent plasterwork and interiors designed by Robert Adam in the late 18th-century.

Sensible choice

Saltram was the film location for *Sense and Sensibility*. You may recognize it as Norland Park, the Dashwoods' home, in the film starring Emma Thompson, Kate Winslet and Hugh Grant, not to mention the dashing Alan Rickman. Sadly, they've all gone now.

What to see

- Fancy ceilings and even fancier Chinese wallpapers.
- Peek at the paintings – including some rather good ones by Sir Joshua Reynolds.
- An orangery, and several strange little buildings in the garden.

What to do

- Imagine sitting down with the Dashwoods (or with Alan or Kate...) in that swanky dining room.
- Explore the good cycle paths and walks in the parkland.
- Visit the art gallery, which sells local arts and crafts.

Special events

Easter trails, craft fairs, summer school holiday activities and Halloween event. Contact us for details.

By the way...

- You'll find baby-changing facilities, a children's play area and children's menu in the licenced restaurant. Wheelchairs can be booked.

Plympton, Plymouth,
Devon, PL7 1UH
01752 333500

OPENING TIMES
House
21 Mar 08–2 Nov 08
12am–4:30pm Mon, Tue, Wed, Thu, Sat, Sun
Park
All year dawn–dusk Mon–Sun
Catering
1 Feb 08–20 Mar 08
11am–4pm Mon, Tue, Wed, Thu, Sat, Sun
21 Mar 08–2 Nov 08
11am–5pm Mon–Sun
3 Nov 08–31 Jan 08
11am–4pm Mon, Tue, Wed, Thu, Sat, Sun
Shop/garden/gallery
1 Feb 08–20 Mar 08
11am–4pm Mon, Tue, Wed, Thu, Sat, Sun
21 Mar 08–2 Nov 08
11am–5pm Mon, Tue, Wed, Thu, Sat, Sun
3 Nov 08–31 Jan 08
11am–4pm Mon, Tue, Wed, Thu, Sat, Sun

Notes
Admission by timed ticket. Open Good Friday. Last admission to house 45 mins before closing. Shop/gallery/garden closed 24–26 Dec and 2 Jan. Catering closed 25 and 26th Dec. House opening date 21 March subject to completion of rewiring project. Please tel. to confirm.

Trelissick Garden

Garden Park Countryside Coastline River Beach

Feock, nr Truro,
Cornwall, TR3 6QL
01872 862090

OPENING TIMES
1 Feb 08–2 Nov 08
10:30am–5:30pm Mon–Sun
3 Nov 08–23 Dec 08
11am–4pm Mon–Sun
27 Dec 08–31 Dec 08
11am–4pm Mon, Tue, Wed,
Sat, Sun
2 Jan 08–31 Jan 08
11am–4pm Mon–Sun
Woodland walks
All year Mon–Sun

Notes
Closes dusk if earlier.

These famous gardens are very special, with tranquil terraces and glorious views. Wander in this peaceful, colourful environment, then pop into the shop, buy a plant or two, and have a sit down at the restaurant.

Plants with attitude
All kinds of exotic plants here, including skunk cabbage (now, guess why!), Australian tree ferns (no, they don't wear cork hats) and lichen-covered logs. Of course, we have lots of nice blossoms too.

What to see
- A babbling brook weaving through the watercress beds in Namphillow Wood.
- Tiny escape ladders for hedgehogs by the cattle grids!
- Many river birds – look out for cormorants sunning themselves to dry their wings. Why not make it a 'green' day out and travel by boat from Truro, Falmouth or St Mawes (May to September)?

What to do
- Find the Celtic Cross Summerhouse. A priest would preach to the fishermen here – do you think they stopped fishing?
- Picnic on the lawns across the bridge from the Dell – it's a particularly lovely spot.
- Work out the time from the sundial in the scented garden. You will need to know your Roman numerals!

Special events
We have family-friendly activities all year, including Easter-egg hunts and theatrical events during the holidays. Call us to find out what's on.

By the way...
- The house isn't open to the public but there is a shop, art gallery, plant sales and self-service restaurant with additional external seating in the courtyard. Pushchairs and back-carriers are fine, and we have changing facilities. Pick up a woodland walk leaflet.

Best of the Rest

A la Ronde

Built with stunning views over the Exmouth estuary A la Ronde was the creative project of two 18th-century ladies well ahead of their time. Jane and Mary Parminter filled the house with curiosities, from cabinets filled with shells, miniatures and even a flea trap, to the drawing room decorated with feathers from game birds and the famous shell gallery – an entire room decorated with shells and feathers so delicate that it can only be fully viewed with the interactive remote cameras. There is a children's trail around the house and family events throughout the year: craft activities, Easter-egg hunt, quiz trails, story telling, Father's Day walks, or you could make a piece of art inspired by the property for exhibition.

Contact: Summer Lane, Exmouth, Devon EX8 5BD. Tel. 01395 265514 **Opening times: Shop/grounds** 15 Mar 08–2 Nov 08, 10:30am–5:30pm, Mon, Tue, Wed, Sat, Sun **House** 15 Mar 08–2 Nov 08, 11am–5pm, Mon, Tue, Wed, Sat, Sun **Tearoom** 15 Mar 08–2 Nov 08, 10:30am–5pm, Mon, Tue, Wed, Sat, Sun **Notes:** Due to the size and unusual layout of the house, small delays may occur at busy times.

Newark Park

A lived-in house with large garden, wonderful views and countryside walks. Families can enjoy a picnic in the wild, romantic garden and go on long walks in the surrounding countryside and spot a wide variety of wildlife including peafowl in the grounds. There is a children's quiz, Easter trail and even a Tiny Tots Teddy Bear hunt and picnic.

Contact: Ozleworth, Wotton-under-Edge, Gloucestershire, GL12 7PZ. Tel. 01453 842644 **Opening times:** 19 Mar 08–29 May 08 11am–5pm Wed, Thu; 1 Jun 08–2 Nov 08 11am–5pm Wed, Thu, Sat, Sun **Notes:** Open BH Mons and Good Fri 11am–5pm. Closes dusk if earlier. Also open Easter Sat and Sun 11am–5pm.

Studland Beach & Nature Reserve

Take the children for a fabulous day out on this friendly sandy beach which stretches three miles from South Haven Point to Old Harry Rocks with shallow bathing water for children. Middle beach, reached from Knoll or Middle car parks, is particularly good for families. Bring a picnic and buckets and spades and spend the whole day on the sands. In the school holidays children's events take place including beach discovery walks.

Contact: Purbeck Estate Office, Studland, Swanage, Dorset BH19 3AX. Tel. 01929 450259 **Opening times: Beach** All year Mon–Sun **Shop/café** 1 Mar 08–20 Mar 08 10am–4pm* Mon–Sun; 21 Mar 08–29 Jun 08 9:30am–5pm* Mon–Sun **Shop** 30 Jun 08–1 Sep 08 9:30am–6pm Mon–Sun **Café** 30 Jun 08–1 Sep 08 9am–7pm Mon–Sun **Shop/café** 2 Sep 08–26 Oct 08 9:30am–5pm Mon–Sun; 27 Oct 08–31 Jan 08 10am–4pm* Mon – Sun **Notes** *Shop/café closes 1hr later at weekends. Shop and café open hours may be longer in fine weather and shorter in poor weather. Visitor centre, shop and café closed 25 and 26 Dec. **Car parks can be very full in peak season**.

Trerice

Trerice has a great reputation for making families feel welcome. Let the staff lead you 'up the garden path' with their garden trail, or do the house quizzes for both young and older children. Rub an Arundell in the brass rubbing room or play Kayles (Cornish skittles) and Slapcock (Tudor badminton) on the bowling green. The gardens and orchard are very pretty, including an award-winning experimental Tudor garden developed by children from the local primary school and an Elizabethan maze mown into the grass. There is an annual Easter-egg hunt and living-history and craft activities on selected days. Check the National Trust website for details of further events.

Contact: Kestle Mill, nr Newquay, Cornwall, TR8 4PG. Tel. 01637 875404 **Opening times: House/shop** 9 Mar 08–2 Nov 08 11am–5pm Mon, Tue, Wed, Thu, Fri, Sun **Notes** Tearoom and garden open from 10:30am. Last serving in tearoom 4:30pm. Garden, tearoom, shop and Great Hall open 6–7, 13–14, 20–21 Dec, 11am–3pm, Sat and Sun.

Coastal Walk – Snapes Point

South Devon

An easy walk in a gentle landscape beside the beautiful Kingsbridge Estuary. This area of coast is known as a ria. It formed when valleys were flooded as sea levels rose in peri-glacial conditions at the end of the last ice age. The deep-water estuary is now used for sailing, safe mooring, other watersports and fishing.

Getting there:

Road: A381 to Salcombe and then local roads. Car park at grid reference SX 739 401.

Foot: Part of South West Coast Path, footpaths from Salcombe.

Bus: 164 Totnes-Knightsbridge; 606 Kingsbridge-Salcombe.

Rail: Totnes, Ivybridge.

For public transport information visit www.traveline.org.uk.

Distance: 2.4km (1½ miles).

Terrain and accessibility: Gentle, easy walking conditions. Height gain of 30m (98ft) over the walk. The beach is not suitable for paddling or swimming.

Directions and points of interest:

Follow the path from the car park down to the river. Continue on this path, following the map shown opposite (the numbers on the map correspond to the numbers below) and look out for the following features:

1. Viewpoint over the estuary. The estuary is particularly sheltered at this point with safe moorings for boats. At low water in winter, wader birds such as redshanks, dunlins and turnstones search for food on the shore.
2. Tosnos Point. The field margins are managed for wildlife under the Countryside Stewardship Scheme. The scheme targets farmland

birds especially cirl buntings, which like to feed for insects and seeds close to the hedges.

3 Viewpoint over the town of Salcombe and Town Quay. At high water, many boats use the quay to drop off and pick up people using the town. There are boat repair yards and chandlers close to the shore.

4 Site of an old carriageway built in 1800 for the Salcombe-Kingsbridge railway. Return to the car park via the path, which passes the Snapes Manor.

Property contact details: 01548 562344

Maps and start grid ref: OS Landranger 202 gr SX 739 401, Explorer 20 E&W.

Facilities available: Car parks, toilets, pubs, shops and cafés available in Salcombe.

National Trust properties nearby: Coastal properties. Houses and gardens include Greenway, Overbeck's and Saltram.

Countryside Walk – Sherbourne Park Estate Gloucestershire

Sherborne Park Estate, set in lovely rolling countryside and the village of Sherborne next to the river Windrush, offers something for all. This sign-posted walk takes you through a woodland sculpture trail, farmland, woods and down to the village of Sherborne. It is a fun walk for people of all ages.

Getting there:
Road: 4.8km (3 miles) east of Northleach; approach from A40 only.
Bus: Swanbrook 53, Oxford to Gloucester, one mile walk to Lodge Park from the bus stop.
Rail: Bus passes Gloucester station and picks up close to Oxford station. For public transport information visit www.traveline.org.uk.

Distance: Approximately 4.8km (3 miles); allow 1½ hours to complete.

Terrain and accessibility: Easy walking over mainly grassy paths.

Directions and points of interest:
Follow the map shown opposite. The numbers on the map correspond to the numbers below.
1 Start at the Sherbourne car park. The paths are colour coded – take the purple route.
2 Visit Sherborne village and the pleasure grounds.
3 Ice house.

4 The trees along this part of the walk are ancient trees, usually called 'veteran trees'.

5 This part of the walk is a great place to spot wildlife, including buzzards, foxes, hares, stoats, weasels and deer.

6 Sculpture Trail. Here the purple route turns right and links with the blue walk to return to the car park.

Property contact: 01451 844257

Maps and start grid ref: OS 163, SP158143

Facilities available: Parking, toilets (when Lodge Park open), post office in Sherbourne for drinks and snacks. In Northleach, 8.5km (5 miles) away, there are pubs, tearooms and public toilets.

National Trust properties nearby: Chedworth Roman Villa, Ebworth Estate, Woodchester Park, Chastleton House, Hailes Abbey, Snowshill Manor, Rodborough and Minchinhampton Commons.

Historic Landscape Walk – Stonehenge Wiltshire

A short self-guided walk exploring the landscape that surrounds the stones at Stonehenge. This 4km (2½ mile) walk is a must if you enjoy wide open spaces and 'big skies'. A circular route takes in the beauty of the Wiltshire downland as well as passing many prehistoric monuments such as the Cursus Barrow site and the King Barrows. Stonehenge Monument is visible in the distance throughout the walk.

Getting there:
Road: Monument 3km (2 miles) W of Amesbury at junction of A303 with A344/A360.
Foot: Start from the Stonehenge car park at the picnic area.
Bus: Wilts and Dorset 3 Salisbury to Stonehenge.
Rail: Salisbury 15km (9½ miles).
Parking: Stonehenge (and car park) is not a National Trust property; a charge may be made for non-National Trust members.
For public transport information visit www.traveline.org.uk.

Distance: 4km (2½ miles); allow two hours to complete.

Terrain and accessibility: Medium walking. Terrain over well-marked stony and grassy paths.

Directions and points of interest:
Follow the map shown opposite (the numbers on the map correspond to the numbers below). This is a World Heritage Site – as you are following the route, look out for the following features:
1 Start.
2 The Cursus Barrows.
3 Mixed woodland and stunning autumn colour.
4 Kings Barrows Ridge. From here you can return to the main car park as shown on the map, and admire the view over the Stonehenge Monument.

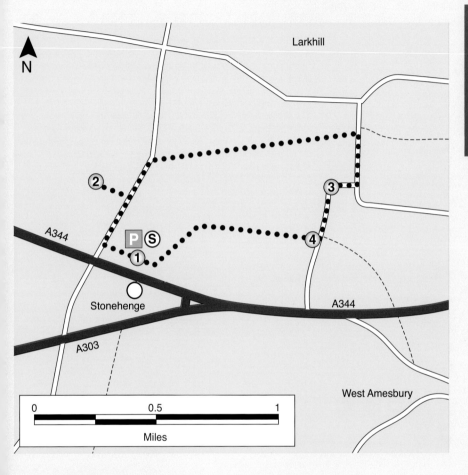

Property contact: 01980 841570

Maps and start grid ref: OS outdoor leisure 184, SU120420

Facilities available: Parking, toilets, shop and refreshments.

National Trust properties nearby: Mompesson House, Stourhead, Little Clarendon, Philipps House, Dinton Woods, Mottisfont Abbey and Avebury.

Ashridge Estate

Countryside Visitor centre

South & South East

Visitor centre, Moneybury Hill,
Ringshall, Berkhamsted,
Hertfordshire, HP4 1LX
01494 755557

OPENING TIMES
Estate
All year Mon–Sun
Visitor centre/shop
15 Mar 08–21 Dec 08
12am–5pm Mon–Sun
Monument
15 Mar 08–26 Oct 08
12am–5pm Sat, Sun
Tearoom
1 Feb 08–29 Feb 08
10am–5pm Tue, Wed, Thu, Fri,
Sat, Sun
15 Mar 08–21 Dec 08
10am–5pm Mon–Sun
31 Dec 08–31 Jan 08
10am–4pm Tue, Wed, Thu, Fri,
Sat, Sun

Notes
Open BH Mons and Good Fri:
12am–5pm. Last admission to
Monument 4:30pm Mon–Fri by
arrangement, weather
permitting. Shop and tearoom
close dusk if earlier than 5pm.

About 2025 hectares (5000 acres) of woodland and open
countryside running along the Herts/Bucks borders in the Chiltern
Hills. Take a stroll, or go for something longer – there are more than
enough splendid walks to tire out even the most energetic legs. Why
not bring a picnic, and scrunch around in the leaves in autumn? A
great place for the whole family to get out and about in the fresh air.

Bridge over troubled water?
The Bridgewater Monument in the grounds (near the visitor centre) was
built in memory of the 3rd Duke of Bridgewater, better known as the
Canal Duke. He built the United Kingdom's first canals to get coal from
his mines to Manchester – although some say he actually built his canal
to take his mind off a recent romance with the Duchess of Hamilton!
From the top of the Monument on a clear day, you can see as far as
London and Canary Wharf.

What to see
- Plenty of flora and fauna including fallow and muntjac deer and, if
  you're very lucky, badgers and woodpeckers. Bluebells carpet the
  area in spring and fallen leaves do the same in autumn.

What to do
- For a small fee, climb up the Bridgewater Monument (only 170 steps
  – what do you mean, 'my legs ache!').
- Go for a nature walk – self-guided walks available from the shop,
  including one for Ivinghoe Beacon with a great view of the Chilterns.

Special events
Please contact us for details of our full programme of events for every
age and interest.

By the way...
- We have a wheelchair available and maps of accessible routes on
  the Estate, as well as a number of PMV vehicles. Booking advisable.
  The shop and visitor centre are fully accessible.

Basildon Park

Historic house Garden Park

Basildon Park, a house built in the 18th-century neoclassical style, is a good choice for a Sunday excursion. There's plenty of space to run around and everyone will enjoy glorious walks through the parkland or on the surrounding downland and in the woods at Streatley Hill.

Sticky fingers
There are objects here that visitors can touch and feel. This is unusual for an National Trust house – fragile items usually need protecting.

What to see
- Monkeys, elephants, a leopard and lots of other beasts on a new jungle mural covering the walls and ceiling of the small tearoom.
- An octagonal room with highly coloured Indian scenes on the walls and a ceiling populated with eastern birds.
- Stone dogs on the lawn, brought back from Italy in the 19th century.

What to do
- Touch the patterns in the Shell Room – very trendy in the 18th century.
- Try one of the walks through the park. You'll find a leaflet in the ticket office, or follow the red posts for a short walk, green posts for a longer one.
- See if there are any mini beasts in the dead tree in Pheasant Park. It's been left there to encourage creepy crawlies.

Special events
Basildon Park holds a variety of family-friendly events, including Easter and Halloween trails, and live theatre. Get in touch.

South & South East

Lower Basildon, Reading, Berkshire, RG8 9NR
0118 984 3040

OPENING TIMES
House
19 Mar 08–26 Oct 08
12am–5pm Wed, Thu, Fri, Sat, Sun
10 Dec 08–14 Dec 08
12am–4pm Wed, Thu, Fri, Sat, Sun
Shop
19 Mar 08–26 Oct 08
11am–5pm Wed, Thu, Fri, Sat, Sun
29 Oct 08–21 Dec 08
12am–4pm Wed, Thu, Fri, Sat, Sun
10 Dec 08–14 Dec 08
11am–5pm Wed, Thu, Fri, Sat, Sun
Restaurant/grounds
As house 11am–5pm Wed, Thu, Fri, Sat, Sun

Notes
Open BH Mons. House and shop closes 7pm on 12 Dec. Property closes at 4pm on 15, 16 and 17 Aug for firework concerts.

Bateman's

Historic house Mill Garden

Burwash, Etchingham,
East Sussex, TN19 7DS
01435 882302

OPENING TIMES
House
15 Mar 08–2 Nov 08
11am–5pm Mon, Tue, Wed,
Sat, Sun
Garden/tearoom/shop
1 Mar 08–9 Mar 08 11am–4pm
Sat, Sun
15 Mar 08–2 Nov 08
11am–5pm* Mon, Tue, Wed,
Sat, Sun
5 Nov 08–23 Dec 08
11am–4pm Wed, Thu, Fri, Sat,
Sun

Notes
Open Good Fri 11am–5pm. The
mill grinds corn most Weds and
Sats at 2pm. ***Shop closes
5:30 March–Oct**. Shop,
tearoom and garden open 22
and 23 Dec.

Did you like the film *The Jungle Book*? You'll be interested in this
Jacobean house, home of Rudyard Kipling, who wrote the book it's
based on. It's been arranged just as it was when he left, with his pen
in the inkwell awaiting new stories. Even his 1928 Rolls Royce
Phantom is outside waiting to rev up.

Why why?
Kipling's elder daughter was called 'Elsie Why?' by the family because
she was always asking questions. Do you know anyone like that?

What to see
- The original illustrations for *The Jungle Book*, Oriental rugs and
  artifacts, brought home by Kipling. Find the sundial in the garden.

What to do
- Visit the water mill, which generated electricity for the whole house.
  We grind corn there most Wednesdays and Saturday, at 2pm.
- Walk round the pond designed by Kipling to be shallow so that
  children could fall in safely, but don't try it!
- Hunt out the Kipling family initials, carved into the porch.

Special events
Recently we have had folk music in the garden, a craft fair and painting
for children, with the cost usually included in the admission price.

By the way...
- We have a dog crèche where you can leave your dog, and a picnic
  area near the car park.
- You can book a wheelchair, but there are some steps.
- There are many interesting objects in the house that you can touch
  (please ask).

Bodiam Castle

Castle Countryside Moat

A real 14th-century castle – with turrets, moat and all – situated by the River Rother in East Sussex. There are medieval battlements and ramparts galore, and spiral staircases to explore. One of the most famous and atmospheric places in Britain, Bodiam will leave a lasting impression on all the family.

My other house is a castle

In 1385 Sir Edward Dalyngrigge was given permission to fortify his house against the invasion of France. But he decided to build a castle near his house instead. That's some extension...

What to see

- Four cylindrical towers at each corner, and four rectangular ones in between.
- Murder holes in the roof of the gatehouse, from which people dropped boiling water on the unsuspecting enemy.
- A World War II pill box where more recent soldiers lay in wait.

What to do

- Climb the towers, walk the battlements and look out for enemy soldiers. Imagine living in the castle or staying in one of the guest rooms. Explore the nooks and crannies around the ruins.
- During school holidays, children can try on replica armour.
- Tracker packs are available for children.

Special events

We often have family and children's activities, including medieval weekends. Steam trains run on the Kent & East Sussex Railway right up to Bodiam, in season (not National Trust).

By the way...

- Dogs in the grounds are fine, but please keep them on a lead. Pushchairs are admitted. Special menus in the tearoom, including dairy-free. Stairs to upper floors and the grounds can be muddy.

South & South East

Bodiam, nr Robertsbridge, East Sussex, TN32 5UA
01580 830196

OPENING TIMES
Castle
1 Feb 08–15 Feb 08
10:30am–5pm Sat, Sun
16 Feb 08–31 Oct 08
10:30am–6pm Mon–Sun
1 Nov 08–31 Jan 08
10:30am–4pm Sat, Sun
Shop/tearoom
1 Feb 08–15 Feb 08
10:30am–4pm Sat, Sun
16 Feb 08–31 Oct 08
10:30am–5pm Mon–Sun
1 Nov 08–24 Dec 08
10:30am–4pm Wed, Thu, Fri, Sat, Sun
27 Dec 08–31 Jan 08
10:30am–4pm Sat, Sun

Notes
Last admission to castle 1hr before closing. Castle closes dusk if earlier than that. Historical re-enactment 5 and 6 July. Additional admission charge for members and non-members.

Box Hill

Countryside Nature reserve Information centre

The Old Fort, Box Hill
Road, Box Hill, Tadworth,
Surrey, KT20 7LB
01306 885502

OPENING TIMES
All year Mon–Sun
Servery
1 Feb 08–29 Mar 08
10am–4pm Mon–Sun
30 Mar 08–26 Oct 08
9am–5pm Mon–Sun
27 Oct 08–31 Jan 08
10am–4pm Mon–Sun
Shop/information centre
1 Feb 08–29 Mar 08
30 Mar 08–26 Oct 08
11am–5pm Mon–Sun
27 Oct 08–31 Jan 08
11am–4pm Mon–Sun

Notes
Closes dusk if earlier. Shop,
information centre and servery
closed 25/26 Dec and 1 Jan 09.

You can't beat flying a kite up here on a billowy day, with gorgeous views over the South Downs and tons of fresh air. Bring a picnic and let the dog off (except where there are sheep), and admire this outstanding area of woodland and chalk downland. Hop up to the top for a peek at a fort dating from the 1890s.

Boxed in?
Box Hill got its name from the box trees which have grown here since at least the 16th century. Unfortunately they do pong a bit if you sniff them – some say it's a bit like tomcats. On a more savoury note – it was here that Jane Austen set the ill-fated picnic in her novel *Emma*.

What to see
- Tons of wildlife, including butterflies, tawny owls and kestrels. Look for the tracks of badgers and foxes, and you might see some if you're lucky.
- See if you can spot tiny bee orchids or wild strawberry plants in June and July.
- Scrunch around in autumn leaves later on in the year.

What to do
- Stretch your legs walking through beautiful woods and grassy areas, or kick a ball around.
- Visit our information centre at the summit and see natural exhibits like a badger's skull or a birds' nest.

Special events
A host of outdoor events take place every year at Box Hill. Get in touch to find out details.

By the way...
- South scarp is very steep. If you have mobility problems, try the accessible paths along the North Downs Way. The servery has snacks and drinks, but isn't a full restaurant. We have baby-changing facilities; pushchairs are fine here, too.

Chartwell

Historic house Garden

The home for 40 years of Sir Winston Churchill, and the place where he and his wife Clementine brought up their children and where they were frequently visited by their grandchildren. The house is full of family mementoes and photographs, while the grounds contain reminders of the many ways in which the Churchills and their guests enjoyed their surroundings. Ducks, geese and black swans still swim on the lakes, and fish like the ones Sir Winston used to feed are in the ponds. The playhouse, which he built for his young daughters, is still there in the kitchen garden, for 'children only' to enter and enjoy.

Prime Minister's pets

Sir Winston had a great love of many pets who gave him pleasure and company when he chose to escape for a while from other people. The gravestones of some of them can be seen in the garden, and one, his cat Jock, held a special place in his affections. Jock was a favourite companion, so much so that Churchill made it known that there should always be a similar marmalade cat living comfortably at Chartwell. Today Jock IV keeps up the tradition, having succeeded Jock III in 2005. Like his predecessors he shares a flat in the house at Chartwell with members of National Trust staff – or perhaps they share it with him – and from there he has the run of the extensive and beautiful grounds from his special cat flat. He is surely a cat who is the envy of all others.

What to see

- The 'Marycot' play house, which Sir Winston Churchill built himself for his young daughters to play in.
- The fish pond with its Golden Orfe, large fish like the ones Sir Winston used to feed from the box beside his seat.
- The pet graves, with the names of two favourite dogs and one very special cat.

What to do

- Follow the special trails through the house, garden and studio. Look out for items, plants and paintings and answer the quiz questions. Enjoy the open spaces of the slopes above the lake and spot the many kinds of birds in or around it.
- Walk through the woods of the Chartwell estate.

Special events

Family picnic days in summer with music on the lawn, displays and children's craft activities. Occasional guided walks with seasonal themes. Father Christmas days in the restaurant at Christmas.

By the way...

- Quizzes are based on observation of features encountered in the course of a visit and are suitable for children and their parents to do together.
- There are many steps, slopes and areas of open water in the grounds (some deep). Adults must accompany children at all times.

Mapleton Road, Westerham,
Kent, TN16 1PS
01732 866368

OPENING TIMES
House/garden
15 Mar 08–29 Aug 08
11am–5pm Wed–Sun
1 Jul 08–31 Aug 08 11am–5pm
Tue, Wed, Thu, Fri, Sat, Sun
3 Sep 08–2 Nov 08 11am–5pm
Wed, Thu, Fri, Sat, Sun
Restaurant
1 Feb 08–14 Mar 08
11am–3pm Wed–Sun
15 Mar 08–29 Jun 08
10:30am–5pm Wed–Sun
1 Jul 08–31 Aug 08
10:30am–5pm Tue–Sun
3 Sep 08–2 Nov 08
10:30am–5pm Wed–Sun
5 Nov 08–21 Dec 08
11am–4pm Wed–Sun
27 Dec 08–31 Jan 08
11am–3pm Wed–Sun
Shop/garden
1 Feb 08–14 Mar 08
11am–3pm Wed–Sun
15 Mar 08–29 Jun 08
11am–5:30pm Wed–Sun

Notes
Admission by timed ticket to house, which should be purchased immediately on arrival but cannot be booked. Open BH Mons. Last admission 45mins before closing. Car park closes 5:30pm (3:30pm from 3 Nov–31 Jan 09) or dusk if earlier and is closed on 25 Dec. Garden open Nov–March, as above, weather and conditions permitting.

Claremont Landscape Garden

Garden Lake Amphitheatre

Portsmouth Road, Esher,
Surrey, KT10 9JG
01372 467806

OPENING TIMES
Garden
1 Feb 08–31 Mar 08
10am–5pm Tue, Wed, Thu, Fri,
Sat, Sun
1 Apr 08–31 Oct 08
10am–6pm Mon–Sun
1 Nov 08–28 Feb 08
10am–5pm Tue, Wed, Thu, Fri,
Sat, Sun
Shop/tearoom
1 Feb 08–24 Feb 08
11am–4pm Fri, Sat, Sun
25 Feb 08–31 Mar 08
11am–4pm Wed, Thu, Fri, Sat,
Sun
1 Apr 08–31 Oct 08
11am–5pm Wed, Thu, Fri, Sat,
Sun
1 Nov 08–21 Dec 08
11am–4pm Wed, Thu, Fri, Sat,
Sun
9 Jan 08–31 Jan 11am–4pm
Fri, Sat, Sun

Notes
Open all year (closed Mons 1
Nov–31 March). Closes dusk if
earlier. Closed 25 Dec. Open 1
Jan 09 10am–4pm. Belvedere
Tower open first weekend each
month April–Oct and New
Year's Day. Late-night openings
14, 21, 28 June until 9pm.
Shop and tearoom close 1hr
before garden, and may close
early in bad weather.

These elegant gardens were begun in around 1715 and there are so
many interesting features to explore in its 20 hectares (50 acres).
There's a lovely serpentine lake, and island with a pavilion on it, a
grotto, and an amphitheatre in the grass.

Gardeners' world
Some of the country's greatest gardeners had a say in designing
Claremont – fortunately not all at the same time. Sir John Vanbrugh,
Charles Bridgeman and 'Capability' Brown, to name a few.

What to see
- Lots of ducks near the lake – conveniently close to the car park.
- The grass amphitheatre – a kind of outdoor auditorium. Try sitting
  down up at the top and getting someone to talk at you from the
  bottom. Open-air concerts are held in summer; ring us for details.

What to do
- Have a picnic, or grab a cuppa in the tearoom.
- Go for a ramble – there are children's trails – and the lake one is
  suitable for buggies.

Special events
Get in touch or visit the National Trust website for details.

By the way...
- Dogs need to be on a lead, and can visit only between Nov and the
  end of March at the moment. There are some steep slopes but we
  have an accessible route. There are baby-changing facilities, and
  pushchairs are fine too.

Claydon House

Historic house Garden Park Countryside Museum Lake

Florence Nightingale was once a regular visitor to this charming Georgian country house, home of the Verney family, and you can see mementoes of her visits. There are also fascinating associations with the Civil and Crimean Wars, including letters from Florrie written during the period. And inside there's some fancy Chinese décor.

You've gotta hand it to him...

A rather gruesome tale, this. Apparently Sir Edmund Verney, the first owner, was King Charles I's standard-bearer. At the battle of Edgehill in 1642, his hand was chopped off by the Roundheads so that they could grab the flag. The rest of his body was never found – some say he's still hanging around in the house, hoping his hand will turn up.

What to see

- Carvings of Asian birds and scaly monsters, and the phoenix in the Verney coat of arms – Harry Potter would be at home here!
- A huge 19th-century gamelan (set of Asian gongs) in the museum.

What to do

- Take a tour of the house with the children's quiz.
- Wander around in the unspoilt countryside outside, and maybe get a picnic hamper from the restaurant
- Have a peek inside All Saints' Church, in the grounds.

By the way...

- Baby-changing facilities and family-friendly guides are available.
- A children's menu is provided in the Carriage House restaurant (not National Trust). Opening hours same as house.
- There's a handling collection of objects to touch and feel.
- Wheelchairs are available – please book – and you get in for half-price if you can't make the stairs to the upper floors.

Middle Claydon, nr Buckingham, Buckinghamshire, MK18 2EY
01494 755561

OPENING TIMES
15 Mar 08–2 Nov 08
1pm–5pm* Mon, Tue, Wed, Sat, Sun
Church/second-hand bookshop
As house 12am–5pm

Notes
Open Good Fri 1pm–5pm.
*Closes dusk if earlier. Private garden (not National Trust – additional charge applies). Special Christmas opening Dec 6/7, 13/14, 20/21 1pm–4pm.

Dapdune Wharf, River Wey & Godalming Navigations

Countryside River Old barge

Navigations Office and
Dapdune Wharf, Wharf Road,
Guildford, Surrey GU1 4RR
01483 561389

OPENING TIMES
15 Mar 08–2 Nov 08
11am–5pm Mon, Thu, Fri,
Sat, Sun

Notes
River trips 11am–5pm
(conditions permitting). Access
to towpath during daylight
hours all year.

Back in 1653 the Wey was one of the first rivers to be made navigable and today, with its narrowboats and well-maintained towpath, it's a great place for a family adventure. You can clamber aboard *Reliance*, a restored barge, at Dapdune Wharf in Guildford, and boat trips are also available. If you'd rather stay on solid ground, there are some lovely walks on the tow path with friendly pubs and a tearoom nearby.

Beats the train?
The Wey Navigation linked Guildford to Weybridge and is over 19 miles (29km) long. Back in those days, getting goods from A to B involved large commercial barges pulled by horses from the towpath.

What to see
- The inside of the big old barge, *Reliance*.
- Lots of wildlife on the towpath, including kingfishers and roe deer.
- Don't miss our award-winning visitor centre.

What to do
- Guide a model barge through the lock in our interactive model.
- Take a 40-minute boat trip on *Dapdune Belle* (extra charge).
- Go fishing – get a permit from the Environment Agency or one of the angling clubs.

Special events
Easter-egg trails, special Thursday activity days in August, lots of guided walks, including bat walks.

By the way...
- Nearly everything is accessible, maybe with a bit of help from a friend. There's a little shop and tearoom at Dapdune Wharf, and some nice riverside picnic areas.
- Please keep dogs on leads around the wharf.

Hughenden Manor

Historic house Garden Park Countryside Wood

Hughenden Manor was the much-loved country home of 19th-century Conservative Prime Minister, Benjamin Disraeli. Enjoy the manor filled with his pictures, books and furniture, and then take the family for a walk in the gardens and surrounding park and woodland. Be warned – it is very hilly in places. There are often extra children's activities going on.

'We authors, Ma'am'
Disraeli was a great favourite with Queen Victoria, unlike the Liberal Prime Minister, William Gladstone, whom she thought addressed her like a public meeting. Both Disraeli and the Queen had written books – he was a very successful novelist, while she published an account of her travels in Scotland.

What to see
- The secret servants' doors in the dining room (if you can find them).
- Disraeli's own books, all 4,000 of them! On the staircase wall is his 'gallery of friendship', with portraits of his many friends, including the Queen and his devoted wife, Mary Anne.
- A marble copy of Mary Anne's foot – the Queen started a craze for this when she had her children's feet sculpted.
- The German forest planted by the Disraelis.

What to do
- Use the fun children's guide to explore the house and garden.
- Try out the Family Story trail – there's a leaflet to guide you on this ½-hour walk round the estate.
- Go to the church and see the monument put up by Queen Victoria to her favourite Prime Minister.
- Enjoy a scrumptious lunch or tea in the Stableyard Restaurant.

Special events
There are lots of great events at Hughenden. For details, contact the Community Learning Officer. There will be a small charge for most events.

By the way...
- For £3 a day you can hire a super-tough, all-terrain buggy to negotiate the bumpy ground on the estate walks.

High Wycombe,
Buckinghamshire, HP14 4LA
01494 755573

OPENING TIMES
House
1 Mar 08–2 Nov 08 1pm–5pm
Wed, Thu, Fri, Sat, Sun
6 Dec 08–21 Dec 08
12am–3pm Mon, Sat, Sun
Garden
1 Mar 08–2 Nov 08 11am–5pm
Wed, Thu, Fri, Sat, Sun
6 Dec 08–21 Dec 08
11am–3:30pm Mon, Sat, Sun
Park
All year Mon–Sun
Shop/restaurant
1 Mar 08–2 Nov 08 11am–5pm
Wed, Thu, Fri, Sat, Sun
Shop
5 Nov 08–5 Dec 08
11am–3:30pm Wed, Thu, Fri,
Sat, Sun
6 Dec 08–21 Dec 08
11am–3:30pm Mon, Sat, Sun
Restaurant
5 Nov 08–5 Dec 08
11am–3:30pm Sat, Sun
6 Dec 08–21 Dec 08
11am–3:30pm Mon, Sat, Sun

Notes
Admission by timed ticket on Sun, BH weekends and other busy days. Open BH Mons. Last entry 4:30pm or dusk if earlier. Manor tours at 11:30am, limited availability. Walled garden open Thur and Fri. Garden taster tours Wed–Fri, 11.30am and 2pm. Occasional early closing for special events and weddings.

Ightham Mote

Historic house Garden Countryside

Mote Road, Ivy Hatch,
Sevenoaks, Kent, TN15 0NT
01732 810378

OPENING TIMES
House
15 Mar 08–2 Nov 08
11am–5pm Mon, Thu, Fri,
Sat, Sun
Estate
All year dawn–dusk Mon–Sun
Shop/restaurant*/garden
15 Mar 08–2 Nov 08
10:30am–5pm Mon, Thu, Fri,
Sat, Sun
8 Nov 08–21 Dec 08
11am–3pm Thu, Fri, Sat, Sun

Notes
Restaurant open for occasional
themed evenings and for
booked functions. Please tel.
01732 811314 for opening
times of Mote Restaurant and
01732 811203 for shop
opening times outside normal
property hours. Booking at
Mote Restaurant advised winter
& evenings. *Except when
function ongoing. Closed Jan
09. Mote Restaurant is available
for wedding receptions.
Shop/restaurant/partial gardens
open 14 Feb–14 Mar
11am–3pm, Thurs–Sun, except
during restaurant functions
when refreshment kiosk will
open. Partial gardens/courtyard
and ground floor access
Nov/Dec weekends,
11am–3pm. Great Hall dressed
for Christmas during Dec.

Ightham Mote is a romantic moated medieval and Tudor manor
house, built around a courtyard. The Mote started life in 1320 but
has been added to by various owners, including the Selby family,
who lived in it from the end of the Elizabethan period right through
to Victorian times. Over the years it has acquired a painted Tudor
ceiling, a Jacobean fireplace, Chinese 18th-century wallpaper and a
19th-century billiards room.

Concealed shoes
The story goes that at Ightham Mote in the 1870s, workmen found a
seated skeleton of a young woman walled up behind the panelling in
the Great Hall. Henry James, the American author, said that during a
Christmas party there, he 'slept in a room with a ghost and an oubliette
(hiding place) – fortunately the former remained in the latter'. Recent
building works at the property have uncovered many concealed shoes
hidden in walls and under floors. The shoes were part of a superstitious
tradition that tried to secure the wellbeing of the building and its
residents from evil spirits. Come and see some of the shoes on display.

What to see
- Perhaps the only house with a Grade I-listed dog kennel, made in
  1890 for Dido, a St Bernard dog who was so big her food had to be
  served in a washing-up bowl.
- All the owners had different building ideas and no building
  restrictions, so look out for several different types of chimney.
- There's a slit in the wall near the entrance gate, known as a parley
  hole. In medieval days people would post letters or speak through it
  to ask if they could come into the building.

What to do
- Squint through the squint window in the Chapel.
- What on earth is a putlog?

74

- Try to hug the massive sweet chestnut trees, which measure over 8m (23ft) around.
- Explore the gardens, which provided the medieval house with food.

Special events

There are many different events during the season, and quite a few are suitable for all the family. Recent activities have included woodcarving and cookery demonstrations and special drawing workshops for children. Some children's activities involve a small additional fee. It's a good idea to phone first to see what's on. Booking is sometimes necessary for these events.

By the way...

- Ightham Mote was the subject of the largest conservation project ever undertaken by the National Trust on a house of this kind, which started in 1985 and was only finished in 2004.
- Contact us in advance for information on the wide range of touchable objects. There are many scented plants in the garden.
- Wheelchairs are available, as well as portable ramps. Some of the grounds and upper floors of the house are not easily accessible.

Needles Old Battery & New Battery

Countryside Coastline Fort

West High Down, Alum Bay,
Isle of Wight, PO39 0JH
01983 754772

OPENING TIMES
Tearoom
12 Jan 08–14 Mar 08
11am–3pm Sat, Sun
Old Battery/tearoom
15 Mar 08–30 Jun 08
10:30am–5pm Tue, Wed, Thu,
Fri, Sat, Sun
1 Jul 08–31 Aug 08
10:30am–5pm Mon–Sun
1 Sep 08–2 Nov 08
10:30am–5pm Tue, Wed, Thu,
Fri, Sat, Sun
Tearoom
8 Nov 08–14 Dec 08
11am–3pm Sat, Sun
10 Jan 08–31 Jan 08
11am–3pm Sat, Sun
Needles New Battery
15 Mar 08–2 Nov 08
11am–4pm Tue, Sat

Notes
Also open Easter Mon and May
BH weekends. Property closes
in high winds – please tel. on
day of visit to check.

This Victorian fort is perched on the tip of the Isle of Wight in a stunning position overlooking The Needles rocks. If you have an interest in guns, ships and military matters, there's a range of things to explore here.

Battered about a bit
Did you know that a Battery is simply a collection of guns and artillery? In 1903 the obsolete guns were thrown over the cliff. Tsk! Later on, early anti-aircraft guns were tried out here and even rocket tests in the 1950s and 1960s. Don't worry, nothing's loaded now.

What to see
- Cartoons by acclaimed comic-strip artist Geoff Campion, which explain what went on at the Old Battery.
- A list of all the ships that have been wrecked on The Needles plus original cannons on display.

What to do
- Climb down the narrow spiral staircase and go through the 55m (180ft) tunnel to the searchlight for a view of the Needles Rocks.
- Experience life as a soldier with the children's explorer pack 'A Soldier's Life'.

Special events
Though we don't have many events we have an exhibition, and you might want to visit the nearby Bembridge Windmill while you're here – you can climb right up to the top.

By the way...
- We're afraid this site is somewhat inaccessible if you have mobility problems. The paths are steep and can be uneven. But the ground floor is accessible. The walk up to the Old Battery is 1.6km (roughly 1 mile) – so be prepared for a bit of a hike.

Polesden Lacey

Historic house Garden Park

Step back into the 1920s, stroll through the house and grounds and imagine you're a house guest of the Hon Mrs Greville, a society hostess who lived here. In 1923 the future King George VI and Queen Elizabeth spent some of their honeymoon in this elegant Regency villa, and must have enjoyed its opulent interiors and beautiful rose garden.

Party party...

Mrs Greville threw many lavish parties for the rich and famous and entertained all kinds of royalty. She came from quite humble origins as the daughter of William McEwan – founder of the brewery. This was just her country home – she had another one for her London parties.

What to see

- Lady G's mementoes from her parties, kept in a special book – you can even find out what her guests had to eat.
- Gleaming gilt-covered walls and a chandelier with nearly 4000 pieces that takes over a week to clean.
- Lovely gardens – find Lady Greville's gravestone in the rose garden.

What to do

- Croquet anyone? Have a go on the croquet lawn – you can hire equipment from us (please book in advance).
- Test your brains with the house quiz.
- Run around the children's play area and try the adventure trail.

Special events

There are often events in the grounds, including sheepdog trials and vintage car rallies. We have fungus forays and other nature walks, as well as a summer festival and children's events.

By the way...

- There are wheelchairs available, and a ramped entrance. There are steps to the upper floors and elsewhere.
- Call first, and we'll arrange touchable objects for you to try.
- Baby-changing facilities, children's menu and hip-carrying child slings available.

Great Bookham, nr Dorking, Surrey, RH5 6BD
01372 452048

OPENING TIMES
House
15 Mar 08–25 Oct 08
11am–5pm Wed, Thu, Fri, Sat, Sun
26 Oct 08–2 Nov 08
11am–4pm Wed, Thu, Fri, Sat, Sun
Garden/tearoom
2 Jan 08–15 Feb 08
11am–4pm Mon–Sun
16 Feb 08–25 Oct 08
11am–5pm Mon–Sun
26 Oct 08–23 Dec 08
11am–4pm Mon–Sun
2 Jan 08–31 Jan 08
11am–4pm Mon–Sun
Shop
5 Jan 08–15 Feb 08
11am–4pm Mon–Sun
16 Feb 08–25 Oct 08
11am–5pm Mon–Sun
26 Oct 08–30 Nov 08
11am–4pm Mon–Sun
1 Dec 08–23 Dec 08
11am–4pm Mon–Sun
2 Jan 08–4 Jan 08
11am–4pm Mon–Sun

Notes
Open BH Mons. Garden closes dusk if earlier. Garden, tearoom and shop closed 5 Feb and 19 Nov for staff training. Garden, tearoom and shop closed 24 Dec–1 Jan 09 incl. Shop closed 16–17 June and 5–6 Jan 09 for stocktaking.

Petworth House & Park

Historic house Park Lake

South & South East

Petworth, West Sussex
GU28 0AE
01798 342207

OPENING TIMES
House
15 Mar 08–5 Nov 08
11am–5pm Mon, Tue, Wed,
Sat, Sun
Shop/restaurant/pleasure grounds
1 Mar 08–12 Mar 08
11am–4pm Mon, Tue, Wed,
Sat, Sun
15 Mar 08–5 Nov 08
11am–5pm Mon, Tue, Wed,
Sat, Sun
12 Nov 08–29 Nov 08
10am–3:30pm Wed, Thu,
Fri, Sat
4 Dec 08–21 Dec 08
10am–3:30pm Thu, Fri,
Sat, Sun

Notes
Open Good Fri. **Please note**:
extra rooms shown weekdays
from 1pm (not BH Mons) as
follows. Mon: White and Gold
Room and White Library.
Tues/Wed: three bedrooms on
first floor.

A magnificent 17th-century house and grounds with landscaping by 'Capability' Brown and more than 1000 fallow deer – probably the largest herd in Britain. The house is full of treasures and has the National Trust's finest collection of paintings – including 19 paintings by Turner, who lived here for a while.

I do, I do, I do – but don't sit down!
Elizabeth Percy, who inherited Petworth in 1682, married three times before she was 16. Her third husband, the Duke of Somerset, was so full of his own importance that he cut one of their daughters out of his will because she dared to sit down while he was asleep! The same family has lived here for over 800 years and you can trace their family history through many portraits.

What to see
- An original Victorian kitchen with copper pans, steamers and jelly moulds.
- Giant trays, which the footmen had to carry over to the dining room in the house.
- The difference between the servants' quarters and the grand mansion.

What to do
- Walk in the park and look out for the famous Petworth herd of fallow deer and old trees.

- Follow the childrens' quiz through the house and use your detective skills – tracker packs are available for young children.

Special events
Packed programme of family events all season – get in touch with us for more information.

By the way...
- There are wheelchairs available, and a ramped entrance. Baby-changing facilities are provided and there is a childrens' menu in the restaurant.

Sheffield Park Garden

Garden Countryside Lake

Sheffield Park, East Sussex
TN22 3QX
01825 790231

OPENING TIMES
2 Feb 08–2 Mar 08
10:30am–4pm Sat, Sun
4 Mar 08–4 May 08
10:30am–5:30pm Tue, Wed,
Thu, Fri, Sat, Sun
5 May 08–1 Jun 08
10:30am–5:30pm Mon–Sun
3 Jun 08–5 Oct 08
10:30am–5:30pm Tue, Wed,
Thu, Fri, Sat, Sun
6 Oct 08–2 Nov 08
10:30am–5:30pm Mon–Sun
4 Nov 08–31 Dec 08
10:30am–4pm Tue, Wed, Thu,
Fri, Sat, Sun
3 Jan 08–31 Jan 08
10:30am–4pm Sat, Sun

Notes
Open BH Mons. Closed 23–26
Dec. Last admission 1hr before
closing time or dusk if earlier.

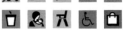

This lovely 'Capability' Brown garden is nowhere near Sheffield.
Sheffield means 'sheep clearing', and the park is actually recorded
first in the Domesday book. The 49 hectares (120 acres) of garden
has trees and shrubs from all over the world. Be a family of plant
hunters as you explore the garden together.

Lady of the lake
According to legend there's a lady ghost between the third and fourth
lakes, known as Upper and Lower Woman's Way Pond. You could
wave, but she wouldn't see you – apparently she has no head.

What to see
- In spring there are tons of daffodils and bluebells, with a rainbow of
  colour in May. Autumn is pretty fantastic too as the garden shows
  off its wonderful leafy colours.
- Don't miss the waterfall, cascades and four large lakes.

What to do
- Explore the garden with one of our family tracker packs or be an
  artist for the day with the artist's pack. The Bluebell Steam Railway
  is just up the road, and there's a joint ticket you can buy to combine
  it with your visit.

Special events
Family events throughout the year, including Teddy Bears Picnic and
family fun days – please call for details.

By the way...
- All-terrain pushchairs or back carriers available for loan.
- No pets, it's just not really suitable.
- Four wheelchairs available and a map of an accessible route. Some
  of the grounds have steep slopes.

Uppark House & Garden

Historic house Garden Countryside

Uppark is a country house and grounds with an original Grand Tour Collection. Quizzes and trails are available around the house and garden. The picturesque style gardens are tranquil and intimate in contrast to the South Meadow with its open sweeping views across the Downs to the sea and an area for children's ball games.

What to see
- Beautiful 18th-century dolls house with original contents & owners still in residence.
- Unspoilt views across the South Downs to the sea.
- Willow sculpture on the woodland walk.

What to do
- Tracker packs with activities to complete in the garden.
- Quizzes for the house and garden.
- Toy box of bats and balls on the South Meadow.

By the way...
- There are photographs in the house show you what the rooms were like after the fire and before the restoration that destroyed much of the interior in 1989.

South Harting, Petersfield, West Sussex, GU31 5QR
01730 825415

OPENING TIMES
House
16 Mar 08–30 Oct 08
12:30pm–4:30pm Mon, Tue, Wed, Thu, Sun
Part of house
6 Dec 08–11 Dec 08
11am–3pm Mon, Tue, Wed, Thu, Sun
Garden/shop/restaurant
16 Mar 08–30 Oct 08
11:30am–5pm Mon, Tue, Wed, Thu, Sun
30 Nov 08–18 Dec 08
11am–3:30pm Mon, Tue, Wed, Sun

Notes
Open Good Fri. On BH Sun and Mons garden/shop/restaurant open 11am–5pm and house 11:30am–4:30pm. Garden Tours 1st Thur of each month and every Thur in July/Aug. Print room open 1st Mon of each month, times as house.

Waddesdon Manor

Historic house Garden Park

Waddesdon, nr Aylesbury,
Buckinghamshire, HP18 0JH
01296 653226

OPENING TIMES
House
19 Mar 08–26 Oct 08
12am–4pm Wed, Thu, Fri
19 Mar 08–26 Oct 08
11am–4pm Sat, Sun
Christmas season in house
12 Nov 08–23 Dec 08
12am–4pm Wed, Thu, Fri
12 Nov 08–23 Dec 08
11am–4pm Sat, Sun
22 Dec 08–23 Dec 08
12am–4pm Mon, Tue
Bachelors' wing
19 Mar 08–26 Oct 08
12am–4pm Wed, Thu, Fri
Coffee bar
19 Mar 08–23 Dec 08
11am–5pm Wed–Sun
Gardens/shops/restaurants
2 Feb 08–16 Mar 08
10am–5pm Sat, Sun
19 Mar 08–23 Dec 08
10am–5pm Wed–Sun
27 Dec 08–31 Dec 08
10am–5pm Mon, Thu–Sun
3 Jan 08–31 Jan 08
10am–5pm Sat, Sun

Notes
Admission by timed ticket only,
incl. National Trust members.
Open BH Mons. Last admission
1hr before closing. Sculpture in
garden uncovered week before
Easter, weather permitting.
Space limited in Bachelors'
Wing and entry cannot be
guaranteed. Coffee bar and
summerhouse open weather
permitting.

Home to the Rothschild family, Waddesdon already has so much to offer young people – beautiful, safe grounds and space to explore, living history, opportunities for learning and fun both outdoors and in. Our woodland playground has been developed using a large wooded area through which an adventurous trail winds, encouraging children to test their dexterity as they swing, slide, balance and climb their way down the slope, exploring and discovering playthings both natural and man-made in the landscape. At the foot of the slope, next to the stables, is a space dedicated to younger children, who can play safe in the knowledge that their families are within sight.

What to see
- Family audio tours of the house.

What to do
- Woodland playground.
- Wildlife Interpretation Trail.
- Living willow sculptures.

Special events
Special children's tours of the house during school holidays. MAD about Waddesdon, an annual music, drama and art festival for children, takes place in the Summer.

The Witley Centre

Countryside Nature reserve Visitor centre Wood Heaths

Here you'll find one of the few remaining fragments of the heath that used to cover much of Southern England. Used as common land over many generations, since the Bronze Age, Witley Common has several ancient burial mounds and evidence of iron working from the 16th and 17th century. Today the commons provide a sanctuary for wildlife and also a chance for you to escape from the hustle and bustle, walk the trails or watch birds at the bird tables while you picnic outside the purpose-built centre.

Left right, left right

During World Wars I and II, the commons were used as a training camp for the army. There were up to 20,000 soldiers marching around on it at one time. A Polish contingent of soldiers planted hawthorn around their barracks to cheer things up a bit. In the late 1940s, the parade ground was broken up, and the land was restored to its pre-war condition. Now the commons are a Site of Special Scientific Interest.

What to see

- The green hairstreak and silver-studded blue. No, they're not punks, they're butterflies!
- Woodpeckers and nuthatches on Witley Common.
- Dartford warblers and nightingales on Milford Common.
- Lizards, adders and roe deer.

What to do

- Bring a picnic and relax.
- Pick up a quiz sheet from the Witley Centre and go on one of the nature trails over heathland and woodland.
- Visit the countryside exhibition and try out the special puzzles and quizzes for the younger members of the family.
- Have a cup of tea and watch the wildlife.

Special events

Get in touch to find out what events we have on. Past activities have included pond dipping for bugs and creepy crawlies, and a night hike for spotting bats. Booking is essential, and children must bring an adult along with them.

By the way...

- The grounds are partly accessible, but it can be a bit muddy in wet weather. There are two wheelchairs available at the Witley Centre, as well as an adapted WC. The shop and picnic tables are accessible.
- There's a touch table of objects that anyone can handle, and a guide in Braille.

Witley, Godalming,
Surrey, GU8 5QA
01428 683207

OPENING TIMES
Centre
4 Mar 08–29 Oct 08
11am–4pm Mon, Tue, Wed, Thu, Fri
Common
All year Mon–Sun

South & South East

83

Best of the Rest

Devil's Dyke

The Dyke is the largest chalkland combe in Britain – a favourite with walkers, energetic children, kite flyers and dogs. Bring your bike or follow a self-guided walking tour. There's a family-friendly pub by the car park, and activities like Orchid Safaris or Devil's Dyke Detectives – get in touch to see what's on.

Contact: West Sussex Downs Property Office, The Coach House, Slindon Estate Yard, Slindon, Arundel, West Sussex BN18 0RE. 01243 814554 **Opening Times:** All year dawn–dusk Mon–Sun.

Greys Court

An intriguing property with lots for families to enjoy. Among the ruins of a medieval fortified manor house, a delightful series of secret gardens are linked by 'doorways' in the walls. There is a brick maze for children to explore and a medieval tower to climb. Pick up a family explorer pack, filled with fun activities throughout the garden. Greys Court hosts events each year, like Easter-egg hunts. Check for details.

Contact: Rotherfield Greys, Henley-on-Thames, Oxfordshire RG9 4PG. Tel. 01491 628529 **Opening times:** 22 Mar 08–27 Sep 08 12am–5pm Tue, Wed, Thu, Fri, Sat **Notes:** Garden open in aid of NGS (National Garden Scheme) 17 May (charge incl. National Trust members).

South Foreland Lighthouse

A striking landmark on the White Cliffs of Dover, this distinctive Victorian lighthouse was the first to display an electrically powered signal and was used in experiments by Faraday and Marconi. Climb the 73 steps in the tower to see spectacular cross-Channel views and view the 100-year-old working clockwork mechanism and optic. Picnic in the grounds, or follow one of our seasonal trails.

Contact: The Front, St Margaret's Bay, Dover, Kent CT15 6HP. Tel. 01304 852463 **Opening times:** 14 Mar 08–3 Apr 08 11am–5:30pm Mon, Fri, Sat, Sun; 4 Apr 08–24 Apr 08 11am–5:30pm Mon–Sun; 25 Apr 08–22 May 08 11am–5:30pm Mon, Fri, Sat, Sun; 23 May 08–5 Jun 08 11am–5:30pm Mon–Sun; 6 Jun 08–17 Jul 08 11am–5:30pm Mon, Fri, Sat, Sun; 18 Jul 08–11 Sep 08 11am–5:30pm Mon–Sun; 12 Sep 08–29 Sep 08 11am–5:30pm Mon, Fri, Sat, Sun; 17 Oct 08–27 Oct 08 11am–5:30pm Mon–Sun **Notes:** Admission by guided tour. Open by arrangement during closed period for booked groups only.

Nymans Garden

A beautiful peaceful garden for children to enjoy. The Messel family who designed it made sure there is a surprise around every corner. Fascinating historic rooms to visit in the house and romantic ruins, as well as 275 acres of woodland to explore. Try the family trail for the garden and house or follow one of the trails in Nymans Woods, where you can see exotic shrubs and trees and beautiful woodlands and lakes.

Contact: Handcross, nr Haywards Heath, West Sussex, RH17 6EB. Tel. 01444 405250 **Opening times:** **Garden/shop/restaurant** 2 Feb 08–16 Mar 08 10am–4pm Wed, Thu, Fri, Sat, Sun; 19 Mar 08–2 Nov 08 10am–5pm Wed, Thu, Fri, Sat, Sun; 5 Nov 08–31 Jan 08 10am–4pm Wed, Thu, Fri, Sat, Sun **House** 19 Mar 08–2 Nov 08 11am–4pm Wed, Thu, Fri, Sat, Sun **Notes:** Property closes at dusk if earlier. Last admission to house 3:45pm. Restaurant closes 30 mins before property. Open BH Mons. Shop open daily in Dec. Christmas lunches in restaurant Tues–Sun. Closed 25/26 Dec and 1 Jan 09.

Standen

Beautiful late Victorian family house designed by renowned Arts and Crafts architect, Philip Webb. The hillside garden and wooded estate provide plenty of opportunities for an interesting and fun day out, and there are trails and quizzes, colouring sheets, Victorian-style toys, art bags, objects to handle, activity packs and puzzles to solve. Why not try the 'Peals of Laughter' exhibition on the Beale family children in the Croxley Room, or a day in the life of a Standen servant in the Cook's Store?

Contact: West Hoathly Road, East Grinstead, West Sussex RH19 4NE. 01342 323029 **Opening times: House** 1 Mar 08–9 Mar 08 11am–4:30pm Sat, Sun; 15 Mar 08–20 Jul 08 11am–4:30pm Wed, Thu, Fri, Sat, Sun; 21 Jul 08–31 Aug 08 11am–4:30pm Mon, Wed, Thu, Fri, Sat, Sun; 3 Sep 08–2 Nov 08 11am–4:30pm Wed, Thu, Fri, Sat, Sun; 8 Nov 08–21 Dec 08 11am–3pm Sat, Sun **Garden/shop/restaurant*:** 1 Mar 08–9 Mar 08 11am–5pm Sat, Sun; 15 Mar 08–20 Jul 08 11am–5pm Wed, Thu, Fri, Sat, Sun; 21 Jul 08–31 Aug 08 11am–5pm Mon, Wed, Thu, Fri, Sat, Sun; 3 Sep 08–2 Nov 08 11am–5pm Wed, Thu, Fri, Sat, Sun; 8 Nov 08–21 Dec 08 11am–3pm Sat, Sun **Notes:** Open BH Mons. *Garden closes at 5:30pm from Mar to early Nov. Some queueing on approach to property may occur on BHs.

Stowe Landscape Gardens

Stowe Landscape Gardens offer families the opportunity to safely explore, discover the gardens and let off steam. The garden buildings all have their own styles, from temples inspired by Ancient Greece to a seating area decorated with a pebble mosaic. Spot grand temples, monuments and a range of wildlife among the hidden corners and amazing views. Search for Queen Elizabeth I and William Shakespeare in the Temple of British Worthies in the Elysian Fields. Who else can you find? After enjoying a walk around the gardens, why not have a picnic under one of Stowe's beautiful trees?

Contact: Buckingham, Buckinghamshire MK18 5EH. Tel. 01280 822850 **Opening times:** 5 Jan 08–2 Mar 08 10:30am–4pm Sat, Sun; 5 Mar 08–2 Nov 08 10:30am–5:30pm Wed, Thu, Fri, Sat, Sun; 8 Nov 08–31 Jan 08 10:30am–4pm Sat, Sun **Shop:** 5 Jan 08–2 Mar 08 10:30am–4pm Sat, Sun; 5 Mar 08–2 Nov 08 10:30am–5:30pm Wed, Thu, Fri, Sat, Sun; 8 Nov 08–19 Dec 08 11am–3pm Wed, Thu, Fri; 12 Nov 08–31 Jan 08 10:30am–4pm Sat, Sun **Tearoom:** 5 Jan 08–2 Mar 08 10:30am–3:30pm Sat, Sun; 5 Mar 08–2 Nov 08 10:30am–5pm Wed, Thu, Fri, Sat, Sun; 8 Nov 08–31 Jan 08 10:30am–3:30pm Sat, Sun **Parkland** All year dawn–dusk Mon–Sun **Notes:** Open BH Mons. Last admission 1½hrs before closing. Gardens closed Sat 24 May.

Wildlife Walk – Ashridge Estate

Hertfordshire

On the main ridge of the magnificent Chiltern Hills, there are over 5000 acres (2023 hectacres) of open countryside, chalk downland and woodland to explore and escape to at Ashridge. The range of habitats means there's plenty of wildlife (the estate is renowned for butterflies and wildflowers). Bluebell displays in spring are superb and you can find lots of grassland flowers like orchids. Autumn is a great time to watch deer rut and enjoy the golden hues of the surrounding countryside.

Getting there:
Bike: Traffic-free and signed cycle route to within 1 mile of the estate. See www.sustrans.org.uk
Buses: For Monument no. 30/31 from Tring (alight Aldbury) stops within half a mile of the estate. For Beacon no. 61 Aylesbury–Luton (passes close to Aylesbury and Luton) Chiltern Rambler 327 from Tring to Monument or Beacon (Sundays, May–September).
Foot: 4.4km (2¾ miles) off The Ridgeway on property.
Rail: Tring is 2.8km (1¾ miles) from Monument, and Cheddington is 6.6km (3½ miles) from Beacon.
Road: Between Berkhamsted and Northchurch, and Ringshall and Dagnall, just off the B4506.

Distance: 3km (2 miles).

Terrain and accessibility: Signposted route, perfect for families.
The walk is linear so you can return at any point. Level surfaces are good for pushchairs and wheelchairs. Maps of accessible routes available. The visitor centre is wheelchair accessible with an adapted WC.

Directions and points of interest:
Follow the map shown opposite. The numbers on the map correspond to the numbers below.

1. Start at the Ashridge visitor centre, near the Bridgewater Monument. Cross the green, taking the path leading off the main track (it has studposts at the entrance).
2. Enter the ancient woodland. In late summer, note that lots of the sycamores along the path have tar spot fungus (black marks) – a good indicator of unpolluted air. Also look for butterflies in sunny openings and signs of badgers. Their tracks are seen in many places as well as holes called 'dung pits' or a 'badger's latrine'.
3. Go over a bridge and you are now on an ancient Drover's path, which was worn away into a ditch by villagers taking their animals to graze on Pitstone Common. Continue to Moneybury Hill, so-called because of the buried coins found here (it is prohibited to use metal detectors on National Trust land).
4. Pass the left-hand mound called Bell Barrow (due to its shape). It is thought to be a Bronze Age burial mound. The wooden lodge on the left is a copy of a Victorian shooting lodge that burned down in 1989.
5. On the right is a huge giant's bench with lovely views of Pitstone Hill and Aldbury Nowers. Continuing along, note the hazel trees that

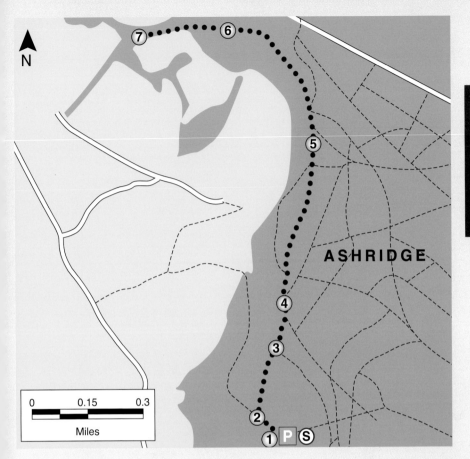

have been coppiced (cut at the ground, then left to grow) to provide a wildlife habitat. The fallen cedar is still alive and growing. As you walk through the pine woodland between here and point 6, enjoy the smells of the conifers.

6 Emerge from the pine trees onto Clipper Down.

7 Either turn around (this is also the turning point for mobility vehicles) and return by the same route, or continue for another mile to Ivinghoe Beacon for more wonderful views.

Property contact: 01442 851227, ashridge@nationaltrust.org.uk

Map and start grid reference: OS Explorer 181: SP970130 (Ashridge visitor centre)

Facilities available:
Free parking 50m (164ft) away, visitor centre, tearoom, National Trust gift shop, WC (not always available), baby changing facilities, short stretch of cycle path, 14.5km (9 miles) on a bridleway. Self-guided walks available.

87

Coastal Walk– East Head

Chichester Harbour, West Sussex

East Head is a natural, constantly evolving sand and shingle spit owned by the National Trust since 1966. The short walk around the Head neatly encapsulates the challenges faced by the Trust in managing a dynamic site under impact of sea-level rise and the possibility of more frequent storms, to retain the processes of evolution of the coast and access for people.

Getting there:
Road: B2179 to West Wittering from the A286 Chichester.
Car parks: Privately managed by West Wittering Estates (WWE).
Foot: From public footpath in West Wittering village.
Bus: (B=bus stop) West Wittering number 52 or 53 from Chichester.
Rail: Chichester. For public transport information visit www.traveline.org.uk.

Distance: 3.2km (2 miles).

Terrain and accessibility: Easy, flat walking conditions with soft sand in places. Height gain of 4–5m (13–16ft) over the walk. If on the beach, beware of strong currents – don't swim at low tides and do not use inflatables.

Directions and points of interest:
Start at the car park. Follow the path from the car park along the front of the beach, keeping the sea on your left, as shown on the map opposite. The numbers on the map correspond to the numbers below. Look out for the following features:

1 Notice the wooden groynes at regular intervals. Beach levels are higher on the east side as material is prevented from migrating along the beach. The groynes help prevent change. However, where they stop and erosion does take place the contrast between man-made and natural coastline is dramatic.

2 Here, the dune has receded, revealing the layers of sand and shingle (sediment) that have been moved by the wind and sea to form the dunes.

3 Since 1966 East Head has doubled in size – this area is growing or accreting sediment that has been eroded in other areas. In the summer, ground nesting birds such as ringed plover nest above the high-tide line.

4 Behind the shelter of East Head where there is little wave action, salt-marsh specialist communities of plants such as glasswort and sea plantain and

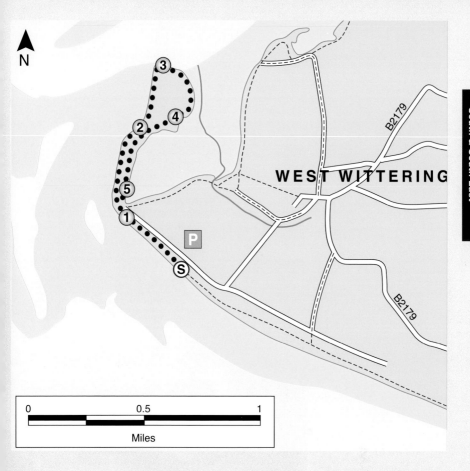

invertebrates live, providing food for wader birds such as redshank and curlew.

5 At the 'hinge' very little sediment is available as the groynes prevent new material getting here to help it build again. However, recently changes have been made to the groyne structure, which may release more sediment on to East Head.

Property contact details: 01243 814554 (West Sussex Downs office).

Maps and start grid ref: OS Landranger 197 gr SZ768981, Explorer 120.

Facilities available: Shop, café and toilets in WWE car park.

National Trust properties nearby: Bosham Quay Meadow and Harting Down.

Ham House & Garden

Historic house Garden

Ham Street, Ham,
Richmond-upon-Thames,
Surrey, TW10 7RS
020 8940 1950

OPENING TIMES
House
15 Mar 08–2 Nov 08
12am–4pm Mon, Tue, Wed,
Sat, Sun
Garden
All year 11am–6pm Mon, Tue,
Wed, Sat, Sun
Shop/café
2 Feb 08–9 Mar 08
11am–3:30pm Sat, Sun
15 Mar 08–2 Nov 08
11am–5:30pm Mon, Tue, Wed,
Sat, Sun
8 Nov 08–21 Dec 08
11am–3:30pm Sat, Sun
Café
3 Jan 08–31 Jan 08
11am–3:30pm Sat, Sun

Notes
Open Good Fri: house
12am–4pm; garden
11am–6pm. Garden: closes at
dusk if earlier; closed 25, 26
Dec and 1 Jan 09. Special
Christmas openings in Dec for
garden/shop/café. Christmas
lunches.

Ham House is unique in Europe as the most complete survival of
17th-century fashion and power. One of a series of palaces and
grand houses along the banks of the Thames, it was built in 1610
and enlarged in the 1670s, when it was at the heart of Restoration
court life and intrigue.

Spooky stories

Ham House was home to the extravagant Duchess of Lauderdale, who
was renowned as a political schemer during the Civil War and
Restoration period. She is said to still haunt its passageways with her
pet dog. In fact, there are so many phantom tales of Ham, that it is
reported to be one of the most haunted houses in England.

What to see

- The lavish 17th-century interiors with a wealth of textiles, furniture
  and paintings.
- The service buildings – see the earliest identified Still House in
  England and the dairy with cast iron 'cows legs'.

What to do

- Family tracker packs throughout the open season both for the house and the garden.
- After-dark 'ghost' tours for Halloween and daytime family ghost tours during school holidays. Booking essential.
- Christmas family events including carol concerts and special weekend openings.

Special events

Easter trails, theatre in the garden and special weekend Christmas openings. Please check the National Trust website for updates or contact the property for more details.

Morden Hall Park

Garden Park Countryside Farm Nature reserve Visitor centre Waterways

London & East

Morden Hall Road, Morden,
London, SM4 5JD
020 8545 6850

OPENING TIMES
Park
All year 8am–6pm Mon–Sun
Shop/café
All year 10am–5pm Mon–Sun
Kiosk
5 Apr 08–26 Oct 08
11am–5pm Sat, Sun
Second-hand bookshop
5 Apr 08–26 Oct 08
12am–4pm Sat, Sun

Notes
Car park by café, shop and
garden centre closes at 6pm.
Shop and café closed 25, 26
Dec and 1 Jan 09. Rose garden
and estate buildings area open
8am–6pm. Snuff Mill
Environmental Education Centre
open last Sun of April–Oct,
12am–4pm. Kiosk also open
every day during school hols,
April–Oct 11am–5pm (unless
the weather is bad).

With its open spaces and tranquil, meandering river, Morden Hall
Park is a rare commodity in south-west London. The rose gardens,
wild meadows and wetlands rich in wildlife, add up to a delightful
haven in the midst of a densely built-up area. Visitors can stroll
along the river to the site of two water mills, which were used until
1922 to grind snuff, and explore other historic estate buildings now
used by a range of local artisans. The original walled kitchen garden
now houses a large, independently run garden centre, and the newly
refurbished riverside gift shop and café is well worth a visit.

The man behind the park
The park was home to local philanthropist Gilliat Hatfeild, remembered
and loved by local people for his many acts of kindness, like holding
tea parties for local school children before the war. Mr Hatfeild was a
great lover of trees and open spaces and shunned the 20th century,
building stables to travel by horse and carriage. His passion for fishing
is seen in the weather vanes on top of several buildings. He passed the
park to the National Trust to preserve it for the local community.

What to see
- Coots, moorhens, mallard ducks and herons on the waterways.
- All kinds of fish in the Capital garden centre's aquaria.
- Outside the mill, two of the millstones used to grind the tobacco.

What to do
- Play games in open parkland, wander by the River Wandle and
  cross the variety of bridges over the river.
- Have a picnic in the fenced dog-free paddock especially for families.
- Visit the independently run Deen City Farm, where you can stroke
  rabbits and guinea pigs, and see baby goats, Jacob sheep and
  Derek, the snow-white peacock. Usually open Tuesday to Sunday.
- In season, smell the roses – there are over 2000 of them so that's
  quite a sniff – or should that be snuff...

Special events
A programme of family events is run in the Snuff Mill. Holiday activities
every Thursday in school holidays and discovery days one Sunday a
month. Please ring us to find out more.

By the way...
- The park is ideal for family cycling because it's flat, and the Wandle
  Trail passes right through it.
- Well-behaved dogs will enjoy a run in the parkland but must be kept
  on leads near buildings and in the rose garden.
- The shop and café are accessible, but some of the paths in the park
  are not. There is recently improved access to the Snuff Mill, as well
  as an adapted WC.
- Braille and large-print guides are available.
- There are baby-changing facilities, and the Riverside Café has a
  children's menu.

Osterley Park & House

Historic house Garden Park Lake

Osterley is a beautiful house and park within easy reach of central London. It is a great place to escape the city and you might see rabbits, squirrels, ducks and even parakeets. Originally a Tudor house, it was transformed in the 18th century into its present elegant appearance.

Heartbreak house

In 1782, Sarah-Anne Child, the 18-year-old daughter of Osterley's owner, ran away to Gretna Green to marry the Earl of Westmorland. Soon afterwards her father died, some say of a broken heart.

What to see

- In the park you can see 400-year-old oak trees and lots of other rare and exotic trees. In the spring there are lots of bluebells and in summer time, Mrs Child's flower garden is full of flowers.
- In the house, look for marigolds in the decorations on the walls and furniture. The marigold was the emblem of the Child family who used to live here.

What to do

- Borrow our family tracker packs for either the house or garden, and discover more about Osterley with lots of fun activities for you to do.

Special events

There are family events throughout the year. The highlight of the summer is the annual Osterley Day, which takes place in early summer. This is a community and arts event, with something for the whole family to enjoy. Other past events include Easter trails and fun days.

By the way...

- Baby slings and hip seats can be borrowed in the house; pushchairs are admitted when visitor numbers allow.
- There are baby-changing facilities available. Children's menu and high chairs available in the tearoom.

Jersey Road, Isleworth,
Middlesex, TW7 4RB
020 8232 5050

OPENING TIMES
House/Jersey galleries
12 Mar 08–2 Nov 08
13pm–4:30pm Wed, Thu, Fri, Sat, Sun
6 Dec 08–21 Dec 08
12:30pm–3:30pm Sat, Sun
Shop
12 Mar 08–2 Nov 08
12:30pm–5pm Wed, Thu, Fri, Sat, Sun
5 Nov 08–21 Dec 08
12am–4pm Wed, Thu, Fri, Sat, Sun
Tearoom
12 Mar 08–2 Nov 08
11am–5pm Wed, Thu, Fri, Sat, Sun
5 Nov 08–21 Dec 08
12am–4pm Wed, Thu, Fri, Sat, Sun
Park
1 Feb 08–29 Mar 08 8am–5pm Mon–Sun
30 Mar 08–25 Oct 08
8am–7:30pm Mon–Sun
26 Oct 08–31 Jan 08
8am–6pm Mon–Sun
Garden
12 Mar 08–2 Nov 08
11am–5pm Wed, Thu, Fri, Sat, Sun.

Notes
Open Good Fri and BH Mons. Car park closed 25 and 26 Dec. Garden open until 7pm 1st Thur in April–Oct

Sutton House
Historic house Art gallery

2 & 4 Homerton High Street,
Hackney, London, E9 6JQ
020 8986 2264

OPENING TIMES
Historic rooms
1 Feb 08–21 Dec 08
12:30pm–4:30pm Thu, Fri,
Sat, Sun
Art gallery/shop/café-bar
1 Feb 08–21 Dec 08
12am–4:30pm Thu, Fri,
Sat, Sun

Notes
Open BH Mons. Closed Good
Fri. Sutton House is a lively
property in regular use by local
community groups. The rooms
will always be open as
advertised, but please tel. in
advance if you would like to visit
the property during a quiet time.

Here's an unexpected gem of a Tudor house, hidden right in the
middle of East London. It's well worth a visit to explore its
atmospheric interior, enjoy the peaceful courtyard and grab a
bite to eat at the cosy café.

Hackney house
Difficult to believe that Hackney was once a pretty village outside
London, but it was in 1535 when the house was built. Sutton House
has been a rich merchant's home, a school, and a recreation centre for
poor working men. Now it's a venue for community events, talks and
exhibitions.

What to see
- Fine Tudor oak panelling and carved fireplaces, aromatic Tudor
  kitchen, Georgian and Victorian rooms, doors and panels which
  open to reveal parts of the original house – including two
  'garderobe' loos (no longer in use). Paintings and artwork by
  local artists.

What to do
- Creep around in the old cellars.
- Explore the exhibition that tells the story of the house.
- Touch (and smell) objects in the authentic Tudor kitchen.

Special events
We have many events, including monthly Family Days full of fun
activities. Come on a ghost tour (if you dare) or enjoy children's
activities at our craft fair.

By the way...
- There's a children's quiz/trail and baby-changing facilities. We have a
  wheelchair – you need to book it – but there are stairs to upper
  floors.
- It's worth checking that we're open to the public before you visit –
  there are sometimes special private events.

Anglesey Abbey, Gardens & Lode Mill

Historic house Mill Garden

Anglesey Abbey house is a 20th-century gentleman's country residence set in 46 hectacres (114 acres) of garden and with an 18th-century watermill. Lord Fairhaven collected many works of art and treasures, which can be seen in the house and around the gardens.

House built on the site of a 12th-century priory
Gardens include channels and hollows of priory fishponds and a pool containing large Chinese carp. Amazing! Lode Watermill first appeared in the Domesday Book and at one time ground cement although now it again grinds wheat into flour.

What to see
- Look out for mythical beasts, Roman emperors and Greek gods around the gardens – all statues, of course.
- In the house go on an animal trail or see if you can spot all of the 37 clocks and track down other curiosities using the children's guide.

What to do
- Turn up on one of the milling days to see the mill in action (please telephone for details).
- Follow the garden trails, do a wildlife or bird survey and explore the fantastic woodland paths.

By the way...
- So that everyone can enjoy the peace and tranquility of the gardens as Lord Fairhaven intended, please do not bring bikes or any ball games or frisbies into the gardens.

Quy Road, Lode, Cambridge, Cambridgeshire, CB25 9EJ
01223 810080

OPENING TIMES
1 Feb 08–16 Mar 08
10:30am–4:30pm Wed, Thu, Fri, Sat, Sun
19 Mar 08–2 Nov 08
10:30am–5:30pm Wed, Thu, Fri, Sat, Sun
5 Nov 08–21 Dec 08
10:30am–4:30pm Wed, Thu, Fri, Sat, Sun
31 Dec 08–31 Jan 08
10:30am–4:30pm Wed, Thu, Fri, Sat, Sun
House
19 Mar 08–2 Nov 08
1pm–5pm Wed, Thu, Fri, Sat, Sun
Lode Mill
As Winter Garden
11am–3:30pm Wed, Thu, Fri, Sat, Sun
19 Mar 08–2 Nov 08
1pm–5pm Wed, Thu, Fri, Sat, Sun

Notes
Open BH Mon and Good Fri. The Gallery: 19 Nov–18 Jan 09 Wed–Sun 11am–3:30pm. Snowdrop seasons: 16 Jan–17 Feb 08 and 21 Jan–22 Feb 09 (days and times as Winter Garden). Summer late openings: restaurant and gardens only, 5 Jun–1 Aug, Thu and Fri until 9pm. NGS days: Sun 22 June and Sun 24 Aug (on these days entry proceeds go to charity. National Trust members are asked to make a donation).

Belton House

Historic house Garden Park

London & East

Grantham, Lincolnshire
NG32 2LS. 01476 566116

OPENING TIMES
House
1 Mar 08–14 Mar 08
12:30pm–4pm Sat, Sun
15 Mar 08–2 Nov 08
12:30pm–5pm Wed–Sun
Garden/park
2 Feb 08–14 Mar 08
12am–4pm Sat, Sun
15 Mar 08–30 Jun
11am–5:30pm Wed–Sun
1 Jul 08–7 Sep 08
10:30am–5:30pm Mon–Sun
8 Sep 08–2 Nov 08
11am–5:30pm Wed–Sun
3 Nov 08–21 Dec 08
12am–4pm Fri, Sat, Sun
26 Dec 08–4 Jan 08
12am–4pm Mon–Sun
Adventure playground
1 Mar 08–14 Mar 08
11am–4pm Sat, Sun
15 Mar 08–30 Jun 08
11am–5:30pm Wed–Sun
1 Jul 08–7 Sep 08
10:30am–5:30pm Mon–Sun

Notes
House open BH Mons. Property
closed 12 July. Open daily in
school hols, 1 March–2 Nov
(adventure playground, parkland
and garden, shop and
restaurant only). Bellmount
Woods open daily, access from
separate car park. Bellmount
Tower open occasionally, tel. for
details. House may close early
in poor light conditions.
Adventure playground may
close in adverse weather
conditions.

This magnificent county house was built in 1685–88 for 'young' Sir
John Brownlow. Stunning rooms are displayed in 17th-century,
Regency, Victorian and 1930s style. Fine furnishings, paintings and
Grinling Gibbons wood-carvings feature inside. Outside, there are 14
hectacres (36 acres) of lovely gardens to explore and a beautiful
lakeside walk.

Belting around Belton
Belton was the film location for the BBC's recent productions of *Jane
Eyre*, *Pride and Prejudice* as well as the children's serial 'Moondial'.
Step back in time and try on Victorian clothing in the activities room.
Let off steam in the National Trust's largest adventure playground.

What to see
- Look out for the sleek, stately Belton greyhound that features on the weathervane, gates and throughout the house. There's a whole menagerie of animals to find too, hidden in the paintings and decorations of the house.

What to do
- Visit the activities room upstairs to try on costumes or come along to the Belton discovery centre.
- Swing, climb and slide away around the mega-sized adventure playground – the less energetic can watch from the picnic area.
- Take one of the trails, available for the house and gardens.

Special events
Get in touch for details of our family fun weekends, activities and trails. We often have special walks, or even a chance to have a go at archery or try your hand at different crafts.

By the way...
- Grab a family guide or activity pack to help you explore. We are very baby-friendly, with facilities and carriers to borrow. Wheelchairs available but there are many steps up to the entrance. Ask for a map of accessible routes in the grounds.

Blickling Hall, Gardens & Park

Historic house Garden Park Countryside Lake

Blickling, Norwich,
Norfolk NR11 6NF
01263 738030

OPENING TIMES
House
15 Mar 08–27 Jul 08
11am–5pm Wed–Sun
28 Jul 08–31 Aug 08
11am–5pm Mon, Wed, Thu, Fri,
Sat, Sun
1 Sep 08–2 Nov 08 11am–5pm
Wed, Thu, Fri, Sat, Sun
Garden
3 Jan 08–14 Mar 08
11am–4pm Thu, Fri, Sat, Sun
15 Mar 08–27 Jul 08
10:15am–5.15pm Wed, Thu,
Fri, Sat, Sun
28 Jul 08–31 Aug 08
10:15am–5.15pm Mon, Wed,
Thu, Fri, Sat, Sun
1 Sep 08–2 Nov 08
10:15am–5.15pm Wed, Thu,
Fri, Sat, Sun
3 Nov 08–31 Jan 08
11am–4pm Thu, Fri, Sat, Sun
Park
All year dawn–dusk Mon–Sun
Plant centre
15 Mar 08–2 Nov 08
10:15am–5.15pm Wed, Thu,
Fri, Sat, Sun
Shop/restaurant/bookshop
As garden

Notes
Open BH Mons and Easter–Aug
incl. During local school hols
(Easter–Oct incl.), all facilities
(incl. cycle hire) open Wed–Mon
incl. Closed 25 and 26 Dec.

Blickling Hall is a very romantic-looking building with an array of gables, turrets, striking brick chimneys and ancient yew hedges. The property was constructed in the early 17th century and is one of England's great Jacobean houses. It has a spectacular Long Gallery and fine collections of furniture, pictures, books and tapestries. Wander in its extensive gardens and parklands, with something to see throughout the year and lots of interesting walks to explore.

Heads or tales
Henry VIII's second queen, poor old Anne Boleyn, lived in an earlier house at Blickling when she was young. Bet she later wished she'd stayed at home instead of marrying Henry, who had her beheaded. Some swear they've seen her headless ghost riding up to the house in a coach pulled by headless horses.

What to see
- Anne Boleyn's life-size carved relief.
- Some very curious beasts hiding in the plaster ceiling in the Long Gallery.
- In the gardens there is a secret garden with a sun dial, a temple and an orangery with citrus trees.
- In the park there's a pyramid. Well, not a real Egyptian one, but a mausoleum built for one of Blickling's owners.

What to do
- Explore the park by following one of three waymarked walks. Dogs can come too if kept on a lead. See if you can spot local wildlife, including woodpeckers, herons and owls. Trails, special tours, tracker packs, cycle hire and croquet to choose from.

Special events
Family-friendly activities include an Easter trail, Halloween events, outdoor concerts, open-air theatre and giant garden games. Get in touch to book or find out more.

By the way...
- At the weekends and during school holidays you can hire bicycles to explore the park. The basement rooms are not accessible except by stairs, but the rest of the house is, and we have wheelchairs available. The garden and other facilities are fully accessible, with maps of special routes. We have Braille and large-print guides, and a handling collection.
- Don't miss the Sitooterie in the garden.

Chilterns Gateway Centre, Dunstable Downs & Whipsnade Estate

Countryside Visitor centre

Dunstable Road, Whipsnade,
Bedfordshire, LU6 2GY
01582 608489

OPENING TIMES
Downs
All year Mon–Sun
Centre
1 Feb 08–17 Mar 08
10am–4pm Mon–Sun
18 Mar 08–28 Oct 08
10am–5pm Mon–Sun
29 Oct 08–31 Jan 08
10am–4pm Mon–Sun

Notes
Chilterns Gateway centre
closed 24/25 Dec. Closes dusk
if earlier in winter.

The Downs are a large area of chalk grassland and farmland that's a haven for wildlife. A great place to stretch your legs and get lots of fresh air. It's the highest spot in Bedfordshire and has wonderful views out over the Vale of Aylesbury and along the Chiltern Ridge. The Icknield Way is possibly the oldest road in England.

Downs in disguise
During World War II the Meteorological Office at Dunstable was camouflaged to look like part of the Downs. The buildings and tennis court were covered with leaves and nets, and one of the buildings was disguised as a haystack!

What to see
- Flying of all kinds – planes on their way to Luton, gliders, paragliders and kites.
- Put your nose to the ground to look for interesting plants and creatures of all kinds.

What to do
- A very popular kite-flying spot. If you don't have one, we sell a large range in the shop.
- Pop into the popular Chilterns Gateway centre.
- Bring your bike – the bridleway is okay for cycling.

Special events
- Check the National Trust website for details.

By the way...
- The centre is fully accessible and a popular family location.

Dunwich Heath: Coastal Centre & Beach

Countryside Coastline Nature reserve Visitor centre Beach Heath

Dunwich Heath is a remote and beautiful place with a unique atmosphere. There are stunning views out over the sea and mysterious heathland walks over the gorse and heather, shady woods and crumbling sandy cliffs. It's a lovely place to walk, and then come back for tea at the old coastguard cottages.

A village in the sea
Perched high on the cliff, fronting the wind, are the white-painted coastguard cottages. Replacing an older, wooden structure, which was lost to the sea, the cottages were built in 1827 and for 80 years were home to frequently changing families of coastguards charged with clearing the coast of smugglers. When the Admiralty finished with the buildings, the cottages became home to holidaymakers.

What to see
- The heathland at Dunwich supports the largest population of Dartford warblers in East Anglia along with other heathland specialists such as the stonechat and meadow pipit, many solitary bees and wasps, and butterflies such as the greyling, brown argus and green hairstreak. The wetland along Dowcra's Ditch has fascinating dragonflies, damselflies and the rare ant-lion. The shingle banks on the beach support many wonderful plants such as yellow-horned poppy and during the summer the air is filled with the calls of sand martins which nest along the cliffs.

What to do
- Splash in the sea or try a bit of beachcombing.
- Explore the heath and its rare wildlife.
- At the new Seawatch stations, search for seals, porpoise or seabirds across Solebay.

Special events
Events leaflet available from March. Please get in touch.

By the way...
- We have holiday flats if you'd like to stay here longer. Heathland Explorers – our Children's Holiday Club – runs every Wednesday throughout the school holidays (April–October). Check for details.

Dunwich, Saxmundham,
Suffolk, IP17 3DJ
01728 648501

OPENING TIMES
2 Feb 08–2 Mar 08 dawn–dusk
Sat, Sun
13 Feb 08–17 Feb 08
Wed–Sun
5 Mar 08–20 Jul 08 Wed–Sun
24 Mar 08–30 Mar 08
Mon–Sun
26 May 08–1 Jun 08 Mon–Sun
21 Jul 08–14 Sep 08 Mon–Sun
17 Sep 08–21 Dec 08 Wed–Sun
27 Dec 08–28 Dec 08 Sat, Sun
31 Dec 08–4 Jan 08 Wed–Sun
10 Jan 08–31 Jan 08 Sat, Sun

Notes
Open BH Mons. Heath open dawn–dusk. Coastguard cottages, shop and tearoom open from 10am. Closing times vary.

Hatfield Forest

Countryside Nature reserve Lake Fishing

London & East

Takeley, nr Bishop's Stortford,
Hertfordshire, CM22 6NE
01279 870678

OPENING TIMES
All Year dawn–dusk Mon–Sun
Refreshments
21 Mar 08–31 Oct 08
10am–4:30pm Mon–Sun
1 Nov 08–31 Jan 08
10am–3:30pm Sat, Sun

Notes
Refreshments available daily in
school hols: summer
10am–6pm; winter
10am–3:30pm.

This ancient woodland is a rare surviving example of a medieval royal hunting forest. Today it is a paradise for walkers and families with young children. With 404 hectacres (1000 acres) to explore, an exciting special events programme, café selling homemade cakes and an 18th-century Shell House, there is something here for everyone. There are miles of grass tracks for cycling, cows roam freely in the summer months and signs of wildlife are apparent everywhere you go. This very special place is ideal for families to come and enjoy 365 days a year.

Feature title
Some of the trees in the forest are over a 1000 years old, and the Doodle Oak in particular was mentioned in the Domesday Book. There is evidence of an Iron Age settlement and the deer that live in the forest are thought to be descendants of the herds introduced by King Henry I.

What to see
- During the summer cattle graze in the forest. Wildfowl can be spotted on the lake and the Shell House is open most weekends.

What to do
- Get a day ticket to go fishing (mid June–mid March).
- Discover the forest by foot with a trail guide or by bike – there are several miles of grass paths available to explore.

Special events
Trusty, the National Trust hedgehog, sometimes comes along to give out stickers, and we have Easter, Halloween and Christmas trails. We have live music and theatre events. Get in touch to see what's on... full events list available.

By the way...
- Hatfield is both a National Nature Reserve and a Site of Special Scientific Interest. The visitor centre is fully accessible.
- It's a great place for picnics – bring one along.

Houghton Mill

Mill Lock River

Enjoy watching the wheels and cogs go round in this last working watermill on the Great Ouse, set on an island in the middle of the river. The impressive five-storey, 18th-century building has operational machinery – you can see flour being produced before your eyes (and buy some to take home too). It's a lovely area to take a walk in, with riverside meadows and a trail around Houghton Village.

Water power

Did you know that along with making flour, and pumping water, mills have also been used to produce paper and even gunpowder? The only milling that goes on at Houghton is of the floury variety although the water also drives a turbine that produces electricity for the building.

What to see
- All the water wheels, grinding stones, cogs and shafts – great if you're interested in how things work.
- Milling (on Sundays and Bank Holidays) – find out what a damsel or hopper was for.
- Look out over the nearby lock.

What to do
- Turn the model millstones and pull the rope to lift a bag of flour.
- Bike or horse ride on the bridleway (but watch out if you're walking!)
- Stay in the nearby caravan and campsite (run by the Caravan Club).

By the way...
- The grounds are fully accessible, as is the ground floor of the mill.
- Phone ahead to make sure we will be milling if you want to see the wheel in action.

Houghton, nr Huntingdon, Cambridgeshire, PE28 2AZ
01480 301494

OPENING TIMES
Mill/bookshop
22 Mar 08–26 Apr 08
11am–5pm Sat
23 Mar 08–27 Apr 08
1pm–5pm Sun
3 May 08–27 Sep 08
11am–5pm Sat
28 Apr 08–28 Sep 08
1pm–5pm Mon, Tue, Wed, Sun
4 Oct 08–25 Oct 08
11am–5pm Sat
5 Oct 08–26 Oct 08
1pm–5pm Sun
Tearoom
As mill 11am–5pm
Walks/car park
All year 9am–6pm Mon–Sun

Notes
Open BH Mons and Good Fri: mill 1pm–5pm; tearoom 11am–5pm. Caravan and campsite open March–Oct. Groups and school parties at other times by arrangement with the Property Manager.

Ickworth House, Park & Gardens

Historic house Garden Park Wood

London & East

The Rotunda, Horringer, Bury
St Edmunds, Suffolk, IP29 5QE
01284 735270

OPENING TIMES
House
15 Mar 08–30 Sep 08
1pm–5pm Mon, Tue, Fri,
Sat, Sun
1 Oct 08–2 Nov 08
1pm–4:30pm Mon, Tue, Fri,
Sat, Sun
Gardens
15 Mar 08–30 Sep 08
10am–5pm Mon, Tue, Fri,
Sat, Sun
1 Oct 08–2 Nov 08 11am–4pm
Mon, Tue, Fri, Sat, Sun
Park
All year 8am–8pm Mon–Sun
Shop/restaurant
15 Mar 08–2 Nov 08
10am–5pm Mon, Tue, Fri,
Sat, Sun
3 Nov 08–23 Dec 08
11am–4pm Mon, Tue, Fri,
Sat, Sun
27 Dec 08–1 Jan 08
11am–4pm Mon, Wed, Thu, Fri,
Sat, Sun
2 Jan 08–31 Jan 08
11am–4pm Mon, Tue, Fri,
Sat, Sun

Notes
Park closes dusk if earlier than
8pm. Park and gardens closed
25 and 27 Dec. Park, gardens,
shop and restaurant open daily
during half-term hols, Easter
and summer hols.

This eccentric stately home, with a big central rotunda and curved corridors, was started in 1795 for an equally eccentric character, the 4th Earl of Bristol. Today, you can see his fine collection of silver and paintings by Titian, Velasquez and Gainsborough. The Italianate garden and 18th-century parkland are also worth exploring, with a vineyard, summerhouse and lakes.

Hervey going

Frederick Augustus Hervey, aka the 4th Earl of Bristol, was Bishop of Derry for 35 years, but also enjoyed living it up. Lord Claremeont said 'His genius is like a shallow stream, rapid, noisy, diverting, but useless'. Lord Chesterfield said of an earlier Hervey, 'At the beginning God created three different species, men, women and Herveys'. With friends like these...

What to see

- The heraldic animal of the Hervey family, the snow leopard or
  ounce, can be spotted in almost every room in the house. Look too
  for silver fish, fans, miniature paintings and lots of other objects.
- Outside, shiver in the spooky gothic atmosphere of the Victorian
  stumpery and marvel at the massive ancient oak trees in the park.

What to do

- Play in the adventure playground.
- Work out with the family on the woodland Trim Trail and family cycle
  route (some steep terrain, helmets advised).
- Borrow a park and garden activity backpack or navigate through
  the park with the family explorer guide.

Special events

Lots of family activities throughout the year including twilight
adventures, den building, archaeology, medieval mayhem, and wartime
Ickworth. Also guided walks, holiday programmes, open-air children's
theatre and seasonal special events such as Easter Bunny Day, Easter-
egg trails and Halloween. Get in touch to see what's coming up.

By the way...

- Contact us to see what special events for families are planned.
- Great facilities for visitors are now open 12 months a year in the
  West Wing (including shop and restaurant).

Oxburgh Hall, Garden & Estate

Historic house Garden Wood Moat

Oxborough, King's Lynn,
Norfolk, PE33 9PS
01366 328258

OPENING TIMES
House
15 Mar 08–30 Jul 08 1pm–5pm
Mon, Tue, Wed, Sat, Sun
31 Jul 08–31 Aug 08 1pm–5pm
Mon–Sun
1 Sep 08–1 Oct 08 1pm–5pm
Mon, Tue, Wed, Sat, Sun
4 Oct 08–2 Nov 08 1pm–4pm
Mon, Tue, Wed, Sat, Sun
Garden/tearoom/shop
2 Feb 08–9 Mar 08 11am–4pm
Sat, Sun
15 Mar 08–30 Jul 08
11am–5pm Mon, Tue, Wed,
Sat, Sun
1 Aug 08–31 Aug 08
11am–5pm Mon–Sun
1 Sep 08–1 Oct 08 11am–5pm
Mon, Tue, Wed, Sat, Sun
4 Oct 08–2 Nov 08 11am–4pm
Mon, Tue, Wed, Sat, Sun
8 Nov 08–21 Dec 08
11am–4pm Sat, Sun
3 Jan 08–31 Jan 08
11am–4pm Sat, Sun

Notes
Open BH Mons and Good Fri:
11am–5pm (incl. house). On
Thu and Fri in Aug, house open
for limited timed tickets tour
only, 1pm–5pm. Gatehouse
open for tours Sat and Sun
12–31 Jan 09. Please tel. for
times.

You might see a swan float past your window in this grand manor house surrounded by a moat, and complete with battlements, where the Bedingfeld family, who are still in residence, have lived ever since the house was built in 1482.

Hidey hole
After the Reformation, Catholic families like the Bedingfelds had a lot to fear, even death. The house has secret doors and a priest's hole, where they or their priest could hide if soldiers came.

What to see
- Look for the ha-ha – a ditch dug on the edge of a field to keep cows and sheep out. You can hardly see it, so don't fall in – ha ha!
- A huge Tudor gatehouse.
- The priests' hole – imagine how scary that would be!

What to do
- Take a peek at the little Catholic chapel in the grounds.
- Take the Woodland Explorer Trail around the garden.
- Check out where the drawbridge used to be.

Special events
We have family events like Easter-egg hunts, and also living-history days when you can meet a variety of characters in Tudor costume. Check with us to see what's on.

By the way...
- There's a secondhand bookshop in the Gun Room, during season.
- Try out the children's quiz/trail and pick up information on self-guided family tours.
- We have a ramped entrance and wheelchairs; there are stairs to other floors. And be careful near the moat!

Sutton Hoo

Archeological site Countryside Museum

Sutton Hoo is one of Britain's most important and atmospheric archeological sites. It was the burial ground of the Anglo-Saxon kings of East Anglia. Visit the award-winning exhibition that explains the burial mounds and tells the story of Anglo-Saxon warriors, treasure and kings.

Underground treasure ship
In 1939 one of the large mounds at the site was excavated, revealing a huge amount of priceless royal treasure inside the remains of a burial chamber in a 27m (90ft) ship. It's one of the most important finds ever found in Britain, and is famous worldwide.

What to see
- Visit the viewing platform to see the large burial mounds, including the 'Treasure Mound'.
- A full-size reconstruction of the ship's burial chamber with copies of its treasures as they may have been.
- Find out how the exquisite jewellery was made.

What to do
- Watch our specially commissioned film conjuring up the world of Anglo-Saxon kings, craftsmen and poets.
- Walk along the River Debden on waymarked trails.
- Have fun in the children's play area, and try out the dressing-up box in the exhibition.

Special events
Our family events have included felt-making demonstrations, Easter trail, Halloween Happenings (very spooky) and crafts. Contact us to find out what's planned.

By the way...
- There is a dressing-up box and a quiz in the exhibition.
- There are some tethering rings and water for dogs too.
- We have wheelchairs and a map of an accessible route; the entrance is level.

Tranmer House, Sutton Hoo, Woodbridge, Suffolk, IP12 3DJ
01394 389700

OPENING TIMES
1 Feb 08–8 Feb 08 11am–4pm Sat, Sun
9 Feb 08–17 Feb 08 11am–4pm Mon–Sun
18 Feb 08–18 Mar 08 11am–4pm Sat, Sun
19 Mar 08–6 Apr 08 10:30am–5pm Mon–Sun
7 Apr 08–20 May 08 10:30am–5pm Wed, Thu, Fri, Sat, Sun
21 May 08–1 Jun 08 10:30am–5pm Mon–Sun
2 Jun 08–24 Jun 08 10:30am–5pm Wed, Thu, Fri, Sat, Sun
25 Jun 08–31 Aug 08 10:30am–5pm Mon–Sun
1 Sep 08–21 Oct 08 10:30am–5pm Wed, Thu, Fri, Sat, Sun
22 Oct 08–2 Nov 08 10:30am–5pm Mon–Sun
3 Nov 08–31 Jan 08 11am–4pm Sat, Sun

Notes
Open BH Mons. Estate walks open daily all year 9am–6pm (except for certain Thur, Nov–Jan incl.).

Tattershall Castle

Castle

Tattershall, Lincoln,
Lincolnshire, LN4 4LR
01526 342543

OPENING TIMES
1 Mar 08–14 Mar 08
12am–4pm Sat, Sun
15 Mar 08–1 Oct 08
11am–5:30pm Mon, Tue,
Wed, Sat, Sun
4 Oct 08–2 Nov 08
11am–4pm Mon, Tue, Wed,
Sat, Sun
3 Nov 08–16 Dec 08
12am–4pm Sat, Sun

Notes
Open Good Fri
11am–5:30pm. Last audio
guide issued 1½hrs before
closing. Castle opens 1pm on
Sats when weddings are
being held (except July/Aug).

You can explore from the cellar to the battlements in this very dramatic medieval tower, with walls as thick as a room. It was built in the 1400s for Ralph, Lord Cromwell, a wealthy adviser to King Henry VI, and over one million locally made bricks were required to build the tower and buildings. There was an earlier fortified castle but this one was really made mostly for show.

It's a moat point
Well two, actually – the original castle on this site had an outer and inner moat, which have been restored. One 'for best' – for entertaining guests and visitors, so they say – and one to keep out nasty enemy gatecrashers.

What to see
- One vast tower – with four great chambers with enormous gothic fireplaces and lots of tapestries.
- The very creepy cellar – go on, we dare you.

What to do
- Dress up and play with Tudor toys and medieval costumes.
- Grab our free audio guide to find out more about 15th-century life.
- Walk over the moats (by way of the bridges, that is).

Special events
Fancy a spot of brass rubbing? On some Sundays we'll let you loose on our collection for a small charge. We also have children's activity days and living-history weekends – get in touch for more detail.

By the way...
- We have some touchable objects and a Braille guide too.
- There are stairs to the upper floors in the castle.

Wimpole Home Farm

Park Farm

Wimpole Hall, Arrington,
Royston, Cambridgeshire,
SG8 0BW
01223 206000

OPENING TIMES
2 Feb 08–12 Mar 08
11am–4pm Sat, Sun
15 Mar 08–16 Jul 08
10:30am–5pm Mon, Tue,
Wed, Sat, Sun
19 Jul 08–31 Aug 08
10:30am–5pm Mon, Tue,
Wed, Thu, Sat, Sun
1 Sep 08–29 Oct 08
10:30am–5pm Mon, Tue,
Wed, Sat, Sun
2 Nov 08–21 Dec 08
11am–4pm Sat, Sun
27 Dec 08–1 Jan 08
11am–4pm Mon, Tue, Wed,
Sat, Sun
3 Jan 08–31 Jan 08
11am–4pm Sat, Sun

Notes
Open BH Mons and Good Fri:
10:30am–5pm. Closed every Fri
except Good Fri. Open
Sat–Thurs during local school
Easter and half-term hols.

Lots to see at this charming farm built by Sir John Soane in 1794 for the 3rd Earl of Hardwicke, who was potty about animals and agriculture. Wimpole is a working farm that's home to all types of rare breeds, which you can look at, touch and even feed. Why not combine your visit with a trip to the Hall, a stunning Georgian mansion. There is also a huge park to explore, with gothic tower and serpentine lakes.

Come in number five!

If you come to Wimpole in April you'll see new-born lambs, and might even see one being born. Once the lambs are born, we give them trendy ear tags (they don't mind them) and mum and her lambs all have the same number sprayed on their sides, so we know who belongs to who. During the rest of the year there is a daily events programme so that you can meet the animals and even help us feed them. In school holidays we have family activity days where you can have a go at making butter and try your hand at all sorts of different crafts. Then why not let off steam in the play area and adventure woodland! A family trail enables mum and dad to get involved in this visit of discovery.

What to see

- Different breeds of sheep with strange names like Logthan, Soays, Portland's and Manx. Cows, pigs, goats, rabbits, chickens... a farm full of four-legged friends (and two-legged ones with beaks).
- Thatched buildings and a Victorian dairy.

What to do

- Go on a wagon ride between Home Farm and Wimpole Hall, pulled by our lovely big Shire Horses – they're such gentle giants. Help feed the goats, groom the ponies or cuddle a bunny in our daily programme of activities. Youngsters can let off steam in the play area or adventure woodland.

Special events

Wimpole Home Farm has a programme of daily events and activities, plus a whole range of special events throughout the year. Lambing time, family activity days and the chance to meet Father Christmas are just a few that our visitors return to again and again. Youngsters can even have their birthday party here – just don't share your cake with the chickens! Visit the National Trust website or give us a call.

By the way...

- Pushchairs and back carriers welcome, and there is a children's play area. Book one of our three wheelchairs or self-drive PMVs but bear in mind that there are some gravel areas.
- Please note that there is a small charge for National Trust members to visit the Home Farm.

Wicken Fen National Nature Reserve

Mill Countryside Nature reserve Visitor centre Cottage

Lode Lane, Wicken, Ely,
Cambridgeshire, CB7 5XP
01353 720274

OPENING TIMES
11 Feb 08–17 Feb 08
10am–5pm Mon–Sun
18 Feb 08–23 Mar 08
10am–5pm Tue, Wed, Thu, Fri,
Sat, Sun
24 Mar 08–31 Oct 08
10am–5pm Mon–Sun
1 Nov 08–31 Jan 08
10am–4:30pm Tue, Wed, Thu,
Fri, Sat, Sun
Fen Cottage
30 Mar 08–19 Oct 08
2pm–5pm Sun

Notes
Café closed Tue 1 Nov–31 Jan.
Reserve closed 25 Dec. Some
paths are closed in very wet
weather. Fen Cottage (showing
the way of life c.1900) open BH
Mons.

One of Britain's oldest nature reserves and a very special and ancient place. Once the whole of East Anglia was covered with fenland, which is a special kind of peaty wetland. Now this is the last 0.1% of natural fenland left. It's a haven for birds, plants, insects and all kinds of wildlife. Explore its lush green paths and visit the hides, or walk along the boardwalk (fine for pushchairs).

Not quite high and dry
Most of the fenland that was part of the Great Fen of East Anglia has now been drained and ploughed. That drainage made the level of the dry land fall, so that Wicken Fen is now left standing like an island, up to 2m (6ft) higher than the land around it.

What to see
- Butterflies, birds, bugs, reptiles and rare plants like fen violet.
- Fen Cottage – a typical workers' dwelling built from fen products.

What to do
- Put on your wellies (it can be wet) and take one of the trails – pick up a guide at the visitor's centre. Bring your binoculars – or hire some from us – to look at the birds from Tower Hide.
- Have a very un-medieval ice cream after your walk.

Special events
We have quite a lot going on. Recently we have had bat and moth detection nights, ghosts walks, wildlife identification and a chance to try your hand at rush weaving.

By the way...
- We have a couple of wheelchairs, and the boardwalk is accessible, as is the café and picnic area.

Woolsthorpe Manor

Historic house Garden Farm Discovery centre

The birthplace and family home of Sir Isaac Newton, the chap who discovered gravity when an apple fell on his head in this very garden. The descendants of this famous apple tree live on in the orchard. It's amazing to think that Newton had some of his most important and famous ideas in this modest little house.

Irritating Isaac

Newton may have been a clever clogs but he was also known to be a bit cantankerous. He disagreed with the Royal Astronomer, and had an argument with famous mathematician Leibniz that lasted over 15 years. Well, nobody said a genius has to be nice.

What to see
- A descendant of the famous apple tree.
- The room where Newton worked.

What to do
- Wander around the orchards and paddocks.
- Visit the farm buildings with rare breed Lincoln Longwool sheep.
- Dip into the science discovery centre, with a chance to look through telescopes, play with pendulums and more.

Special events

We have an apple day (well, we would...) and we have family activity and workshop days. Get in touch to see what's coming up.

By the way...
- There's a family guide and quiz/trail for you to have a go at, or pick up a leaflet to do a village walk.
- There are baby-changing facilities, but bear in mind the café is small and has a limited selection. You can book a wheelchair, though there are stairs to the upper floors.

Water Lane, Woolsthorpe by Colsterworth, nr Grantham, Lincolnshire, NG33 5PD
01476 860338

OPENING TIMES
1 Mar 08–23 Mar 08 1pm–5pm Sat, Sun
26 Mar 08–29 Jun 08 1pm–5pm Wed, Thu, Fri, Sat, Sun
2 Jul 08–31 Aug 08 1pm–5pm Wed, Thu, Fri
2 Jul 08–31 Aug 08 11am–5pm Sat, Sun
3 Sep 08–28 Sep 08 1pm–5pm Wed, Thu, Fri, Sat, Sun
4 Oct 08–26 Oct 08 1pm–5pm Sat, Sun

Notes
Open BH Mons and Good Fri.

Best of the Rest

London & East

Felbrigg Hall, Garden & Park

Felbrigg is a fine 17th-century house surrounded by a park with some stunning trees and plenty of space to run around in. Find the bath which got you clean without the servants getting the slightest glimpse of your private parts. Spot the false door in the dining room and look up inside a dovecote full of white doves. Events include Victorian living history days when you could have a go at butter-making, writing with quill pens – and even laundry work. There are musical evenings, plays and a host of other activities. Wonderful walks to the lake, woods, church and across the estate are great for nature spotting – this has been designated an Area of Outstanding Natural Beauty.

Contact: Felbrigg, Norwich, Norfolk NR11 8PR. Tel. 01263 837444 **Opening times: House** 3 Mar 08–2 Nov 08 11am–5pm Mon, Tue, Wed, Sat, Sun **Gardens** 3 Mar 08–26 Oct 08 11am–5pm Mon, Tue, Wed, Sat, Sun; 26 May 08–1 Jun 08 11am–5pm Mon–Sun; 21 Jul 08–31 Aug 08 11am–5pm Mon–Sun; 27 Oct 08–2 Nov 08 11am–5pm Mon–Sun; 27 Dec 08–31 Dec 08 11am–4pm Mon, Tue, Wed, Sat, Sun **Shop/restaurant/tearoom/ bookshop/plant sales:** 3 Mar 08–2 Nov 08 As gardens Mon, Tue, Wed, Sat, Sun; 3 Nov 08–14 Dec 08 11am–4pm Thu, Fri, Sat, Sun; 27 Dec 08–31 Dec 08 11am–4pm Mon, Tue, Wed, Sat, Sun; 5 Jan 08–31 Jan 08 11am–4pm Sat, Sun **Estate walks:** All year dawn–dusk Mon–Sun **Notes:** Open BH Mons and Good Fri. Timed tickets may be in operation 11am–1pm.

Melford Hall

Come to Melford Hall and be a spy! It's 1786 ... A few years ago, Captain Hyde Parker captured a Spanish galleon. It was stuffed with treasure on its way to the King of Spain. The loot was divided up and Sir Hyde Parker sent his share back to England. Now the King of Spain wants his treasure back! His spies hint that Melford Hall is a good place to start – come and sneak into the Great Hall, slip into the Library, tiptoe to the Cabinet Corridor and creep up the stairs. Tiptoe through the other rooms of the house looking for an ivory statue and lots of china and jewels along the way.

Contact: Long Melford, Sudbury, Suffolk CO10 9AA. Tel. 01787 379228 **Opening times:** 22 Mar 08–30 Mar 08 1:30pm–5pm Mon, Wed, Thu, Fri, Sat, Sun; 5 Apr 08–27 Apr 08 1:30pm–5pm Sat, Sun; 1 May 08–28 Sep 08 1:30pm–5pm Wed, Thu, Fri, Sat, Sun; 4 Oct 08–26 Oct 08 1:30pm–5pm Sat, Sun **Notes:** Open BH Mons.

Orford Ness

The largest vegetated shingle spit in Europe, the Reserve contains internationally important flora and fauna including shingle, saltmarsh, mudflat, brackish lagoons and grazing marsh. It provides an important location for breeding and passage birds as well as for the coastal shingle flora and wildlife, including a large number of nationally rare species. The Ness was a secret military test site from 1913 until the mid-1980s. Visitors follow a 8.8km (5½ mile) route, which can be walked in total or in part.

Contact: Quay Office, Orford Quay, Orford, Woodbridge, Suffolk, IP12 2NU. Tel. 01728 648024 **Opening times:** 22 Mar 08–28 Jun 08 Sat; 1 Jul 08–27 Sep 08 Tue, Wed, Thu, Fri, Sat; 4 Oct 08–25 Oct 08 Sat **Notes:** The only access is by National Trust ferry from Orford Quay, with boats crossing regularly between 10am and 2pm and the last ferry leaving the Ness at 5pm.

Peckover House & Garden

Explore the fascinating home of the Peckovers, the Quaker banking family who lived here for 150 years. This is a hands-on house with a 'cabinet of curiosities', dressing-up clothes for children of all ages, and three floors revealing the lives of both the family and their servants. Built c.1722, this is one of England's finest townhouses with superb rococo plaster and wood decorations. Outside, discover the hidden wonders of the 0.8 hectares (2 acres) of beautiful Victorian garden, with its orangery, summerhouse, roses, fernery and manicured croquet lawn, as well as a 17th-century thatched barn and Georgian stables. There are stunning displays of daffodils, narcissi and tulips in spring and roses in summer.

Contact: North Brink, Wisbech, Cambridgeshire PE13 1JR. Tel. 01945 583463 **Opening times: House/shop/bookshop:** 15 Mar 08–2 Nov 08 1pm–4:30pm Mon, Tue, Wed, Sat, Sun **Garden/restaurant:** 15 Mar 08–2 Nov 08 12am–5pm Mon, Tue, Wed, Sat, Sun **Notes:** Open BH Mons and Good Fri: 12am–5pm. Also open 3 and 4 July for Wisbech Rose Fair.

Constable Country Walk –
Flatford & Dedham Vale Suffolk

London & East

Explore the picturesque Stour Valley and Dedham Vale made famous by the paintings of 18th-century England's foremost landscape artist. John Constable painted idyllic views of the area in his famous six-foot canvases, scenes that remain easily recognisable today.

Getting there:

Train: Regular service to Manningtree station – London Liverpool Street to Ipswich line.

Bus: Services to Manningtree station and Dedham from Colchester and Ipswich.

Cycling: The Painter's Trail cycle route passes through the Stour Valley to Manningtree station.

Road: Car park at Manningtree station, Flatford and Dedham.

Distance: 6.4km (4 miles) return from Manningtree to Flatford. Optional loop to Dedham adds another 5km (3 miles).

Terrain and accessibility: Generally flat grass and gravel paths with some moderate slopes. Can be muddy after wet weather – take care when walking on riverside sections of the route.

Directions and points of interest:

Leave Manningtree station exit and descend a ramp to the right. The footpath starts from the end of the ramp in the car park. After leaving the car park turn right along a track, and then turn right again under a railway bridge. Follow the map shown opposite. The numbers on the map correspond to the numbers below.

1 Follow the path until you reach the river and turn left along a streamside path through the Cattawade Marshes, where the fresh water of the Stour meets the tidal estuary. The Cattawade Marshes are a great place to spot waterfowl and waders. The little egret can be seen fishing in streams and ditches downstream of Flatford.

2 Walk behind Fifty Six Gates, an old flood-defence barrier, and follow the path on the bank to the hamlet of Flatford.

3 This little riverside hamlet is the setting for some of Constable's most famous paintings, such as *The Hay Wain*, *The Mill Stream*, *Boat-building Near Flatford* and *The White Horse*. The Bridge Cottage is now home to a small exhibition on Constable, a National Trust tearoom and shop. Take a detour to see Flatford Mill and Willy Lott's House – these are owned by the National Trust but leased to the Field Studies Council, which runs arts-based courses there. Return to Manningtree by the same route or continue on to Dedham.

4 Walk up Tunnel Lane from Bridge Cottage. Turn left at the top of the lane and after 100m (110yd) take the footpath parallel to the road.

5 Panoramic views over the vale can be seen from the top of the hill and are captured in the painting *Dedham Vale Morn*. Turn left into Fen Lane. Look out for the landscape that inspired *The Cornfield* when walking along Fen Lane towards Dedham.

6 Shortly after crossing a bridge turn right along a tree-lined footpath. Cross riverside meadows, until reaching a bridge at Dedham.

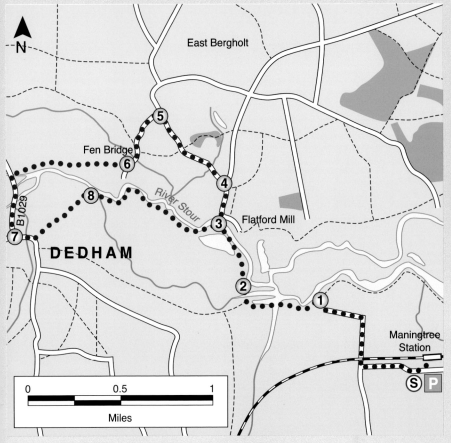

Dedham is a pretty village with the Church of St Mary the Virgin, home to an original Constable painting. *The Ascension* is one of his religious works painted in the same year as *The Hay Wain*.

7 Leave the village on a footpath after the drive to Dedham Hall. Follow this to Flatford, bearing left at the National Trust sign to Dedham Hall Farm.

8 The river leads back to Bridge Cottage across water meadows. A kissing gate marks the site of the stile featured in *The Leaping Horse*.

Property contact: 01206 298260 (Flatford Bridge Cottage)

Map and start grid ref: OS Landranger 168, Explorer 196, TM 093 322

Facilities available: WC at Manningtree station, Flatford and Dedham villages. National Trust riverside tearoom and shop at Flatford, other shops and pubs at Dedham. Flatford Bridge Cottage exhibition on Constable.

National Trust properties nearby: Bourne Mill, the Suffolk estuaries, Thorington Hall.

Attingham Park

Historic house Park Farm

Shrewsbury, Shropshire
SY4 4TP
01743 708123

OPENING TIMES
House
1 Mar 08–9 Mar 08 1pm–4pm
Sat, Sun
13 Mar 08–26 Oct 08
1pm–5:30pm Mon, Tue, Wed,
Fri, Sat, Sun
27 Oct 08–2 Nov 08 1pm–4pm
Mon, Tue, Thu, Fri, Sat, Sun
House tours
As house 11am–1pm
Park/shop/reception
1 Feb 08–12 Mar 08 9am–4pm
Mon–Sun
13 Mar 08–31 Oct 08
9am–6pm Mon–Sun
1 Nov 08–31 Jan 08 9am–4pm
Mon–Sun
Tearoom
1 Mar 08–9 Mar 08
10:30am–4pm Sat, Sun
13 Mar 08–26 Oct 08
10:30am–5pm Mon, Tue, Thu,
Fri, Sat, Sun
27 Oct 08–2 Nov 08
10:30am–4pm Mon, Tue, Thu,
Fri, Sat, Sun
8 Nov 08–31 Jan 08
10:30am–4pm Sat, Sun

Notes
Open BH Mons and Good Fri.
Last admission 1hr before
closing. Closed Christmas Day.
House: 27 Oct–2 Nov, behind
the scenes; special Christmas
weekend openings 13/14 and
20/21 Dec. Kiosk open during
local school hols. Tearoom:
open 9–17 Feb; Christmas
opening 27 Dec–4 Jan 09,
10:30am–4pm.

An elegant 18th-century mansion with a grand façade and swanky
Regency interiors – originally the home of the 1st Lord Berwick – set
in a grand park with nice river walks. See how the other half lived as
you admire the silver, furniture and paintings here. The Home Farm,
on the edge of the estate, is a working farm where children can feed
the animals.

Bigging it up...
There were lots of tricks to make the house seem bigger. The drive is
winding, and goes by especially positioned trees, so that the grounds
seem larger. The Main Drawing Room has mirrors at either end, to
make the room go on forever. And there are false doors to give the
illusion of extra rooms.

What to see
- The Boudoir Room – for the ladies to retreat to. Round and with five
  doors (two fakes), it is decorated with romantic cupids.
- The Picture Gallery by John Nash. Look at the picture of Queen
  Charlotte, whose face ages as you walk past it from left to right.
- The Octagon Room – once Lord Berwick's private 'quiet room'.

What to do
- Imagine being a servant who had to answer when one of the bells in
  the Bell Room went off – there was one for every room in the house.
- See the biggest salmon ever caught in Britain in the Tenant's Parlour.
- Dress up, learn to lay a fire or play games of the times in the Family
  Activity Room.

Special events
Food fayres, parkland tractor rides and Christmas fun are just some of
our recent events, as well as special trails during holiday times. Get in
touch to find out more.

By the way...
- There's a children's play area, baby-changing and feeding facilities
  and you can borrow a child sling. Children's menu in the tearoom.
- Visit the Environmental discovery room in the park to find out about
  the deer and birds.
- Ask for the alternative entrance if you have mobility problems; we
  have wheelchairs available. Handling collection is available, and there
  are things to touch in the house.

Baddesley Clinton

Historic house Garden Park Lake

In Elizabethan times this house was riddled with secret hidey holes to conceal the hounded Catholic Ferrers family and their friends. See if you can spot them, then stretch your legs on the many walks and trails in the grounds.

Not the most pleasant paddle
When Protestant Elizabeth I was on the throne, the house became a refuge for Catholic priests on the run. In 1591 a priest's hole in the drains saved nine catholic priests, who stood knee deep in water while the Queen's soldiers searched the house.

What to see
- The Ferrers family coat of arms in the 16th-century stained glass.
- Look carefully by the library fireplace to find a bloodstain from a murder that took place in 1485. Listen for ghostly whispering too!
- A 16th-century garderobe or loo, that hides the entrance to one of the secret hiding places.

What to do
- Find another priest's hole – ask a steward to help you find it.
- Have a look at the moat – but don't fall in!
- Listen out for the chiming turret clock, and cosy up to our log fire in February, March, April, October and November.

Rising Lane, Baddesley Clinton Village, Knowle, Solihull, West Midlands, B93 0DQ
01564 783294

OPENING TIMES
House
9 Feb 08–2 Nov 08 11am–5pm Wed, Thu, Fri, Sat, Sun
Grounds/shop/restaurant
9 Feb 08–2 Nov 08 11am–5pm Wed, Thu, Fri, Sat, Sun
5 Nov 08–21 Dec 08 11am–4pm Wed, Thu, Fri, Sat, Sun

Notes
Admission by timed ticket to house; visitors may then stay until house closes if they wish. Open BH Mons.

Central

continued...

119

Special events
Typical events are bug hunts, Easter-egg trails and other family activities – get in touch for more information.

By the way...
- The public bridleway is also a cycle path.
- We can loan you a baby or infant sling, and we have changing facilities, level entrance and four wheelchairs available. There are some stairs.

Berrington Hall

Historic house Garden

Wander around inside this elegant late 18th-century house designed by Henry Holland, with its nursery, Victorian laundry and Georgian dairy. Or stroll in the equally attractive gardens designed by 'Capability' Brown, with sweeping views to the Brecon Beacons.

Dressing up

Flip through this book to Snowshill Manor (see p.136), and you'll realise why Charles Wade didn't have room for his costume collection there. A lot of it is housed here instead, and some is always on display.

What to see

- Two commodes in the very elegant white and gold drawing room (not very private).
- Dolls, dolls' houses and a lovely rocking chair in the Victorian nursery.

What to do

- Visit the children's play area or try out the children's quiz. Hands-on activities are arranged most weekends during the season.

Special events

Family activity days, annual plant fair, World War II weekend and Apple Weekend. Get in touch for details of special activities during holidays.

By the way...

- There's a lovely living willow tunnel in the children's play area.
- Baby-changing facilities, and baby slings for loan.
- We have wheelchairs, but should warn you that there are many steps to enter the house.

nr Leominster,
Herefordshire, HR6 0DW
01568 615721

OPENING TIMES
House
1 Mar 08–16 Mar 08 1pm–5pm
Sat, Sun
17 Mar 08–2 Nov 08 1pm–5pm
Mon, Tue, Wed, Sat, Sun
Garden/shop/tearoom
2 Feb 08–24 Feb 08
11am–4pm Sat, Sun
11 Feb 08–13 Feb 08
11am–4pm Mon, Tue, Wed
1 Mar 08–16 Mar 08
11am–5pm Sat, Sun
17 Mar 08–2 Nov 08
11am–5pm Mon, Tue, Wed,
Sat, Sun
6 Dec 08–21 Dec 08
12am–4:30pm Sat, Sun
Park walk
1 Mar 08–16 Mar 08
11am–5pm Mon, Tue, Wed,
Sat, Sun
17 Mar 08–2 Nov 08
12am–4:30pm Sat, Sun
6 Dec 08–21 Dec 08
12am–4:30pm Sat, Sun

Notes
Open Good Fri. House tours 11am–1pm. Access to parkland restricted 1 Mar–16 June (due to nesting birds). Park Walk closed 2 and 3 Aug. House ground floor only open 6/7 Dec.

Brockhampton Estate

Historic house Garden Park Countryside Farm

Greenfields, Bringsty, nr
Bromyard, Herefordshire
WR6 5TB
01885 482077

OPENING TIMES
House
3 Mar–1 Apr 12am–4pm
Sat, Sun
4 Apr–30 Sep 12am–5pm Wed,
Thu, Fri, Sat, Sun
3 Oct–28 Oct 12am–4pm Wed,
Thu, Fri, Sat, Sun
Estate
All year dawn–dusk Mon–Sun
Tearoom
As house, Wed, Thu, Fri,
Sat, Sun
1 Jul–31 Aug 12am–5pm
Mon–Sun
1 Dec–30 Dec 12am–4pm
Sat, Sun

Notes
Open BH Mons. Good Fri:
12am–5pm. Last orders in
tearoom 30mins before house
closes.

This fairytale medieval moated manor house has a lovely crooked gatehouse and ruined Norman chapel and is set in extensive areas of woods and traditionally farmed land. We're sure there are some tree sprites in the garden – there are certainly some fun wooden sculptures on the woodland walks.

That's a Great Hall

Inside the house you can see an immense Great Hall, open up to the rafters, which are made from wood from the estate. Many of those ancient oaks and beeches are still standing.

What to see

- Harold the Shire – a full-size replica shire horse made from a windblown oak.
- In the house, spot a carved wooden lion, and leather fire buckets from the 19th century.
- Sculptures showing scenes from working life in the past.

What to do

- Follow the Nursery Rhyme Trail or visit the wildflower meadow.
- Take one of the waymarked walks – Ash, Holly, Beech or Oak. Dogs can come too, under strict control.
- Buy local crafts and produce from The Granary at Lower Brockhampton.

By the way...

- Wonderful place for picnics.
- Farm tours and guided walks by arrangement.
- Pushchairs admitted. Fairly accessible, but parkland can be uneven and muddy so watch out.

Calke Abbey

Historic house Garden Park Farm Nature reserve

Calke was built in 1701–4 and isn't really an Abbey; for years it was home to the eccentric Harpur Crewe family, who never threw much away. It hasn't changed much since the 1880s, and gives an amazing glimpse of 19th-century life. It's also a magical and especially child-friendly place, with some special trails.

Invisible servants

The owners were a funny lot – they didn't want to see their servants so they built secret corridors and tunnels for them to use. If a servant bumped into a member of the family, they had to turn their face to the wall and pretend to be invisible!

What to see

- Some rather weird collections – cannonballs, shells and stones, and even an alligator skull.
- An aviary with pheasants in it.
- A stunning Chinese silk bed.

What to do

- Find the Old Man of Calke who is 1,000 years old. Become a detective around the house. Find the Ice House for a chilling experience. Take a tracker pack and explore the park.

Special events

Easter-egg hunts, Apple Day, Pumpkin Party and Father Christmas. There's always something special happening at Calke. To find out more please call us or visit the National Trust website.

Ticknall, Derby,
Derbyshire, DE73 7LE
01332 863822

Central

OPENING TIMES
House
1 Mar 08–9 Mar 08
12:30pm–5pm Sat, Sun
15 Mar 08–2 Nov 08
12:30pm–5pm Mon, Tue, Wed,
Sat, Sun
Garden/stables
1 Mar 08–9 Mar 08 11am–5pm
Sat, Sun
15 Mar 08–2 Nov 08
11am–5pm Mon, Tue, Wed,
Sat, Sun
3 Jul 08–5 Sep 08 11am–5pm
Mon–Sun
Restaurant/shop
1 Feb 08–15 Mar 08
11am–4pm Mon, Tue, Wed,
Sat, Sun
15 Mar 08–2 Nov 08
10:30am–5pm Mon, Tue, Wed,
Sat, Sun
21 Mar 08–18 Apr 08
10:30am–5pm Mon–Sun
3 Jul 08–5 Sep 08
10:30am–5pm Mon–Sun
3 Nov 08–3 Dec 08 11am–4pm
Mon, Tue, Wed, Sat, Sun
4 Dec 08–21 Dec 08
11am–4pm Mon–Sun

Notes
House and garden open
Good Fri.

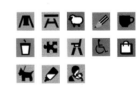

continued...

By the way...

- Calke is very popular, so it can take a while to get in on Bank Holidays.
- There are wheelchairs available. There is quite a lot to see on the ground floor, but stairs to the other floors.
- Ask the Room Steward to show you what items can be touched, or get a list from the entrance hall.
- There's no shaded parking, so think before bringing the dog.

Charlecote Park

Historic house Garden Park Farm

A grand Tudor house with a landscaped deer park and a formal garden by the River Avon. It's been in the Lucy family for at least 700 years. The imposing Elizabethan gatehouse made from pink brick provides a warm welcome and the rest of the house was largely restored in the 19th century and is in 'Elizabethan Revival' style, complete with ornate ceilings and vaulting.

Deer me
A certain William Shakespeare was allegedly caught poaching in the deer park. Perhaps his plays weren't doing so well at the time. Another famous visitor – this time invited – was Queen Elizabeth I, who stayed at Charlecote for two nights in 1572.

What to see
- A fascinating collection of carriages and other vehicles.
- Look out for the Lucy family's unusual symbol – a fish. It's all around the house.
- Elizabethan stained-glass windows in the Great Hall, and a famous table covered with marbles and semi-precious stones.

What to do
- Visit the austere Victorian kitchen and scullery, the laundry room and the brew house – kitted out with original equipment like washtubs and vats.
- Spot herds of fallow deer and Jacob sheep roaming capably in 'Capability' Brown's parkland.
- Explore the children's maze in the play area – don't get lost!

Special events
We cater well for families, and have had bat walks, kite festivals, spinning and weaving demos as well as storytelling and spooky Halloween activities. Get in touch for more information.

By the way...
- There's a ramped entrance, and the ground floor is accessible. We've wheelchairs you can borrow.
- Baby-changing facilities, and carriers for loan, and a children's menu in the restaurant.

Warwick, Warwickshire
CV35 9ER. 01789 470277

OPENING TIMES
House
1 Mar 08–28 Oct 08
12am–5pm Mon, Tue, Fri, Sat, Sun
6 Dec 08–21 Dec 08
12am–4pm Sat, Sun
House tours
1 Mar 08–28 Oct 08
11am–12am Mon, Tue, Fri, Sat, Sun
Park and gardens*
2 Feb 08–24 Feb 08
10:30am–4pm Mon, Tue, Fri, Sat, Sun
1 Mar 08–28 Oct 08
10:30am–6pm Mon, Tue, Fri, Sat, Sun
31 Oct 08–31 Jan 08
10:30am–4pm Mon, Tue, Fri, Sat, Sun
Restaurant
2 Feb 08–24 Feb 08
11am–4pm Sat, Sun
1 Mar 08–28 Oct 08
10:30am–5pm Mon, Tue, Fri, Sat, Sun
1 Nov 08–21 Dec 08
11am–4pm Sat, Sun
Shop
1 Mar 08–28 Oct 08
10:30am–5:30pm Mon, Tue, Fri, Sat, Sun
1 Nov 08–21 Dec 08
11am–4pm Sat, Sun

Notes
Parts of the house only open Dec. *Restricted access to gardens Feb and Nov–Jan 09.

Central

125

Clumber Park

Garden Park Countryside

The Estate Office, Clumber
Park, Worksop,
Nottinghamshire, S80 3AZ
01909 476592

OPENING TIMES
Park
All year dawn–dusk Mon–Sun
Kitchen garden
31 Mar 08–30 Sep 08
10am–6pm Sat, Sun
2 Apr 08–28 Sep 08
10am–5pm Mon, Tue, Wed,
Thu, Fri
**Shop/restaurant/plant
sales**
31 Mar 08–30 Sep 08
10am–6pm Sat, Sun
2 Apr 08–28 Sep 08
10am–5pm Mon, Tue, Wed,
Thu, Fri
1 Oct 08–29 Feb 08
10am–4pm Mon–Sun

Notes
Main facilities open BH Mons,
closed 25 Dec. Chapel open
as shop but closed Feb–Apr
for cleaning. Cycle hire open
as shop except Oct–March,
when open weekends and
school hols only. Interpretation
centre open all year round.
183-berth caravan site run by
Caravan Club open to non-
members (tel. 01909 484758).

Wander around Clumber and you'll find 1500 hectares (3800 acres)
of woods, open heath and rolling farmland. In the middle is a superb
serpentine lake. Formerly home to the Duke of Newcastle, the house
was demolished in 1938 but there is still a chapel and a fascinating
walled kitchen garden with some spectacular glass houses.

How many dukes does it take to change a lightbulb?
Can't help you there, but we do know that the district is called 'The
Dukeries' because it once had five ducal residences: the Dukes of
Newcastle, Kingston, Portland, Norfolk and Leeds. Clumber was the
estate of the Dukes of Newcastle for nearly 300 years.

What to see
- The longest greenhouse owned by the National Trust – that's 137m
  (450ft) long.
- The longest avenue of lime trees in Europe – that's 3km (2 miles).
- Clumber Chapel, made as a mini gothic cathedral.

What to do
- Whether it be cycling, orienteering or a gentle walk through the park
  with your dog, Clumber offers it all. Those less active can picnic,
  shop, find out more about Clumber's wildlife in the conservation
  centre, where you can stick your hands in the feeling box, or simply
  enjoy the views over a cup of tea in our restaurant.
- Discover Clumber's history and landscape in 'The Clumber Story' at
  our interpretation centre.

Special events
Organised throughout the year, please contact the Estate Office.

By the way...
- Wheelchairs and PMVs are available. Adapted cycles, tandems and
  trikes can be hired. There is a ramped entrance to the chapel and
  the walled kitchen garden.

Coughton Court

Historic house Garden

Coughton Court is one of England's finest Tudor houses. Home to the Throckmorton family since 1409, the house boasts fantastic collections of family portraits, Catholic treasures and porcelain. A house and garden of intrigue and discovery.

Priest holes, a tower and a gunpowder plot!
See if you can spot the secret hiding places used to hide away Catholic priests. If you fancy a breath of fresh air, run around the woodland walk and bog garden – watch out for mini beasts and insects!

What to see
- The Throckmorton coat made between sunrise and sunset.
- Priest hole hidey holes.
- Mary Queen of Scot's death mask and chemise (shirt).
- Spot the elephant in the panelled dining room.

What to do
- Climb the tower stairs and take to the roof – how far can you see?
- Go to the rose labyrinth – don't get lost though!
- Run around the play area or indulge in a cooling ice cream from the restaurant while the older folks enjoy a cream tea.
- Take part in the 'Spot Trusty' trail.

Special events
Childrens family learning events throughout the year – ring us for details. Easter-egg trails are a springtime favourite.

By the way...
- There's a childrens house trail/quiz and pocket money goodies in the shop. We can loan you a baby sling, and we have baby changing facilities. Children's packed lunch packs or smaller children's portions on all cooked meals can be provided. Wheelchairs are available.

nr Alcester, Warwickshire
B49 5JA
01789 400777

Central

OPENING TIMES
House
15 Mar 08–29 Jun 08
11am–5pm Wed, Thu, Fri,
Sat, Sun
1 Jul 08–31 Aug 08 11am–5pm
Tue, Wed, Thu, Fri, Sat, Sun
3 Sep 08–28 Sep 08
11am–5pm Wed, Thu, Fri,
Sat, Sun
4 Oct 08–2 Nov 08 11am–5pm
Sat, Sun
Garden/shop/restaurant
As house 11am–5:30pm
Walled garden
As house 11:30am–4:45pm

Notes
Closed Good Fri. Closed 14 June and 6 Sept. Admission by timed ticket on very busy days. Open BH Mons and Tues.

Croome Park

Garden Park Countryside

Croome D'Abitot,
Worcestershire, WR8 9DW
01905 371006

OPENING TIMES
1 Mar 08–30 Mar 08
10am–5:30pm Wed, Thu, Fri,
Sat, Sun
31 Mar 08–31 Aug 08
10am–5:30pm Mon–Sun
3 Sep 08–26 Oct 08
10am–5:30pm Wed, Thu, Fri,
Sat, Sun
1 Nov 08–21 Dec 08
10am–4pm Sat, Sun
26 Dec 08–1 Jan 08
10am–4pm Mon–Sun
Tearoom/shop
As park

Notes
Open BH Mon. Croome church
open in association with The
Churches Conservation Trust
(which owns it). Last admission
45mins before closing. Tel.
estate office for out-of-hours
openings.

Croome Park is the ideal place to run off lots of energy. There are plenty of events and activities for children of all ages and a fantastic family trail. Croome Park was 'Capability' Brown's first commission, it was here where he made his reputation that changed landscapes all over the world.

For kids of all ages
In and around the parkland there are many things to see and do. The story of 'Capability' Brown and how he created the park is all brought to life through a wide range of family trails and events. You can find out more about the role that Croome played in World War II in the exhibition room of our RAF buildings – the last remaining set of complete sick quarters in the UK.

What to see
- The parkland that 'Capability' Brown created has some fantastic features including a grotto, Temple Greenhouse, Island Temple, and eye-catcher follies, which are all linked by paths. Over the years, lots of wildlife creatures have made Croome Park their home and this is all brought to life through activities, walks and trails.

What to do

- The family trail is superb fun. Kids are sent on a mission to spy on Lord and Lady Coventry to see how their park was created. The trail takes in the wider parkland, the miles of culverts that feed into the lake and river, the stories of the plant collectors and visitors who used the Pleasure Grounds in Georgian times (we've also included a booklet for adults to use – just in case you get a little stuck).
- There is also a walks leaflet, which takes in different parts of the park and surrounding areas. Rather than just spot the outer eye catchers from the park, you can go and visit them instead.

Special events

There's something going on during most weekends. There are lots of great guided walks – looking at different parts of the park – its wildlife, trees, nuts and berries. There's hands-on activity events, kite flying, the annual dog show (Pooches n' Croome) and Trusty the Hedgehog is a regular visitor. During the summer school holidays we're open every day – so come along and run around.

By the way...

- We recommend that you wear sturdy shoes. The park is very accessible with paths all the way through the Pleasure Ground and mown paths through the meadows.
- If you don't fancy sampling our 1940s style canteen then you're more than welcome to bring a picnic and lay out your rug wherever you like – enjoy lunch by the lake or tea by the temple.

Hardwick Hall

Central

Doe Lea, Chesterfield,
Derbyshire, S44 5QJ
01246 850430

OPENING TIMES
Hall
1 Mar 08–2 Nov 08
12am–4:30pm Wed, Thu,
Sat, Sun
6 Dec 08–21 Dec 08
12am–4:30pm Sat, Sun
Hall tours
1 Mar 08–2 Nov 08
11am–12am Wed, Thu, Fri,
Sat, Sun
Garden
1 Mar 08–2 Nov 08
11am–5:30pm Wed, Thu, Fri,
Sat, Sun
6 Dec 08–21 Dec 08
11am–5:30pm Sat, Sun
Parkland gates
All year 8am–6pm Mon–Sun
Old Hall (English Heritage)
1 Mar 08–2 Nov 08
10am–5:30pm Wed, Thu, Fri,
Sat, Sun
Shop/restaurant
1 Mar 08–2 Nov 08 11am–5pm
Wed, Thu, Sat, Sun
Stone centre
1 Mar 08–2 Nov 08 11am–4pm
Wed, Thu, Sat, Sun
6 Dec 08–21 Nov 08
11am–4pm Sat, Sun
Kiosk
1 Mar 08–2 Nov 08
10am–4:30pm Mon–Sun

Notes
Open BH Mons and Good Fri:
12am–4:30pm. Kiosk open
between Christmas and New
Year. Park gates shut 6pm in
summer, at dusk in winter.

Hardwick Hall is a truly spectacular Tudor house, one of the most complete in Britain. It presides over the Derbyshire countryside with the same grandeur that its builder, Bess of Hardwick, did.

The Queen's rival
Elizabeth Hardwick, known as Bess of Hardwick, was the second most powerful and wealthy woman in Tudor England – she rivaled Queen Elizabeth I. Ambitious in her choice of husbands, she even married off one of her daughters to Charles Stuart, brother of the late husband of Mary Queen of Scots, who had both Royal Tudor and Stuart blood in his veins. Their daughter, Arbella Stuart, was in direct line for the throne of England.

What to see
- See how this powerful Tudor aristocrat would have lived – Hardwick remains virtually unchanged since Bess lived here.
- Learn about the rare breeds of sheep and cattle.
- Visit the 'Threads of Time' exhibition.
- Outstanding 16th- and 17th-century tapestries and embroideries.

What to do
- Have a picnic in the stunning parkland.
- Take a walk around the Elizabethan walled courtyards, visit the orchard and spot different apple varieties. Take a tour of the stonemason's yard.
- Search through the undergrowth on a fungi foray, dress up as a witch for Halloween and take part in the bat hunt or pumpkin competition, or go on a haunted tour of the house.

Special events
Easter-egg trails, family fun days, Elizabethan weekend, costume days, Halloween activities and lambing walks.

By the way...
- Have fun on our new You-balance Trail at Hardwick Ponds.

Kedleston Hall

Historic house Garden Park Lake Paintings

A really sumptuous Palladian mansion, built between 1759 and 1765 for the Curzon family. The property contains magnificent state rooms designed by Robert Adam, loads of paintings, a museum with weird objects from Lord Curzon's travels in Asia and walks in the restored 18th-century pleasure grounds – complete with a lakes and cascades. A very grand day out with lots to enjoy.

Out of my way!
Sir Nathaniel Curzon, who inherited Kedleston in 1758, thought the village spoilt the view from where he wanted his new house to go. So he had the village moved, stone by stone.

What to see
- Look out for the amazing domed ceiling and sprung floor in the saloon – perfect for parties!
- A replica model of the Taj Mahal in the Eastern Museum.
- A summer house and sculptures hiding in the gardens.
- Lots of wildlife to spot in the park – in the summer months see if you can see the shy highland cattle in the Wilderness.

What to do
- Count the amazing alabaster columns in the Marble Hall as you go inside the house. Then look up at that saloon ceiling – wow!
- Look out for the grand bed decorated with ostrich feathers.
- Have a go at the children's trail.

Special events
Contact us for details or pick up a copy of our property leaflet when you visit. In the past we've had theatre shows, living history demonstrations, spinning demonstrations and craft activities.

By the way...
- The parkland is a great place to romp, and dogs on leads are very welcome.
- There's an alternative entrance avoiding the steps, and we have wheelchairs available. The upper floor can only be reached by a flight of 22 steps.

Derby, Derbyshire, DE22 5JH
01332 842191

OPENING TIMES
House/church
1 Mar 08–2 Nov 08 12am–5pm
Mon, Tue, Wed, Sat, Sun
Garden
1 Mar 08–2 Nov 08 10am–6pm
Mon–Sun
Park
1 Mar 08–2 Nov 08 10am–6pm
Mon–Sun
3 Nov 08–31 Jan 08
10am–4pm Mon–Sun
Shop/restaurant
1 Mar 08–2 Nov 08 11am–5pm
Mon, Tue, Wed, Sat, Sun
24 Jul 08–29 Aug 08
12am–4pm Mon–Sun
3 Nov 08–31 Jan 08
11am–3pm Sat, Sun

Notes
Open Good Fri. Church opens at 11am. Park: occasional day restrictions may apply in Dec/Jan 09. Closed 25/26 Dec. Last entry to Hall 4:15pm. 25min introductory tour of Hall at 11am.

Mr Straw's House

Historic house Garden

7 Blyth Grove, Worksop,
Nottinghamshire, S81 0JG
01909 482380

OPENING TIMES
15 Mar 08–1 Nov 08
11am–5pm Wed, Thu, Fri, Sat

Notes
Admission by timed ticket only
for all visitors (incl. National
Trust members), which must be
booked in advance. All
bookings by tel. or letter (with
sae) to Custodian. On quiet
days a same-day tel. call is
often sufficient. Last admission
4pm. Closed Good Fri. Due to
its location in residential area,
property is closed on BHs as a
courtesy to neighbours.

This house is unique. It's an ordinary suburban semi, but when you
cross the threshold you are plunged back into the 1930s.
Grandparents particularly enjoy visiting with younger ones so they
can reminisce about the past. Children will be amazed to see a 20th-
century house with no TV, CD player, fridge or telephone...

A bit nutty...
The Straws were definitely eccentrics. There is a light fitting that has no
bulb in it – the original bulb fell into William Straw's meal and he was so
annoyed he never replaced it. On the kitchen table you can see where
the family kept their knives and forks in the same basket as their
hammer and chisel.

What to see
- Uniforms and other costumes and accessories. Mr Straw was a
  millionaire but his hairbrush looks as though he didn't have two
  pennies to rub together!

What to do

- Spot the old domestic brand names and designs. Children will easily pick out the Heinz baked beans cans, the design of which has hardly changed.

By the way...

- There is no access to Mr Straw's House without advance booking. We are sorry, there isn't room for pushchairs in the house. Please carry babies.

Shugborough Estate

Historic house Mill Garden Park Countryside Farm

Milford, nr Stafford,
Staffordshire, ST17 0XB
01889 881388

OPENING TIMES
House/farm/servants'
quarters/grounds/tearoom
14 Mar 08–24 Oct 08
11am–5pm Mon–Sun
Shop
14 Mar 08–25 Oct 08
11am–5pm Mon–Sun
26 Oct 08–23 Dec 08
11am–4pm Mon–Sun

Notes
Opening times and prices may
vary when special events held.
Tel. or see website.

See the complete working historic estate of Shugborough where you
can get stuck in – cheese-making, dolly-pegging, baking, milling,
mangling, growing, tasting and exploring. Shugborough, set in 364
hectacres (900 acres) of great, open grassy spaces and gardens, is
the perfect place to let the whole family loose to enjoy a fun day out
packed with living history.

Ahhhh!
The farm at Shugborough has been going since 1805 and is home to
some rare breed farm animals, like Snowdrop the miniature Dexter
cow. Her baby calf was only 30cm (12in) tall when he was born! Meet
Mrs Wheelock at the farm who always needs a hand baking for the
hungry estate workers. Roll up your sleeves and help out in the dairy
before meeting the miller, William Bailey, who will be happy to show off
his working watermill. No visit to the farm would be complete without
meeting the animals and there's Pudding the donkey, Iris the Cow,
Patch and Bluely the rabbits to name but a few.

What to see
- After a short ride on Lucy the train or a stunning walk across the
  parkland, the story continues at the servants' quarters where cooks
  and kitchen maids scurry about preparing food on the range,
  starching the whites in the laundry and brewing Shugborough ale in
  the brewery.

What to do
- Have fun in the children's play area, and climb aboard Lucy the train
  for a free ride from the ticket office to the farm.
- Try and crack the code under the 'Shepherds' monument in the
  grounds. Nobody has yet!
- Watch the working historic watermill in action.

- The fine mansion house is massive with loads of rooms filled with treasure. Costumed characters Lord and Lady Anson are probably in residence so be on your best behaviour!
- Have lunch in our tearooms and try the weird-sounding courgette and chocolate cake. It's delicious and a favourite with children.
- Meet the gardeners in the walled garden, they will be chatting to visitors and might ask you to help out digging and planting the beds using old tools.

Special events

There is a range of events throughout the year from our Easter Eggstravaganza to family fun Bank Holidays in May, historic food fayres and spectacular Christmas evenings – where it always snows!

By the way...

- Baby-changing and feeding facilities are provided. Hip-carrying infant seats are available for loan and there's a children's play area.
- Farm gives children the chance to see domestic and rare breeds.
- Games gallery in corn mill plus children's guide and quiz.
- The 'first person' guides and experiences are unique and children love it. Pushchairs are admitted to the farm.

Snowshill Manor

Historic house Garden

Snowshill, nr Broadway,
Gloucestershire, WR12 7JU
01386 852410

OPENING TIMES
Manor
19 Mar 08–2 Nov 08
12am–5pm Wed, Thu, Fri,
Sat, Sun
Garden
19 Mar 08–2 Nov 08
11am–5:30pm Wed, Thu, Fri,
Sat, Sun
Shop/restaurant/grounds
19 Mar 08–2 Nov 08
11am–5:30pm Wed, Thu, Fri,
Sat, Sun
8 Nov 08–14 Dec 08
12am–4pm Sat, Sun

Notes
Admission by timed ticket at
busy times. Tickets issued at
reception on a first-come, first-
served basis and cannot be
booked. Tickets often run out at
peak times; please arrive early
to avoid disappointment. Last
admission: manor 4:20pm;
gardens 5pm. Open BH
weekends.

The house of architect and craftsman Charles Paget Wade, who
was a passionate collector. There are thousands and thousands of
objects to peruse, from Samurai armour to toys and games. The
organically run hillside garden has a magical combination of terraces
and ponds forming little outdoor rooms.

Crowded house
When Charles saw the house advertised in a magazine, he knew it
would be the perfect place to keep his amazing collections. He himself
lived in the cottage next door. Imagine having a whole house just for all
your stuff!

What to see
- Musical instruments, clocks, toys, masks, bicycles, books, cabinets,
  model ships, paintings, buckets. And that's just for starters...

What to do
- Explore the rooms each named by Wade to reflect what is in them.
  Our favourite is One Hundred Wheels – are there really?
- Pick up a tracker pack or quiz sheet and explore the garden.

Special events

Check with us – we've had a Neptune treasure hunt, an Easter bunny trail, Ugly Bug Ball, a Teddy Bears' Picnic plus Samurai martial arts. Who knows what might be on the cards in the future?

By the way...

- We can loan a baby sling or carrier to go round the manor. It's a 15-minute walk to the house along a bumpy path.
- Touchable objects available – ask about our handling collection.

Sudbury Hall & the National Trust Museum of Childhood

Historic house Garden Museum

Sudbury, Ashbourne,
Derbyshire, DE6 5HT
01283 585337

OPENING TIMES
Hall
21 Mar 08–2 Nov 08 1pm–5pm
Wed, Thu, Fri, Sat, Sun
School visits/taster tours
As hall 11am–1pm
Museum/tearooms/shop
21 Mar 08–27 Jul 08
11am–5pm Wed, Thu, Fri,
Sat, Sun
28 Jul 08–7 Sep 08 11am–5pm
Mon–Sun
10 Sep 08–2 Nov 08
11am–5pm Wed, Thu, Fri,
Sat, Sun
8 Nov 08–21 Dec 08
10:30am–3:30pm Sat, Sun
**Christmas event in the
museum**
6 Dec 08–21 Dec 08
10:30am–3:30pm Sat, Sun
Grounds
15 Mar 08–21 Dec 08
10:30am–5pm Mon–Sun

Notes
Open BH Mons and Good Fri.
Hall may close dusk if earlier
than 5pm. Daily tours
11am–12am. Tel. 01283
585305 for confirmation of the
opening date of the 'new'
Museum.

Sudbury Hall offers visitors a range of state rooms, domestic rooms and below-stairs experiences. The Hall is over 300 years old and features decorative plasterwork, exquisite wood carvings and painted murals, all designed to bring the nature of outdoors into this family home. The Museum of Childhood (opening again in 2008 after a £2.2m redevelopment project) traces the fun and fascinating experience of childhood over the last 200 years. Find something for everyone in the eight new themed galleries, including captivating object displays, exciting activities for the whole family, personal histories, archive film, temporary exhibitions and lots, lots more.

Recognise anything?
The BBC used some rooms in the Hall to film *Pride and Prejudice* – can you tell which scenes were filmed where? Visitors can also explore the Willow Walk and make their way to the discovery centre at the Boat House, picnic on the meadow and watch the swans swim by. Enjoy the newly redeveloped Museum of Childhood after it was closed for refurbishment in 2007.

What to see
- Explore the Hall with our new children's activity sheets and treasure chests, and pick up self-guided garden and village trails.
- In the Museum of Childhood, there are eight newly themed galleries taking you on a journey of memories through your childhood.

What to do
- In the Hall, discover life 'below stairs' with our Meet the Butler tours.
- 'Touch the past' by using our treasure chests.
- Pick up a 'character card' and explore the Hall through another guise.
- Re-live your childhood by taking children into the Museum.

Special events
Join us for family activities and fun in the school holidays and weekends, Wednesdays to Sundays from 12–4pm.

By the way...
- Avoid a dull day if you want to see the paintings clearly – we don't have very bright lighting, as we wish people to enjoy the paintings and furnishings for a few more hundred years, and light can cause a lot of damage.

The Workhouse, Southwell

Historic building   Gardens

Upton Road, Southwell,
Nottinghamshire, NG25 0PT
01636 817250

OPENING TIMES
1 Mar 08–16 Mar 08
11am–4pm Sat, Sun
17 Mar 08–31 Mar 11am–4pm
Wed, Thu, Fri, Sat, Sun
1 Apr 08–30 Sep 08
12am–5pm Wed, Thu, Fri,
Sat, Sun
1 Oct 08–2 Nov 08 11am–4pm
Sat, Sun
Tours
2 Aug 08–31 Aug 08
11am–12am Wed, Thu, Fri,
Sat, Sun

Notes
Open BH Mons and Good Fri.
Last admission 1hr before
closing. 2–31 Aug guided tours
at 11am (except 25 Aug when
open at 11am, but no tours.

The Workhouse is one of the least-altered examples of a kind of 'welfare' brought about by the New Poor Law of 1834. Paupers – poor people who had no work, or had fallen into debt or disgrace – lived in grim conditions here, as in other workhouses. It's worth a visit to see just how life has changed.

Or has it?
You can see a full re-created 19th-century dormitory with replica beds here. But next door there is also a re-creation of a bedsit, to remind you that the building's most recent welfare use was as housing for the temporarily homeless in the 1970s.

What to see
- A film to start with, where the Reverend Becher will introduce the Workhouse and bring it to life.
- The old workshops and dormitories.
- Segregated rooms for women and men – and segregated stairways too!

What to do
- Follow the excellent audio guide, which is based on archive records and brings the building to life.
- Interact with displays that tell you about poverty through the years.
- Play 'The Master's Punishment' game.

Special events
A variety of special events, living history re-enactments and workshops are held throughout the year – including rag-doll making, fun days, family history courses, craft and creative performances. Contact us for further details.

By the way...
- There's food in the local villages, but no café on site (it's a very authentic workhouse!) although you can picnic here.
- Baby-changing facilities and pushchairs are fine, though you can borrow a hip-carrying infant seat.
- Get in touch if you would like to use one of our wheelchairs. The house is not suitable for motorised wheelchairs.

Best of the Rest

Central

Canons Ashby House

Visitors enjoy the intimate atmosphere of this delightful Elizabethan manor house. Look heavenwards and count the number of animals on a Jacobean ceiling with the aid of the children's discovery trail sheet. Explore the remains of the medieval village, just humps in the ground now, and cross the medieval ridge and furrow fields in the park to the 'castle' mound. There is a paddock for children to run around in and a 30-hectare (70-acre) park to explore. Easter-egg trails, Step Back in Time weekend, bat walks and a history walk are all activities we offer.

Contact: Canons Ashby, Daventry, Northamptonshire NN11 3SD. Tel. 01327 860044 **Opening times: House** 1 Mar 08–14 Mar 08 1pm–5pm Sat, Sun; 15 Mar 08–30 Sep 08 1pm–5pm Mon, Tue, Wed, Sat, Sun; 1 Oct 08–2 Nov 08 1pm–4pm Mon, Tue, Wed, Sat, Sun; 6 Dec 08–21 Dec 08 12am–4pm Sat, Sun **Gardens/park/church** 1 Mar 08–14 Mar 08 11am–5:30pm Sat, Sun; 15 Mar 08–30 Sep 08 11am–5:30pm Mon, Tue, Wed, Sat, Sun; 1 Oct 08–2 Nov 08 11am–4:30pm Mon, Tue, Wed, Sat, Sun; 8 Nov 08–21 Dec 08 11am–4pm Sat, Sun **Shop/tearoom:** 1 Mar 08–14 Mar 08 12am–5pm Sat, Sun; 15 Mar 08–30 Sep 08 12am–5pm Mon, Tue, Wed, Sat, Sun; 1 Oct 08–2 Nov 08 12am–4pm Mon, Tue, Wed, Sat, Sun **Notes:** Open Good Fri 1pm–5pm. Closes dusk if earlier. Tearoom open 11am (15 Mar–30 Sept).

Carding Mill Valley & the Shropshire Hills

Carding Mill Valley is the ideal spot for a family outing in the fresh air. Enjoy breathtaking views over Shropshire and Cheshire and spot grazing sheep (and lambs in the spring), birds and insects around the valley's streams and bogs. Cycle along the bridlepaths with a picnic on a sunny day, or tramp about in your wellies – and enjoy it.

Contact: Chalet Pavilion, Carding Mill Valley, Church Stretton, Shropshire, SY6 6JG. Tel. 01694 723068 **Opening times: Heathland** All year Mon–Sun **Tearoom/shop** 11 Feb 08–31 Mar 08 11am–4pm Mon–Sun; 1 Apr 08–26 Oct 08 11am–7pm Mon–Sun; 1 Nov 08–30 Nov 08 11am–4pm Mon, Tue, Sat, Sun; 6 Dec 08–31 Jan 08 11am–4pm Sat, Sun **Notes:** WCs open 9am–7pm in summer and 9am–4pm in winter. Tearoom opens 10:30am Feb–March, Nov and Dec–Jan. Tearoom and shop closed 17 June and 20–25 Dec, open 27 Dec–4 Jan 09 (weather dependent).

Croft Castle & Parkland

A day of fun and adventure with 607 hectacres (1500 acres) of countryside to explore and a fascinating 400-year-old castle with family trails and ghosts! There are 1000-year-old trees, wildlife and farm animals in the parkland and a room where you can dress up or design your family crest. Special events include a spooky Halloween, Easter trails, August craft fair, theatre, guided walks, family nature days and more.

Contact: Yarpole, nr Leominster, Herefordshire HR6 9PW. Tel. 01568 780246 **Opening times: Castle** 3 Mar–1 Apr 1pm–5pm Sat, Sun; 4 Apr–30 Sep 1pm–5pm Wed, Thu, Fri, Sat, Sun; 3 Oct–4 Nov 1pm–4:30pm Wed, Thu, Fri, Sat, Sun **Gardens/shop/tearoom** 7 Mar–2 Nov 12am–5pm Wed, Thu, Fri; 3 Mar–4 Nov 11am–5pm Sat, Sun **Park** All year 8am–9pm Mon–Sun **Notes:** Open BH Mons. Park closes dusk if earlier. Taster tours 11am–1pm in the Castle, Sat and Sun. Christmas at Croft Castle 1/2, 8/9, 15/16 Dec 12am–4pm.

Dudmaston

A house full of art works amassed by the previous owners, Sir George and Lady Labouchère, with a collection of 20th-century sculpture and painting. Terraced lawns with oaks and cedars stretch down to the 'Big Pool' lake. Enjoy a dally in the Dingle (a wooded valley) or a walk through the flower gardens.

Contact: Quatt, nr Bridgnorth, Shropshire, WV15 6QN. Tel. 01746 780866 **Opening times: House** 23 Mar 08–30 Sep 08 2pm–5:30pm Tue, Wed, Sun **Garden** 23 Mar 08–30 Sep 08 12am–6pm Mon, Tue, Wed, Sun **Shop** 23 Mar 08–30 Sep 08 1pm–5:30pm Tue, Wed, Sun **Tearoom** 23 Mar 08–30 Sep 08 11:30am–5:30pm Mon, Tue, Wed, Sun **Notes:** Open BH Mons. St Andrew's church, Quatt, open same time as house. Snowdrop walks 2, 3, 9 and 10 Feb. Please check our website or get in touch to check events before visiting.

Hanbury Hall

A delightful country house with 8 hectacres (20 acres) of formal garden, a sunken parterre, orchards and wilderness. Discover Snobs Tunnel – built so the servants wouldn't be seen scurrying to the kitchens – and see how it feels to be a servant in the mushroom and ice houses. In the summer, become a member of the family and play on the bowling green. There are themed family activity days during school holidays.

Contact: School Road, Hanbury, Droitwich Spa, Worcestershire, WR9 7EA. Tel. 01527 821214 **Opening times: Garden/park/tearoom/shop*** 1 Mar 08–16 Mar 08 11am–5:30pm Sat, Sun; 17 Mar 08–30 Jun 08 11am–5:30pm Mon, Tue, Wed, Sat, Sun; 1 Jul 08–31 Aug 08 11am–5:30pm Mon–Sun; 1 Sep 08–29 Oct 08 11am–5:30pm Mon, Tue, Wed, Sat, Sun; 1 Nov 08–31 Jan 08 11am–5:30pm Sat, Sun; 26 Dec 08–1 Jan 08 11am–5:30pm Mon–Sun **House tours** As house 11am–1pm Sat, Sun **House** 1 Mar 08–16 Mar 08 1pm–5pm Sat, Sun; 17 Mar 08–29 Oct 08 1pm–5pm Mon, Tue, Wed, Sat, Sun **Notes:** Admission by timed ticket on BH weekends. Open Good Fri. Closes dusk if earlier. *Shop and tearoom close at 5pm. Garden, park, tearoom and shop open seven days a week during Easter school holidays, 26–30 May and 27–31 Oct. House open 13/14 Dec 11am–4pm.

Ilam Park

Beautiful open park and woodland on the banks of the River Manifold, where many farmers earn their living and there are sheep everywhere. Walk down the avenue of trees known as 'Paradise Walk', look out for newts and frogs in the dew pond, spot the pepperpot tower and visit the education centre. Recent events have included children's theatre shows, nature days and a Trusty treasure trail.

Contact: Ilam, Ashbourne, Derbyshire DE6 2AZ. Tel. 01335 350503 **Opening times: Park** All year Mon–Sun **Shop/tearoom** 1 Feb 08–29 Feb 08 11am–4pm Sat, Sun; 1 Mar 08–31 Oct 08 11am–5pm Mon, Tue, Fri, Sat, Sun; 30 Jun 08–31 Aug 08 11am–4pm Sat, Sun; 1 Nov 08–21 Dec 08 11am–4pm Sat, Sun; 3 Jan 08–31 Jan 08 11am–4pm Sat, Sun **Notes:** Hall is let to YHA and not open. Caravan site run by National Trust, open to Caravan Club/National Trust members Mar–Oct (tel. caravan-site booking office in season or estate office Nov–Feb).

Wildlife Walk – Calke Abbey & Park Derbyshire

As well as a grand Baroque mansion with a large natural-history collection, Calke has secret walled gardens and 243 hectares (600 acres) of parkland, much of which is a National Nature Reserve. The park is a rich and varied landscape of grassland, ponds and wood pasture – one of the rarest habitats in Europe. You'll also find majestic veteran trees and some great bug-watching sites. There are no public roads at Calke so it's perfect for a peaceful walk.

Getting there:
Bike: National Cycle Network traffic-free route 8km (5 miles) away. See www.sustrans.org.uk.
Buses/Rail: no. 69/A Derby–Swadlincote bus (passing close to Derby station), alight Ticknall, then 2.4km (1½ mile) walk through park to house. Burton-on-Trent station is 16km (10 miles) away.
Road: 16km (10 miles) south of Derby on A514 at Ticknall between Swadlincote and Melbourne. Access from M42/A42 exit 13 and A50 Derby South.

Terrain and accessibility: Stepped and stone paths, kissing gates and a stile. Enquire at property for more accessible routes.

Distance: 2.5km (1½ miles).

Points of interest:
Begin at the main overflow car park and walk down the steps to the ponds. Follow the map shown opposite. The numbers on the map correspond to the numbers below. Look out for the following features:
1. At Mere pond, look for dragonflies in the summer. Turn right and follow the deer fencing to the top of the hill, until it meets the old park boundary wall. Fallow deer inhabit the estate and are distinguished by their white spots. See males locking horns, calling females and scent marking during the autumn rut.
2. Turn left away from the deer fence and follow the path near the wall through the open parkland and then along through the Serpentine Wood. This is a good place to see bluebells in spring. Also look for signs of badgers (paths, tracks and diggings).
3. Go through the kissing gate and follow the woodland path.
4. Come out of the wood into the Fisherman's car park. The oldest tree in the park, The Old Man of Calke, is a short way beyond the car

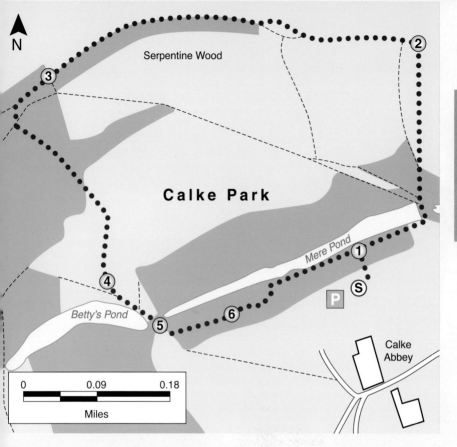

park through the wooden gate. This ancient oak is over 1000 years old but still grows healthily.

5 Follow the stepped path down from the car park to Betty's Pond, go between the two ponds, then bear left over the stile. A number of Calke's ancient trees (some over 400 years old) can be seen around Betty's Pond. Veteran trees sometimes have hollow trunks that can be seen when the main truck has broken or 'opened'. Tree holes provide nesting sites for woodland birds including great spotted and green woodpeckers, tree creepers, nuthatches, starlings and tits.

6 Follow the line of horse chestnuts all the way back to the car park.

Property contact: 01332 863822; calkeabbey@nationaltrust.org.uk

Map and start grid ref: OS Landranger 128: SK367226

Facilities available: National Trust shop, children's guide/quiz/trail, family activity packs, parking, licensed restaurant and kiosk (when busy). Separate parking for those with wheelchairs, adapted WC; shop and restaurant with level entrances, partly accessible grounds.

National Trust properties nearby: Kedleston Hall, Sudbury Hall and Museum of Childhood and Shugborough Estate.

Wildlife Walk – Brockhampton Estate Herefordshire

Brockhampton in Herefordshire is a special place to visit throughout the year with its orchards, meadows and woods that change with the seasons and attract different wildlife. Listen for the deep croak of ravens and to woodpeckers tapping trees, and enjoy the bluebells, primroses, wild daffodils and the eye-catching insects associated with the old trees on the estate.

Getting there:
Buses: no. 418/420 from Worcester of Hereford stops at the estate boundary near Bromyard.
Rail: Malvern Link station is the nearest, 13km (8 miles) away, but you can take a train to Hereford station or Worcester station, then a bus (see above) to the estate boundary.
Road: 3.2km (2 miles) east of Bromyard and between Worcester and Hereford, just off the A44.

Distance: 2.5km (1½ miles).

Terrain and accessibility: Holly Walk is a signposted trail along woodland paths that are surfaced but can be muddy and slippery after rain. There are some protruding roots and a few short, steeper sections. The zigzagged part of the walk (see map) is suitable for many wheelchair users. Other circular walks at Brockhampton include the 1.6km (1 mile) Heart Walk and the 7.25km (4½ mile) Oak Walk.

Directions and points of interest:
To begin this walk from main estate car park follow the Beech or Oak way-marked paths (yellow and green respectively). Both lead to the disabled car park, point 1 on the map shown opposite. The numbers on the map correspond to the numbers below.

1 From Hollybank car park (marked at S on the map opposite), follow the red Holly Walk signs.

2 As the path weaves its way through the woods, look for the first sculpture of the walk – an archway. Its carvings of woodland creatures were created with school children. The left-hand path further on has a shorter, surfaced trail called the Ash Walk.

3 The next sculpture was modelled on a local shire horse called Harold and is made from a huge storm-fallen oak.

4 There are many ancient oak trees here holding up to 300 different species of wildlife, some of which were planted around the time of Henry VIII.

5 Stone Bridge crosses the stream here; it's a place that links Brockhampton House to the other buildings on the estate.

6 Cross straight over the junction to view Lawn Pool on the right. This landscape feature was created so that the Brockhampton House inhabitants could fish and shoot. Coots, moorhens and kingfishers can be seen, along with carp, frogs and toads.

7 After the path that zigzags away from the pool, you come across a picnic table sculpture designed by artist Neil Spencer. The shape reflects the carriage wheels that used to work in the forests here.

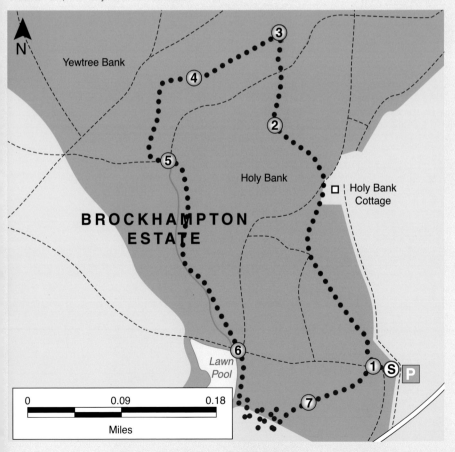

Property contact details: 01885482077;
brockhampton@nationaltrust.org.uk

Map and start grid ref: OS Landranger 149: SO682546. Maps of
circular walks are available at the estate.

Facilities available: The Holy Bank car park shown on this map is
for disabled visitors only. The main estate car park is at Brockhampton's
stable yard, a 10-minute walk away from the start of this trail. The
tearoom at the main car park sells homemade lunches and cakes.
Walk leaflets are also available here. Dogs are allowed in the parkland
(on leads) and in the woods.

National Trust properties nearby: Berrington Hall, Croft Castle,
Croome Park, The Greyfriars and The Weir.

N

Yewtree Bank

③

④

②

⑤

Holy Bank

☐ Holy Bank
Cottage

**B R O C K H A M P T O N
E S T A T E**

⑥

*Lawn
Pool*

① Ⓢ P

⑦

0	0.09	0.18

Miles

Beatrix Potter Gallery & Hill Top

Gallery Walks Historic House Garden

Beatrix Potter Gallery
Main Street, Hawkshead,
Cumbria, LA22 0NS
01539 436355

Hill Top House
Near Sawrey, Hawkshead,
Ambleside, Cumbria, LA22 0LF
01539 436269

OPENING TIMES
Gallery
15 Mar 08–2 Nov 08
10:30am–4:30pm Mon, Tue,
Wed, Thu, Sat, Sun
Shop (gallery)
9 Feb 08–24 Feb 08
10am–4pm Mon–Sun
25 Feb 08–14 Mar 08
10am–4pm Wed–Sun
15 Mar 08–2 Nov 08
10am–5pm Mon–Sun
3 Nov 08–24 Dec 08
10am–4pm Wed–Sun
27 Dec 08–31 Dec 10am–4pm
Mon, Tue, Wed, Sat, Sun
Hill Top House
15 Mar 08–2 Nov 08
10:30am–4:30pm Mon, Tue,
Wed, Thu, Sat, Sun
Shop/garden (house)
9 Feb 08–24 Feb 08
10am–4pm Mon–Sun
1 Mar 08–15 Mar 08
10am–4pm Sat, Sun
16 Mar 08–2 Nov 08
10:30am–5pm Mon–Sun
3 Nov 08–24 Dec 08
10am–4pm Mon–Sun

Notes
Admission to gallery by timed
ticket issued on arrival. Open
Good Fri. Gallery shop is open
occasional extra days in winter.
Please enquire before making a
special journey. Last entry for
Hill Top at 4pm. Limited number
of timed tickets available daily.

Hill Top is the Lakeland farmhouse that was the real setting for some of Beatrix Potter's most enchanting tales. The house and garden are just as she left them and you can see many items which feature in her illustrations. At the Beatrix Potter Gallery you'll find a fascinating exhibition on the life of the children's author, including original illustrations for her books. It's housed inside a 17th-century Lakeland town house that was the model for Tabitha Twitchitt's shop and was once the office of Beatrix's husband, William Heelis.

Hill Top House

The house where Beatrix wrote many of her stories, left much as it was when she lived in it. There's something from one of her books in each room – see if you can spot them. Characters in Beatrix Potter's books like Peter Rabbit and Tom Kitten are based on pets she had as a child. Beatrix had quite a lonely childhood, and was taught at home by a governess, but had many animal friends to keep her company.

What to see

- Watercolours and sketches that Beatrix Potter drew to illustrate her enchanting books.
- The lovely Lakeland countryside that inspired her.
- The house she lived in.
- Try to find Mr Samuel Whiskers' front door and look out for Peter Rabbit's red spotted handkerchief, or see if Jemima Puddle Duck has laid an egg in the rhubarb patch.

What to do

- Pick up a leaflet and take a walk around Beatrix Potter country. Try the children's activity sheets and get a goodie bag from the gallery.
- Take a walk around the village to spot more scenes from the tales and view the breathtaking scenery, which Beatrix wanted to preserve for future generations.

Special events

Get in touch for special events.

By the way...

- Sorry, no WC at the gallery. But there's one nearby in the main village car park 200 yards away. You do need to manage a flight of stairs to get to the exhibition.
- Hill Top can get extremely busy at peak times and visitors may have to wait to enter – early sell-outs are also possible. It is always possible to see the garden and shop during opening hours.

Dunham Massey

Historic house Mill Garden Park

Altrincham, Cheshire,
WA14 4SJ
0161 941 1025

OPENING TIMES
House
8 Mar 08–2 Nov 08 12am–5pm
Mon, Tue, Wed, Sat, Sun
Garden
8 Mar 08–2 Nov 08
11am–5:30pm Mon–Sun
Park
8 Mar 08–2 Nov 08
9am–7:30pm Mon–Sun
3 Nov 08–31 Jan 08 9am–5pm
Mon–Sun
Restaurant/shop
8 Mar 08–2 Nov 08
10:30am–5pm Mon–Sun
3 Nov 08–31 Jan 08
10:30am–4pm Mon–Sun
Mill
8 Mar 08–2 Nov 08 12am–4pm
Mon, Tue, Wed, Sat, Sun

Notes
House open Good Fri and BH
Sun and Mon 11am–5pm.
Property closed, including park,
25 Dec. Also closed 27 Feb
and 19 Nov for staff training.

Outside, it's an early Georgian house, built around a Tudor core.
Inside, it's a wonderful example of a sumptuous Edwardian interior,
with fascinating servants' quarters. The deer park has beautiful
avenues and ponds, and a newly restored Tudor mill in working
order. The garden is charming and has an orangery to explore.

Motte or not?
There's a flattened mound in the garden, which might be the remains of
a Norman motte – an extremely old castle. An 18th-century painting of
a bird's-eye view of the garden shows it clearly visible – but rather
dressed up, with terraces cut into it and a gilded urn on top.

What to see
- A huge collection of Huguenot silver – the finest in Britain.
- A bark house and a well house in the garden.
- The mill; originally it ground corn but now it's a sawmill.

What to do
- Spot the tower and the sundial.
- Pick up a childrens' quiz and trail.
- Eat your sandwiches in our extensive picnic area – but not in the
  deer park, please.

Special events
We have family tours and activities and special family activities in the
holidays. At Christmas and other times you can experience the hustle
and bustle of a Victorian kitchen, or meet the butler face to face – so
mind your Ps and Qs! Give us a call for more details.

By the way...
- There are many touchable things, and wonderful scents and sounds
  in the gardens.
- Although there are a lot of stairs, we do have wheelchairs.
- Baby-changing facilities, child-carrier loan and children's menu
  are available.

Fell Foot Park

Park Lake Boats

This wonderful park on the shores of Lake Windermere is open all year round. It doesn't cost a penny to visit and is a great place for a family afternoon out. You can hire rowing boats to splash about in or take a ferry to Lakeside Pier. Or you can sit back with your picnic and enjoy the view of the Lakeland fells.

Fell Foot fell down
Fell Foot Park was once the estate of a large house that has now been demolished.

What to see
- Go on a (pushchair-friendly) walk to identify monkey-puzzle and giant redwood trees.
- Pleasure boats going by on Lake Windemere.

What to do
- Hire a rowing boat – but don't drop the oars!
- Spend the whole day here, swimming and picnicking.
- Go mad on the huge adventure playground, with a special area for children under seven.

Special events
We have a busy summer activities and events programme including children's open-air theatre and Shakespeare in the park. Please call for further details.

By the way...
- Always supervise children while swimming and watch out for danger warnings. Staff-driven mobility vehicles are available during the season. Trusty the Hedgehog lunch boxes in the licensed tearooms.

Newby Bridge, Ulverston,
Cumbria, LA12 8NN
01539 531273

North West

OPENING TIMES
Park
All year 9am–5pm Mon–Sun
Shop/tearoom
15 Mar 08–2 Nov 08
11am–5pm Mon–Sun

Notes
Site closed 25 and 26 Dec.
Closes dusk if earlier. Facilities, such as rowing-boat hire (buoyancy aids available), 1 April–28 Oct: daily 11am–4pm (last boat), must be returned by 4:30pm.

Formby

Countryside Coastline Wood Beach

Victoria Road, Freshfield,
Formby, Liverpool, L37 1LJ
01704 878591

OPENING TIMES
All year dawn–dusk Mon–Sun

Notes
Closed 25 Dec.

The red squirrels are often easy to see and some may come very close to you on the Squirrel Walk. There are wide sandy beaches, ideal for beach games and sandcastles. The landscape is beautiful with high sand dunes and pine woodland.

Squirrel these facts away...
Did you know that the red squirrel is native to Britain, but is being forced out of its natural habitat by the strong American grey squirrel? Red squirrels have sharp ears and a very bushy tail, which they use to steer when they're leaping in the air. They squirrel their food away for the winter, and you can see them sniffing the ground to find it again later, when food is scarce.

What to see
- Rare red squirrels chasing each other up and down tall pine trees.
- At low tide search for footprints left by prehistoric humans and wild animals in hard-baked mud uncovered by erosion on some parts of the beach.
- Wading birds on the shore, like oystercatchers and sanderlings.

What to do
- Sit very still and a squirrel may come very close to you (get some squirrel food from the kiosk).
- Take a paddle in the sea.
- Have a picnic in one of the woodland picnic sites.
- Enjoy an ice cream from the van.
- Head out on wonderful walks along the improved Sefton Coastal Path – many sections suitable for people of all abilities.

Special events
Please get in touch to find out what's on, or check our website.

By the way...
- The beach access has steep sand dunes, not good for people with mobility difficulties. Baby-changing facilities are provided. Picnic areas – no barbecues, please. A good dog-walking place, but please keep dogs on the lead in the squirrel walks.

Lyme Park

Historic house Garden Park Countryside

Originally a Tudor house, Lyme Park was transformed into a huge Italianate palace in the 18th century, but some of the Elizabethan interiors remain. The garden has many features to explore, including a ravine garden and a conservatory. And the surrounding 570 hectares (1400 acres) of parkland is a medieval deer park.

Mr Darcy's wet shirt
Lyme Park's starring role came as the place where Darcy (played by actor Colin Firth) emerged from the lake in the 1995 BBC TV version of *Pride and Prejudice*. Other members of the family may be more interested in the adventure playground.

What to see
- Deer in the medieval parkland, which also has an 18th-century hunting tower.
- Paintings of the huge Lyme mastiff hunting dogs bred here and given as presents.
- Intricate wood carvings done by Grinling Gibbons.

What to do
- Explore the moorland and woodland in the park. Dogs can come too if kept under control.
- Visit The Cage, a grand former hunting lodge in the park – used for watching the hunt and for banquets.
- Scramble on the adventure playground.

Special events
We're especially good at holiday activities such as Crafty Creations, the Terrible Tudors, walks and trails round the park and house and Let's Go Fly a Kite. Call or check our website for information.

By the way...
- There's an alternative entrance to the house, avoiding steps, and we have wheelchairs. There are stairs, though we're very child-friendly. Baby-changing and feeding facilities, bottle warming and slings to borrow. There's also a children's menu in the restaurant.

Disley, Stockport,
Cheshire, SK12 2NX
01663 762023

OPENING TIMES
House/restaurant/shop
1 Mar 08–9 Mar 08 11am–5pm
Sat, Sun
15 Mar 08–2 Nov 08
11am–5pm Mon, Tue, Fri,
Sat, Sun
Park
1 Apr 08–12 Oct 08
8am–8:30pm Mon–Sun
13 Oct 08–31 Jan 08
8am–6pm Mon–Sun
Garden
1 Mar 08–9 Mar 08 11am–5pm
Sat, Sun
15 Mar 08–2 Nov 08
11am–5pm Mon–Sun
8 Nov 08–21 Dec 08
12am–3pm Sat, Sun
**Timber yard plant
sales/shop**
1 Mar 08–9 Mar 08 11am–4pm
Sat, Sun
15 Mar 08–2 Nov 08
10:30am–5pm Mon–Sun
3 Nov 08–30 Nov 08
11am–4pm Sat, Sun
1 Dec 08–4 Jan 08 11am–4pm
Wed, Thu, Fri, Sat, Sun

Notes
Closed Christmas Day. 1st and 2nd weekend in March: Conservation in Action tours (restricted numbers) 11am–5pm. 15 March–02 Nov: House tours (restricted numbers) 11am–1pm.

153

Mr Hardman's Photographic Studio

Historic house

59 Rodney Street, Liverpool,
Merseyside, L1 9EX
0151 709 6261

OPENING TIMES
15 Mar 08–2 Nov 08
11am–4:15pm Wed, Thu, Fri,
Sat, Sun

Notes
Admission by timed ticket only,
incl. National Trust members.
Open BH Mons. Visitors are
advised to book in advance by
tel. or email to property. Tickets
on the day subject to availability.

This magnificent mid-Georgian terrace house has been fully restored to illustrate how a professional portrait photographer's studio would have looked in the 1950s at a period in time when many people chose to have their family photographs taken. Dark rooms, other work spaces and an interactive discovery room bring this lost art to life. The house also contains personal belongings of the Hardmans, including food from the World War II rationing period.

Smile and say cheese!
On display for younger visitors are the toys that Mr. Hardman used to hold the attention of children who had to stay still for a long time in a hot studio while having their photograph taken. A programme of themed events including family days, costumed tours and specialist evening tours runs throughout the year. You can listen to short audio recordings from people who used to work in the studio and dark rooms, as well as those who came to have their photograph taken.

What to see
- A short DVD is shown at the start of the tour describing the work of Mr Hardman and the type of people who came to have their photograph taken.
- Examples of the landscape photographs he and his wife, Margaret, enjoyed taking in this country and in Europe can be seen throughout the house.
- Our interactive discovery room explains the secrets of the photographic process.
- Old cameras, huge lights, smelly dark rooms, which all add to the atmosphere of this unusual house.

What to do
- Sit in the studio and have your very own black-and-white photograph taken – yours to keep!
- Handle old cameras and equipment in the discovery room.
- See if you can sit still for long enough in front of our special camera – it's not that easy!

Special events
Family focus days, with trails and activities, run at times during the season. Ring us in advance to find out more about forthcoming events.

By the way...
- There are steep staircases to climb in the house. A virtual tour of the house is available for loan. Some of the rooms are very small, so group sizes are kept to a maximum of six persons. There is no need to book your tour in advance, just turn up and go. Car parking and catering facilities can be found in the immediate vicinity of the Anglican Cathedral – a two minute walk away. Baby changing facilities are available.

Quarry Bank Mill & Styal Estate

Mill Garden Countryside Village Living history

Where did our great grandparents work? How did they live? Experience something of the noise and hardship in their lives as you trace the story of cotton through the mill. Demonstrators and hands-on exhibits bring the past to life in this unique insight into Britain's industrial heritage.

Home from work

Styal Village was built especially for the people who worked at the mill. The Apprentice House was built as somewhere for the 90 pauper children who worked in the mill to live. There was no excuse for being late for work...

What to see

- Europe's most powerful working water wheel in action
- See demonstrations of spinning and weaving.
- Look up the main mill chimney – it's a long way!
- New for 2008 – the mill owner's secret garden against the backdrop of the family house.

What to do

- Visit the secret garden and watch its restoration taking place.
- Go on a tour of the Apprentice House with a costumed guide to learn what sort of conditions children who worked here experienced (limited during term time).
- Watch the two steam engines in the mill, used from around 1810.
- Pick up a leaflet and walk in the woods, or picnic in the meadow.

Special events

Easter-egg trails, family activities in the mill during the school holidays. Telephone for information, or look at our website.

By the way...

- There are interactive exhibits and opportunities for touching and handling objects.
- Many steps, with handrail, to the entrance. Chair lift access and wheelchairs are available.

Styal, Wilmslow,
Cheshire, SK9 4LA
01625 445896

OPENING TIMES
Mill/shop
1 Mar 08–31 Oct 08
11am–5pm Mon–Sun
1 Nov 08–31 Jan 08
11am–4pm Wed, Thu, Fri, Sat, Sun
Apprentice House
1 Mar 08–31 Oct 08 (see notes)
Mon–Sun
1 Nov 08–31 Jan 08 (see notes)
Wed, Thu, Fri, Sat, Sun
Garden
1 Mar 08–31 Oct 08
11am–5pm Mon–Sun
Estate
All year 7am–6pm Mon–Sun
Restaurant
1 Mar 08–31 Oct 08
11am–5pm Mon–Sun
1 Nov 08–31 Jan 08
11am–4pm Wed, Thu, Fri, Sat, Sun

Notes
Open BH Mons, Boxing Day and New Year's Day. Closed 25 Dec. Mill: last admission 1hr before closing. Apprentice House: limited availability – timed tickets only, available from the mill on arrival. Garden: timed tickets may be introduced during busy periods. Apprentice House closed 17 March.

155

Rufford Old Hall

Historic house Garden

North West

200 Liverpool Road, Rufford, nr
Ormskirk, Lancashire, L40 1SG
01704 821254

OPENING TIMES
House
24 Mar 08–28 Oct 08
1pm–5pm Mon, Tue, Wed,
Sat, Sun
Garden
1 Mar 08–9 Mar 08 12am–4pm
Sat, Sun
24 Mar 08–28 Oct 08
11am–5:30pm Mon, Tue, Wed,
Sat, Sun
7 Nov 08–21 Dec 08
12am–4pm Fri, Sat, Sun
Shop/restaurant
1 Mar 08–9 Mar 08 12am–4pm
Sat, Sun
24 Mar 08–28 Oct 08
11am–5pm Mon, Tue, Wed,
Sat, Sun
7 Nov 08–21 Dec 08
12am–4pm Fri, Sat, Sun

Notes
Open Good Fri. Christmas gifts
available Weds and Thurs in
Dec 12am–4pm.

The Great Hall looks just like the one on Scooby Doo and it's even got the scary suits of armour and lots of weapons. You can take delight at the flowers in the formal garden or let off steam exploring the woods and grounds. You can even watch a narrowboat glide by on the canal and feed the ducks.

Two's company, three's a (ghostly) crowd
Rufford is supposed to be haunted by not one but three ghosts. The 'Grey Lady', a man dressed in Elizabethan clothes, and Queen Elizabeth I – who has been seen pottering about in the dining room, but vanishes if you try to say hello. Well, how rude!

What to see
- The very large Great Hall with an intricate carved screen. Some think Shakespeare acted here.
- Coats of arms of the powerful local families of the time.
- 16th-century suits of armour that seem very small – would they fit Dad?

What to do
- Find the huge fireplace in the Great Hall, where a secret chamber was found – perhaps to hide Catholic priests from sight.
- Enjoy the late-Victorian grounds with topiary and sculpture.
- Have a picnic or enjoy a tasty snack from the Old Kitchen tearoom.

Special events
We have magic days, summer craft activities, Tudor games, visits from birds of prey and wacky insects and we can't forget our world-famous gnome hunt. Get in touch to see what we have planned.

By the way...
- We love kids – we provide baby-changing facilities, slings for loan, a bottle-warming service and Early Learning toys to play with.
- Allow time; the car park can get very busy.
- Tie your dog up outside the shop; we'll provide fresh water.
- There are wheelchairs, but some steps inside. Everywhere else is pretty accessible with a bit of help from a friend.

Sizergh Castle & Garden

Historic house Garden Park Countryside

You'll enjoy exploring this small castle with its original 14th-century tower built to protect the Strickland family from the Scots.

What to see

- The 14th-century tower with walls 2m (6ft) thick in places. At the very top of the tower is a turret where the garderobes (lavatories) used to be.
- The winding staircase with its sharp turns to the right. This made it difficult for an attacker to wield his sword – try it!
- Beautiful inlaid panelling, which has recently returned from the Victoria & Albert Museum.

What to do

- Imagine 14th-century ladies of the house sewing in the window seat of the tower.
- Have a go at the house quiz, suitable for a variety of ages.
- Explore the rock garden – there are waterfalls and pools here and 200 species of ferns.

Special events

Please get in touch – there are often special activities on.

By the way...

- Sizergh Castle is not open on Friday or Saturday.

Sizergh, nr Kendal,
Cumbria, LA8 8AE
01539 560951

OPENING TIMES
Castle
17 Mar 08–2 Nov 08 1pm–5pm
Mon, Tue, Wed, Thu, Sun
Garden
17 Mar 08–2 Nov 08
11am–5pm Mon, Tue, Wed,
Thu, Sun
Café/shop
1 Feb 08–16 Mar 08
11am–4pm Sat, Sun
17 Mar 08–2 Nov 08
11am–5pm Mon, Tue, Wed,
Thu, Sun
8 Nov 08–21 Dec 08
11am–4pm Sat, Sun

Notes
The estate is open daily 10–25 Feb, 10:30am–3:30pm. Café/shop (only) open daily Feb 08 half term and 26 Dec–2 Jan 09.

Speke Hall, Gardens & Estate

Historic house Garden Countryside Moat

North West

The Walk, Liverpool,
L24 1XD
0151 427 7231

OPENING TIMES
House
15 Mar 08–2 Nov 08
1pm–5:30pm Wed, Thu, Fri,
Sat, Sun
8 Nov 08–14 Dec 08
1pm–4:30pm Sat, Sun
Grounds
15 Mar 08–2 Nov 08
11am–5:30pm Tue, Wed, Thu,
Fri, Sat, Sun
4 Nov 08–31 Jan 08
11am–dusk Tue, Wed, Thu, Fri,
Sat, Sun
Home Farm/restaurant/shop
15 Mar 08–13 Jul 11am–5pm
Wed, Thu, Fri, Sat, Sun
15 Jul 08–14 Sep 08
11am–5pm Tue, Wed, Thu, Fri,
Sat, Sun
17 Sep 08–2 Nov 08
11am–5pm Wed, Thu, Fri,
Sat, Sun
8 Nov 08–14 Dec 08
1pm–4:30pm Sat, Sun

Notes
Open BH Mons. Grounds
(garden and estate) closed
24–26 Dec, 31 Dec, 1 Jan 09.

One of the most famous Tudor manors in Britain, this rambling pile has an atmospheric interior that covers many periods. The oldest parts date from 1530, but there is also a fully equipped Victorian kitchen, not to mention William Morris wallpapers in some rooms.

Only in America
There is a copy of the Hall in California, built in 1912 as a weekend getaway by Percy T. Morgan, and designed to withstand earthquakes. The Tudors would be proud!

What to see
- The 19th-century 'thunderbox' loo. This was supposed to be an improvement on the rather basic Tudor garderobes, but both designs 'deposit' straight into the moat.
- Adam and Eve, two majestic yew trees that are as old as the house.
- A spy hole in one of the bedrooms.

What to do
- Try our children-friendly trails, tracker packs and new MP3 audio tours of the Hall. Then search for the secret priests' hole. The Norris family who lived here were a Catholic family, living in a period of religious persecution.
- The Home Farm visitor centre, which has a children's outdoor play area and picnic space. This was an original 'model farm' (the farm animals are no longer here).
- Enjoy views from the 'Bund', an earth bank, across the airport and the River Mersey to the Welsh Hills in the distance.

Special events
We have events for all the family including Easter trails, outdoor theatre, Halloween, Christmas and costumed tours.

By the way…
- Dogs on lead – but in the grounds only please.
- You can book a wheelchair, and there's a vehicle to take people from Home Farm to the house – they're a short distance apart.

Wordsworth House

Historic house Garden

William Wordsworth's childhood home is great fun for families with a working Georgian kitchen, items to touch and use, and servants to meet and play with. An amazing insight into children's lives 230 years ago.

What to see
William lived here with his three bothers and sister Dorothy for his first eight years. He later referred to this period in his poetry, especially the garden terrace walk which overlooks the River Derwent.

What to see
- See the servants at work in the house and help with their daily routine. Try cooking in the Georgian kitchen with the maid-of-all-work, see the nursemaid spinning or get the manservant to play skittles with you.
- Relax, play or picnic in the beautiful walled garden which supplies the house with flowers, fruit, herbs and vegetables.

What to do
- Play with replica 1770s toys and try on Georgian clothes in the children's bedroom.
- Try writing with a quill pen under supervision of the clerk.
- Read some of William's poetry or even help with the cooking.

Special events
Family activities in school holidays, trails, art and craft activities such as making posies or pastry fish, games, poetry competitions and storytelling.

By the way...
- There is a small grassed area for picnics.
- Refreshments are available from nearby cafés.

Main Street, Cockermouth,
Cumbria, CA13 9RX
01900 820884

OPENING TIMES
House
12 Mar 08–1 Nov 08
11am–4:30pm Mon, Tue, Wed,
Thu, Fri, Sat
Shop
5 Mar 08–23 Dec 08
10am–5pm Mon, Tue, Wed,
Thu, Fri, Sat
2 Jan 08–26 Jan 08
10am–4pm Wed, Thu, Fri, Sat

Notes
Admission by timed ticket available from visitor reception. Open BH Mons: 11am–4:30pm. Education groups: 27 March–27 Oct: Tues, Wed and Thur 9:30am–11am and at other times by arrangement. Booking essential.

159

Best of the Rest

Gawthorpe Hall

Take the family for a visit to Gawthorpe Hall and travel back in time. The house was built in the early 1600s by the Shuttleworth family, and restored in the mid-19th century; there are fascinating objects from both periods of history. Stewards are always happy to explain the house and its contents but children will probably be most intrigued by the giant wooden fish lurking in the grounds or the wild swans and a grey heron on the pond. During the summer there are events for all ages, including open-air theatre. On occasion, the Victorian basement kitchens are opened to the public and you can meet the 19th-century mistress of Gawthorpe, Lady Blanche Shuttleworth and her servants, or let the children's I-spy sheet lead you to treasures such as the four-poster bed covered in carvings.

Contact: Padiham, nr Burnley, Lancashire BB12 8UA. Tel. 01282 771004 **Opening times: Hall/tearoom** 1 Apr 08–29 Oct 08 1pm–5pm Tue, Wed, Thu, Sat, Sun **Garden** All year 10am–6pm Mon–Sun **Notes:** Tearoom opens 12:30pm. Open BH Mons and Good Fri.

Little Moreton Hall

This crooked Tudor building seems to come straight out of a fairy tale but is Britain's most famous timber-framed manor house. The Hall has tiny windows because glass was so expensive. In fact rich Elizabethans sometimes took their windows with them when they travelled so they wouldn't get stolen. Wander through the cobbled courtyard, explore the Long Gallery and the Elizabethan knot garden and look out for the fish and ducks in the moat. We have a children's quiz that will help you explore the Hall but you can also touch the displays upstairs. You can have a picnic on the front lawn – or visit at Christmas time and experience a house decorated in traditional Tudor style.

Contact: Congleton, Cheshire, CW12 4SD. Tel. 01260 272018 **Opening times:** 1 Mar 08–16 Mar 08 11:30am–4pm Sat, Sun; 19 Mar 08–2 Nov 08 11:30am–5pm Wed, Thu, Fri, Sat, Sun; 8 Nov 08–21 Dec 08 11:30am–4pm Sat, Sun **Notes:** Open BH Mons. Closes dusk if earlier. Access during Yuletide celebrations restricted to ground floor, garden, shop and restaurant. Special openings at other times for booked groups.

Tatton Park

Tatton Park is one of the most complete historic estates in the country. Each attraction at Tatton Park is ideal for families and special events are held during the year. Set in 405 hectacres (1000 acres) of parkland with fallow deer, there is plenty of space for family walks, wildlife spotting or cycling and there is a superb adventure playground with new integrated rides suitable for all ages. Take the fun children's quiz at the neo-classical mansion and escape from the maze. Visit the historic rare breeds on the working farm and feed the goats and chickens or step back in time at Tatton's 'Hidden Gem', the Tudor Old Hall. Family events held throughout the year include boredom-buster days during school holidays, themed Easter festival, Medieval Fayre in June, Viking Sunday in August, Halloween Hauntings and car shows, theatre and outdoor concerts.

Contact: Knutsford, Cheshire, WA16 6QN. Tel. 1625 374435 **Opening times: House** 15 Mar 08–28 Sep 08 1pm–5pm Tue, Wed, Thu, Fri, Sat, Sun **Gardens/park/shop** 15 Mar 08–28 Sep 08 10am–6pm Tue, Wed, Thu, Fri, Sat, Sun; 30 Sep 08–31 Jan 08 11am–4pm Tue, Wed, Thu, Fri, Sat, Sun **Restaurant** 15 Mar 08–28 Sep 08 10am–6pm Mon–Sun; 30 Sep 08–31 Jan 08 11am–4pm Tue, Wed, Thu, Fri, Sat, Sun **Notes:** Open BH Mons. Shop open 10:30am–5pm 15 Mar–28 Sept. Park closes 1hr later than garden. Last admission 1hr before closing. House: special opening Oct half term and Christmas events in Dec. Guided tours Tues–Sun 12am by timed ticket (available from garden entrance after 10:30am) on first-come, first-served basis. Limited number of tickets per tour. For prices and opening times for other attractions please contact Tatton Park. Opening hours will be extended during Aug. Tel. 01625 374400 or visit www.tattonpark.org.uk. Closed 25 Dec.

Townend

Townend tells the story of the Brownes, a well-off farming family who lived here from 1626. Their obsessive record-keeping of bills and even shopping lists means a lot is known about them and you can get a good sense of their everyday life through the centuries. Today you can see the wooden carved furniture, some of which was made by George Browne. Look for dates carved into the wood and the Brownes' emblem, a double-headed eagle. See the round chimneys, characteristic of many of the older Lakeland houses. Ask the last George Browne about life at Victorian Townend – phone for details of when he's around. Help make an old-style rag rug, which is slowly being completed by visitors, and use the children's guide to explore the house.

Contact: Troutbeck, Windermere, Cumbria, LA23 1LB. Tel. 015394 32628 **Opening times:** 15 Mar 08–30 Mar 08 1pm–4pm Wed, Thu, Fri, Sat, Sun; 2 Apr 08–26 Oct 08 1pm–5pm Wed, Thu, Fri, Sat, Sun; 29 Oct 08–2 Nov 08 1pm–4am Wed, Thu, Fri, Sat, Sun **Notes:** Open BH Mons. May close early due to poor light.

Wildlife Walk – Arnside Knott

Situated on the edge of Morecambe Bay, this shapely 152m (500ft) limestone hill is a distinctive and beautiful part of the north-west countryside that has fine views of the Lake District. The key to the Knott's diversity is its limestone landscape, which was sculpted by glaciers in the Ice Ages. Over time, the rock, wind-blown soil and man's intervention have created a mosaic of habitats including woodland and flower-studded grassland. This 3km (2 mile) walk takes you through a magical place with many orchids and butterflies.

Getting there:

Bike: Signed on-road cycle route about 3km (2 miles) away. See www.sustrans.org.uk.
Bus: Bus stop in village, 1.6km (1 mile) away.
Foot: Many footpaths, this walk and a bridleway run through the area.
Rail: Arnside station is approximately 1.6km (1 mile) away via footpaths.
Road: M6 (J36); A65 towards Kendal; B6385 to Milnthorpe then B5782 to Arnside.

Distance: 3km (2 miles).

Terrain and accessibility: Easy walking conditions, but steep in places with a height gain of 70m (230ft) over the walk.

Directions and points of interest:

Turn left out of the National Trust car park and take the short walk along the entrance track, following the map shown opposite. The numbers on the map correspond to the numbers below.

1 Climb up the bank on your right to a mountain indicator. There are great views over the Kent Estuary towards the Lake District here.
2 Keep zig-zagging up the hillside to a stone topscope and a breathtaking panorama. If you're lucky you may see the strange-looking Arnside bore – a tidal wave that rolls from the bay into the estuary a couple of hours before high tide. The slopes here are made of frost-shattered limestone, with areas of distinctive, rare blue moor grass, yew and juniper.
3 Bear left on the path and climb through woodland up to open grassland (a good spot for picnics) along the crest of the ridge.
4 Reach the highest point on the walk at a bench. Continue a short way and head right, downhill, with a wall on your left.
5 The route angles right before reaching a gate to enter Redhills Wood. Soon after, turn left at a crossroads and tour the woodland,

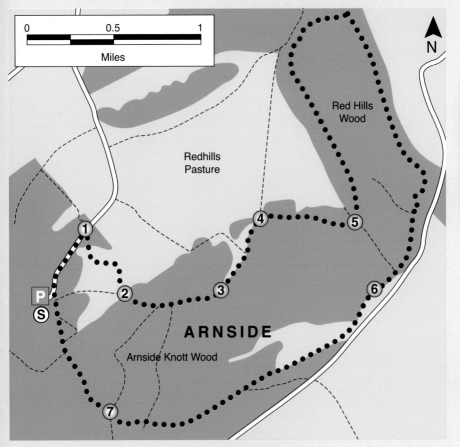

always following paths round to the right.This area is home to a fantastic range of trees and plants, such as dog's mercury, dog's violet and primrose. Look out for the very pretty peach blossom moth and listen for the song of marsh tits (a loud 'pitchoo' sound).

6 Silverdale Road appears down to your left as you emerge on to open hillside. Pass the Shilla Slopes (steep limestone screes created by Ice Age glaciers). Only some plants like marjoram and thyme can anchor in this rubble. They both attract butterflies too.

7 Take the broad uphill track back to the car park. Go through several gates, avoiding left-hand turns to Heathwaite and Copridding Wood.

Property contact details: 01524 701178

Map and start grid ref: OS Landranger 97:SD450774; OS Explorer OL7

Facilities available: Shops, cafés, pubs, toilets in Arnside village and National Trust car park. Walk leaflets available in local shops.

National Trust properties nearby: Heathwaite, Silverdale and much of the Lake District's finest countryside.

Red Squirrel Walk – Formby

Merseyside

This 2.9km (1¾ mile) walk through the pinewoods of Formby is the ideal place to see the famous Formby red squirrels. It is also a great starting point for walks along the Sefton Coastal Path. The squirrels are present throughout the Sefton Coast Pinewoods and there are stunning views of Sefton's natural coast with its golden sand dunes and wide sandy beeches.

Getting there:

(National Trust reserve at Formby is at the west end of Victoria Road).
Road: 3km (2 miles) west of the A565, follow brown signs from the end of Formby by-pass.
Car parks: National Trust car park (pay and display) at Victoria Road, Freshfield, Formby.
Foot: Access at Victoria Road or along the Sefton Coastal Path.
Bus: Cumfy Bus to Victoria Road, Formby; circular nos: 160/1/2/3/4/5.
Rail: Regular services on Merseyrail network to Freshfield Station.
For public transport information visit www.traveline.org.uk.

Distance: 2.9km (1¾ miles).

Terrain and accessibility:

Easy walking conditions on a surfaced path for most of the route, with a few short steep slopes near Victoria Road. The return section to point 5 is a natural woodland path and is more difficult for buggies. Short steep slopes near to Victoria Road.

Directions and points of interest:

Start the walk at point 1, as shown on the map opposite (the numbers on the map correspond to the numbers below). Look out for the following points of interest:

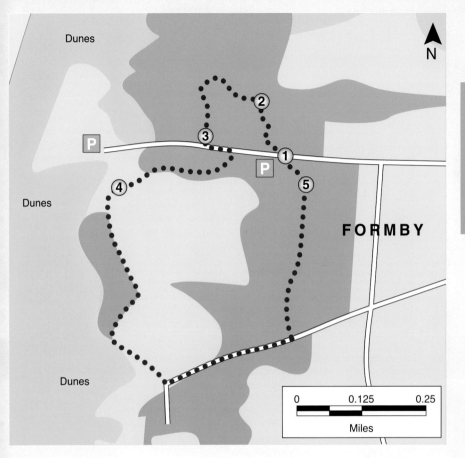

1 The Cornerstone Walk is on the north side of the road opposite the main notice board. Follow the path.
2 The bench seat here provides a pleasant rest among mixed woodland, good for watching red squirrels and woodland birds.
3 Picnic site. A good place for close views of red squirrels.
4 Enjoy views across former asparagus fields from the bench seat here. A small flock of Herdwick sheep graze here in summer.
5 This viewing area is the most popular site for watching red squirrels.

Property contact details: 01704 878 591

Maps and start grid ref: SD 281 082, OS Explorer 285

Facilities available: Parking, toilets, baby changing facilities, three picnic areas, ice cream and soft drinks available.

National Trust properties nearby: 20 Forthlin Road, Mr Hardman's Photographic Studio, Mendips, Rufford Old Hall and Speke Hall.

Beningbrough Hall & Gardens

Historic house Garden

Beningbrough, York,
North Yorkshire, YO30 1DD
01904 472027

OPENING TIMES
House
1 Mar 08–30 Jun 08
11am–3:30pm Mon, Tue, Wed,
Sat, Sun
1 Jul 08–31 Aug 08
11am–3:30pm Mon, Tue, Wed,
Fri, Sat, Sun
1 Sep 08–26 Oct 08
11am–3:30pm Mon, Tue, Wed,
Sat, Sun
Grounds/shop/restaurant
2 Feb 08–3 Feb 08
11am–3:30pm Sat, Sun
9 Feb 08–17 Feb 08
11am–3:30pm Mon, Tue, Wed,
Fri, Sat, Sun
23 Feb 08–24 Feb 08
11am–3:30pm Sat, Sun
1 Mar 08–30 Jun 08
11am–5:30pm Mon, Tue, Wed,
Sat, Sun
1 Jul 08–31 Aug 08
11am–5:30pm Mon, Tue, Wed,
Fri, Sat, Sun
1 Sep 08–26 Oct 08
11am–5:30pm Mon, Tue, Wed,
Sat, Sun
1 Nov 08–21 Dec 08
11am–3:30pm Sat, Sun
10 Jan 08–31 Jan 08
11am–3:30pm Sat, Sun

Notes
Open Good Fri. Closed 27, 28
Dec and 3, 4 Jan 09.

A grand 1716 Georgian mansion with an impressive baroque interior, set in park and gardens. There are more than a hundred 18th-century portraits and seven new interpretation galleries, designed in partnership with the National Portrait Gallery. There is a fully equipped Victorian laundry, with wet and dry rooms, a delightful functioning walled garden supplying the Walled Garden restaurant. There are many family facilities including the wilderness play area.

Picture perfect

In partnership with the National Gallery, Beningbrough houses over 100 famous paintings and has seven new portrait interpretation galleries. Younger visitors can also put themselves in the picture with the aid of computers, clothes and 18th-century props.

What to see

- A fully equipped Victorian laundry – how did posh people keep their clothes clean before washing machines? Servants, of course!
- Discover why bedrooms were such busy places in the 18th century and what it was like to live without bathrooms.

What to do

- Let off steam in the brilliant wooden wilderness play area, with new 'Beningbrough Fort'.
- Explore the grounds and look for the wooden sculptures.
- Visit seven portrait interpretation galleries, with hands-on activities including dressing up to create a computer portrait that can be emailed to yourself.

Special events

We often have family event days, including art activities, trails and theatre. Please contact us for details.

By the way...

- There are some cycle paths through the parkland.
- Wheelchairs are available and there is a lift to all floors of the house. The grounds have some cobbles.

Brimham Rocks

Countryside Moor

Come and explore these strange and fantastic rock formations, nearly 300m (987ft) above the surrounding countryside – they are perfect for hide-and-seek. You'll often see more experienced rock climbers attempting challenging climbs. Early Victorians believed the rocks were created by ancient Druids, but in fact the strange shapes are formed by entirely natural weathering.

Lovers and legends

There is a story that two young lovers leapt off a rock here because the girl's father wouldn't let them marry. As they leapt, they were miraculously saved by the wind and put down safely. It's been known as Lover's Leap ever since.

What to see

- Birds nesting in the rocks, and listen out for jackdaws
- On a clear day the view is 64km (40 miles) across the countryside.
- If you're lucky, rabbits, grouse or even red deer.

What to do

- Look for the wishing stone with a hole in it, and put your hand in to make a wish.
- Pick bilberries in the summer.
- Count the different kinds of lichen on the rocks.

Special events

Recent events include ghostly stories and wildlife trails, as well as family walks. Give us a call to see what's on.

By the way...

- Good footwear is a must, and wrap up warm in colder weather. In July and August it is very busy here.
- Dogs have to go on a lead between April and June so that ground-nesting birds are safe.
- There's a path from the car park to the main rocks; the rest is a bit rough and has slopes.

Summerbridge, Harrogate, North Yorkshire, HG3 4DW
01423 780688

OPENING TIMES
All year 8am–dusk Mon–Sun
Shop/exhibition/kiosk
9 Feb 08–17 Feb 08
11am–5pm Mon–Sun
15 Mar 08–18 May 08
11am–5pm Sat, Sun
24 May 08–5 Oct 08
11am–5pm Mon–Sun
11 Oct 08–2 Nov 08
11am–5pm Sat, Sun
9 Nov 08–21 Dec 08
11am–dusk Sun

Notes
Facilities may close in bad weather. Shop, kiosk and exhibition room open daily during local school holidays, also BH weekends, 26 Dec and 1 Jan 09, weather permitting.

Cragside

Historic house Garden Park Lake River Wood

Rothbury, Morpeth,
Northumberland, NE65 7PX
01669 620333

OPENING TIMES
House
15 Mar 08–5 Oct 08
1pm–5:30pm Tue, Wed, Thu,
Fri, Sat, Sun
7 Oct 08–2 Nov 08
1pm–4:30pm Tue, Wed, Thu,
Fri, Sat, Sun
Gardens/estate/shop/
restaurant
15 Mar 08–2 Nov 08
10:30am–5:30pm Tue, Wed,
Thu, Fri, Sat, Sun
5 Nov 08–21 Dec 08
11am–4pm Wed, Thu, Fri,
Sat, Sun

Notes
Open BH Mons. On BH
weekends the property can be
crowded. Last admission to
house 1hr before closing.
Gardens and estate close at
7pm (dusk if earlier); last
admission 5pm (15 Mar–2 Nov),
3pm (Nov–Dec). Last serving in
restaurant 5pm.

We can guarantee that you will be amazed by the late 19th-century home of inventor and engineer William Armstrong. He was obsessed with water and what it could do, and there are all sorts of intriguing contraptions in his enormous house and estate. Kids will enjoy tumbling about in the adventure playground and the whole family can go on wonderful walks through the woods.

Water wizard
In 1880 Cragside was the first house in the world to glow with hydro-electric lighting. Water also powered a passenger lift and even the spit in the kitchen.

What to see
- Armstrong made sure his inventions were helpful to the servants too. Can you find any of these gadgets when you visit? There's an early version of the dishwasher, the water-driven spit, the dumb waiter, the electric gong, which the butler rang to warn guests to dress for dinner.
- Imagine lazing happily in the sunken Turkish bath located in the basement. This is part of a suite of rooms devoted to relaxation – for men only!
- Marvel at the enormous marble fireplace weighing 10 tonnes, built especially for the visit of the Prince and Princess of Wales in 1884.

What to do

- Try one of the walks through the estate. The circular Armstrong Trail Walk explores Armstrong's hydraulic and hydro-electric machinery.
- Generate electricity using the interactive models in the power house.
- Get tangled up in Nelly's Labyrinth, a tricky maze in the rhododendron bushes.
- Enjoy the swings, slides and tunnels at the adventure playground in Crozier car park or test yourself on our Trim Trail – not for the fainthearted!

Special events

During the school holidays there are family trails, quizzes and tracker packs. Contact us for information on the various activities on offer.

By the way...

- Cragside is a large property with uneven ground, steep drops, lakes and streams so please take care. Don't run off too far and get lost.

Cherryburn

Historic house Garden Farm River

Station Bank, Mickley, nr
Stocksfield, Northumberland
NE43 7DD
01661 843276

OPENING TIMES
Public opening
15 Mar 08–2 Nov 08
11am–5pm Mon, Tue, Thu, Fri,
Sat, Sun
Booked groups
17 Mar 08–31 Oct 08
10am–4pm Mon, Tue, Wed,
Thu, Fri
3 Nov 08–31 Jan 08
10am–3pm Mon–Sun

Notes
Shop open at other times by
arrangement. Open Feb half
term, tel. for details.

The sweet little cottage was the birthplace of Thomas Bewick (1753–1828), one of Northumberland's greatest artists and wood engravers, and you can see an exhibition about him and sometimes demonstrations of engraving and handprinting, to get a taste of how he worked. Walk along the River Tyne, where he was inspired by the wildlife and natural beauty all those years ago, and enjoy a picnic at the farm with some friendly farmyard animals to meet.

Birdman Bewick

Thomas Bewick didn't do that well at school, and left quite early on to become apprentice to an engraver, helping to engrave the designs on banknotes. But his real love was birds and wildlife, and one of his most famous books of engravings was *The Birds of Britain*. He'd have been extremely pleased to know that the beautiful Bewick's Swan was named in his memory.

What to see

- Some of Bewick's engravings, cut into wood – nowadays we can just take a photo instead.
- Demonstrations of hand printing and engraving.
- A secret garden.
- Chickens, rabbits, lambs and donkeys living in the cobbled farmyard.

What to do

- Bring a picnic and enjoy it in the garden (we don't have a café, but we sell lovely cakes, snacks, tea, coffee and soft drinks).
- Pick up some prints that have been made from Bewick's original engravings at the shop.
- Take a stroll along the beautiful River Tyne.

Special events

Recently we've had folk music and country dance in the farmyard, drawing workshops, and engraving demonstrations. Usually the cost is included in the admission price, and there's something going on most Sunday afternoons.

By the way...

- If you contact us in advance, we can provide touchable objects and help to make your visit more accessible. There are some steps to get in and out of the building, and the farmyard is cobbled.
- We can provide a Braille guide, and there's an adapted WC.

East Riddlesden Hall

Historic house Garden Maze Pond

This intimate 17th-century manor house is in the heart of Brontë country. Back in the 1600s, it was one of 19 houses owned by wealthy royalist James Murgatroyd – an entrepreneur, who was also involved in coal mining, cloth manufacture and farming. He remodelled the house with flamboyant gothic architecture and some ornate plasterwork ceilings. In the summer, guides in authentic costume will help you to feel that you've gone back in time.

That's one hefty heifer

The Airedale Heifer is depicted in an 1830 painting at Riddlesden, and was a legendary creature in nearby Keighley. It was supposedly 3.3m (11ft) long and weighed more than 1270kg (1¼ tons). People used to come from miles around to see it.

What to see

- A room with a bricked-in window so that ladies didn't have to look at the outside loo.
- A 17th-century kitchen, with no mod cons.
- Intricate tapestries and embroideries that would have taken hours to make, which is why the ladies would have needed the big fireplaces and cosy wood paneling.
- An enormous 17th-century oak-framed barn.

What to do

- Visit the Airedale Heifer playground and grass maze, with swings, slides and animal rockers.
- Chat to the ducks on the pond.

Special events

Get in touch to see what we have on. We have spooky Halloween activities, school-holiday fun and Easter activities for children.

By the way...

- We have a handling collection of 17th-century items, and there are scented plants in the garden, as well as a Braille guide.
- There are some steps, but the ground floor is accessible, and we have wheelchairs. The grounds are fully accessible and we have portable ramps. There are quite a few steps to the café.

Bradford Road, Keighley,
West Yorkshire, BD20 5EL
01535 607075

OPENING TIMES
House/shop/tearoom
15 Mar 08–2 Nov 08
12am–5pm Mon, Tue, Wed,
Sat, Sun

Notes
Open Good Fri. Tearoom open from 11am on Suns. Shop and tearoom may open weekends in Nov/Dec. Please tel. for details.

Fountains Abbey & Studley Royal Water Garden

Historic house Mill Garden Park Abbey ruins Visitor centre

Fountains, Ripon, North
Yorkshire, HG4 3DY
01765 608888

OPENING TIMES
Abbey/garden/visitor
centre/shop
1 Mar 08–31 Oct 08
10am–5pm Mon–Sun
1 Nov 08–31 Jan 08
10am–4pm Mon, Tue, Wed,
Thu, Sat, Sun
Restaurant
1 Feb 08–30 Apr 08
10am–4pm Mon–Sun
1 May 08–31 Oct 08
10am–5pm Mon–Sun
1 Nov 08–31 Jan 08
10am–4pm Mon, Tue, Wed,
Thu, Sat, Sun
St Mary's
1 Apr 08–30 Sep 08
12am–4pm Mon–Sun
Deer park
All year dawn–dusk Mon–Sun
Mill
1 Mar 08–31 Oct 08
10am–5pm Mon–Sun
1 Nov 08–31 Jan 08
10am–4pm Mon, Tue, Wed,
Thu, Sat, Sun

Notes
Please note: whole estate
closed 24/25 Dec and on Fri in
Nov, Dec, Jan 09. Estate open
on Fri in Feb. Studley Royal
shop and tearoom: opening
times vary, check at property.

Yorkshire's first World Heritage Site offers a great day out for all the family. Explore the passages, staircases and towers in the dramatic Abbey ruins, dress in monks' robes and join a guided tour, visit the interactive exhibition at the water mill or walk the high ride and brave the spooky Serpentine Tunnel. Enjoy the stunning landscaped Georgian Water Garden complete with neo-classical temples, statues and follies which leads to the medieval deer park, home to 500 deer and other wildlife. Children's activities and trails in school holidays and a full programme of events throughout the year.

Woolly wealth

The monks were so busy praying that all the day-to-day labour was done by ordinary 'lay' folk, whose chief role was to look after the Abbey's vast flocks of sheep, who nibbled the Abbey's rich grassland west into the Lake District and north into Teeside. Based on the production of wool, the monks' economic empire grew, making it one of the richest monasteries in the country with buyers from as far afield as France and Italy.

What to see

- Dramatic abbey ruins with gothic arches and towering columns.
- Troughs where the monks washed their feet – they only had full baths four times a year!
- The River Skell flowing beneath the Abbey ruins and, if you're lucky, a bat whizzing by your ear.
- Ducks and swans paddling by the statues in the Water Garden and wild geese on Studley lake.

What to do

- Play hide and seek in the Abbey ruins, grind your own corn at the mill or see if you can identify the different species of wild deer.
- Discover the unusual small buildings – called follies – from temples to rotundas in the Water Garden.
- Go exploring and find the Serpentine Tunnel, Hermit's Grotto and Half Moon pond. Try the five walking trails including walking up to Anne Boleyn's seat, a folly with a surprising view.

Special events

Children's trails and craft workshops in school holidays. Summer open-air theatre, including Shakespeare and children's classics. Concerts in the Abbey on Saturday nights in the autumn. Medieval re-enactments. Autumn Drive In. Christmas entertainment and religious services.

By the way...

- Some areas of the grounds are less accessible, but we have maps of level routes. Wheelchairs are available (please book in advance) and the entrance to Fountains Hall has steps with handrails.

Farne Islands

Coastline Nature reserve Boat trip Wildlife

Northumberland
01665 720651

OPENING TIMES
Both islands
1 Apr 08–30 Apr 08
10:30am–6pm Mon–Sun
Staple
1 May 08–31 Jul 08
10:30am–1:30pm Mon–Sun
Inner Farne
1 May 08–31 Jul 08
1:30pm–5pm Mon–Sun
Both islands
1 Aug 08–30 Sep 08
10:30am–6pm Mon–Sun
Centre/shop
22 Mar 08–30 Jun 08
10am–5pm Mon–Sun
1 Jul 08–31 Aug 08
10am–5:30pm Mon–Sun
1 Sep 08–30 Sep 08
10am–5pm Mon–Sun
1 Oct 08–31 Oct 08
11am–4pm Mon–Sun
1 Nov 08–21 Dec 08
11am–4pm Wed, Thu, Fri,
Sat, Sun
3 Jan 08–31 Jan 08
11am–4pm Wed, Thu, Fri,
Sat, Sun

Notes
Only Inner Farne and Staple
Islands can be visited. Visitors
to Inner Farne in June should
wear hats. Information
centre/shop open half-term hols
10am–5pm.

The Farne Islands on the windswept Northumberland coast are a haven for seabirds and seals, and a thrilling place for a family outing. Kids will love the boat trip to get there.

Watch out, birds about!
The birds are well used to children and are usually quite friendly. Take care in late May, June and early July, though, when the terns have a nasty habit of dive bombing innocent visitors as they protect their young. Bring a hat!

What to see
- There are over 100,000 pairs of bird living here. Children particularly love the puffins with their waddling walk. You'll also see eider ducks, the fun-sounding kittiwake and four species of tern.
- Shoals of Atlantic grey seals, which are fun to watch as they lounge contentedly on the rocks.

What to do
- The only way to visit the islands is to take a boat on a 3-hour round trip from Seahouses to Staple Island in the morning or Inner Farne in the afternoon. On a breezy day the ride is exhilarating.
- Have a chat with a warden to find out more about the creatures in their care.

By the way...
- If fresh air makes your family hungry, stock up on your own snacks – there are no refreshments on the islands. Lavatories are available on Inner Farne only.
- The boat will not make the journey in bad weather.
- You can take your dog on the boat and leave it with the boatman.

Gibside

Park Countryside Nature reserve River Wood

A beautiful, forested landscape garden that was created in Georgian times. Gibside is a designed landscape that was made out of the natural woodlands in the Derwent Valley. You can explore this designed landscape on the network of pathways connecting each part of the garden, and explore the garden buildings in special places. There are also lots of wild areas to explore.

The unhappy (and green-fingered) Countess

Over two hundred years ago, a girl called Mary Eleanor Bowes lived at Gibside. She was an only child and grew up to be very rich. She loved plants and as a child she had her own garden. Later, she built a Green House, which you can visit, though it's now a ruin, where she kept all her special exotic plants from around the world. She is said to have been unhappy because her first husband died young, and her second was cruel to her. Luckily it turned out all right in the end.

What to see

- In summer, swallows nesting in the stables. See into their nest with the 'swallow cam'.
- The Column to Liberty rising high above the tree tops.
- Look out for the beautiful red kites.

What to do

- Can you run the mile? Run down the tree-lined Long Walk as far as you can.
- Have a go at the activities in the stables.
- Wildlife spotting – visit the wildlife hide for inspiration.

Special events

Lots of events through the year including children's days, wildlife walks and open-air theatre for families.

By the way...

- Bring your dog but please keep him on a lead. There are baby-changing facilities and a children's menu. Some areas are more accessible than others. Contact us for more details.

nr Rowlands Gill, Burnopfield, Newcastle upon Tyne, Tyne & Wear, NE16 6BG
01207 541820

OPENING TIMES
10 Mar 08–2 Nov 08
10am–6pm Mon–Sun
3 Nov 08–31 Jan 08
10am–4pm Mon–Sun
Chapel
15 Mar 08–2 Nov 08
11am–4:30pm Mon–Sun
Stables
1 Feb 08–9 Mar 08
11am–3:30pm Mon–Sun
10 Mar 08–2 Nov 08
11am–4:30pm Mon–Sun
3 Nov 08–31 Jan 08
11am–3:30pm Mon–Sun
Shop/tearoom
1 Feb 08–9 Mar 08 11am–4pm Mon–Sun
10 Mar 08–2 Nov 08
11am–5pm Mon–Sun
3 Nov 08–31 Jan 08
11am–4pm Mon–Sun
Grounds
1 Feb 08–9 Mar 08 10am–4pm Mon–Sun

Notes
Closed 22–26 Dec and 29 Dec–2 Jan 09. Last admission times: 1 Feb–9 March 3:30pm; 10 March–2 Nov 4:30pm; 3 Nov–31 Jan 09 3:30pm. Shop and tearoom open 10am weekends. Last entry to tearoom 15mins before closing.

175

Hadrian's Wall & Housesteads Fort Countryside Museum Roman ruins

North East

Bardon Mill, Hexham,
Northumberland, NE47 6NN
01434 344363

OPENING TIMES
1 Apr 08–30 Sep 08
10am–6pm Mon–Sun
1 Oct 08–31 Jan 08
10am–4pm Mon–Sun

Notes
Closed 24–26 Dec and 1 Jan.
Opening times subject to
confirmation by English
Heritage. Tel. for details or visit
www.english-heritage.org.uk.

A wild and evocative World Heritage Site offering a taste of the Roman soldier's life – communal loos and all. The wall was built around AD 122, when the Roman Empire was at its height. Even now the ruins are impressive, and looking after the wall is a full-time job. Housesteads Fort is one of the best-preserved of the sixteen forts along the Wall.

It's cold up north

Soldiers from sunnier climes were brought in to guard the Wall – the Roman name for Housesteads was *Vercovicium*, which means 'effective fighters'. But some of those foreign soldiers were pretty miserable up on their cold lookout posts – and you might want to bring a sweater, too.

What to see

- Ruins of Roman granaries, barracks, a hospital and some of the first flushing toilets.
- A model of the fort as it would have been.
- Wonderful views across the countryside.

What to do

- Walk like a Roman... march alongside the wall, repelling imaginary Picts and Scots.
- If it's a bit chilly, grab a drink and a sandwich at the kiosk, and sit inside to warm up.
- Have a look in the Museum, to find out more on the history of the Wall.

Special events

Get in touch or have a look at our website for further details of activities and events.

By the way...

- The paths are a bit uneven at Housesteads and on the wall but there's a ramped access to the Wall at Steel Rigg.
- You can drive right up to the museum.
- Please keep dogs on a lead because there are sheep and ground-nesting birds nearby.

Hardcastle Crags

Mill Countryside Wood

North East

Hollin Hall, Crimsworth Dean,
Hebden Bridge, West Yorkshire,
HX7 7AP
01422 844518

OPENING TIMES
1 Oct 08–31 Oct 08
11am–4:30pm Tue, Wed, Thu,
Sat, Sun
1 Nov 08–31 Jan 08
11am–3:30pm Sat, Sun
Hardcastle Crags
All year Mon–Sun
Gibson Mill
15 Mar 08–30 Sep 08
11am–4:30pm Thu, Sat, Sun
1 Oct 08–31 Oct 08
11am–3:30pm Thu, Sat, Sun
1 Nov 08–31 Jan 08
11am–3:30pm Sat, Sun
Muddy Boots Café
1 Mar 08–6 Apr 08
11am–4:30pm Sat, Sun
7 Apr 08–30 Apr 08
11am–4:30pm Tue, Wed, Thu,
Sat, Sun
1 May 08–30 Sep 08
11am–3:30pm Tue, Wed, Thu,
Sat, Sun

Notes
Mill & café: open Sat–Thurs;
closed Fri for all local school
hols (except Good Fri and 26
Dec). If limited power, café or
parts of mill may close.

Over 400 acres of beautiful woodland, one of the top ten Yorkshire beauty spots, with more than 30km (18½ miles) of meandering trails to explore. Follow the river, discover the waterfalls, enjoy dancing and dressing up at Gibson Mill.

Sustainable mill
At the heart of Hardcastle Crags is Gibson Mill, the flagship sustainable building for the National Trust and Sustainable Building of the Year 2006. With lots of hands-on games, dressing up, dancing and fun to be had, it also sells fantastic cakes too.

What to see
- Gibson Mill visitor and art exhibition centre, tumbling streams and cascading waterfalls.
- Fields of spring bluebells, summer dragonflies, glorious autumnal colours, naturally frozen winter ice sculptures.

What to do
- Try one of our way-marked walks, the easier Slurring Rock Saunter or the more energetic Crags Constitutional. Let your dog enjoy a scramble, too.

Special events
You can book a guided walk or a special orienteering course. We've had prehistoric survival days for older kids, and bat walks and dawn chorus. Get in touch for details of forthcoming events.

By the way...
- Parking is limited with congestion at busy times. Come by bus!
- Disabled parking is possible – ask if you want to park at Gibson Mill.
- Picnicking is allowed.

Lindisfarne Castle

Castle Garden Coastline Nature reserve

Lindisfarne Castle sits dramatically on a rocky crag on Holy Island, looking out over the Northumberland coast. Once the island was the home of an early monastery, but Viking raids forced the monks off. You reach it by driving across a 5km (3 mile) causeway, which is great fun, but only at low tide.

An Englishman's home is his castle

The castle was originally a Tudor fort, but in 1903 it was converted into a private house for a friend by the young Edwin Lutyens. He added very typical touches like arched windows, brick herringbone floors and an early 20th-century portcullis.

What to see

- A warren of tiny rooms in the house, with its nooks and crannies.
- The remains of Lindisfarne Priory (owned by English Heritage), built in 1082 in the village of Holy Island.

What to do

- Tramp up and down the windy battlements, or visit the walled garden designed by Gertrude Jekyll. Enjoy a cup of tea in Holy Island village. Interactive quizzes and trails available.

By the way...

- No large packs or pushchairs allowed in the castle, and access is steep. Flat shoes are advised! To avoid disappointment, check safe crossing times before making a long journey – the causeway closes two hours before high tide until three hours after.

Holy Island,
Berwick-upon-Tweed,
Northumberland, TD15 2SH
01289 389244

OPENING TIMES
16 Feb 08–24 Feb 08
10am–3pm Mon–Sun
15 Mar 08–2 Nov 08 times vary
Tue, Wed, Thu, Fri, Sat, Sun
30 Dec 08–2 Jan 08
10:30am–3pm Wed, Thu, Fri
Garden
All year 10am–dusk Mon–Sun

Notes
Open BH Mons (incl. Scottish BHs). Lindisfarne is a tidal island accessed via a 5km (3 mile) causeway at low tide. Therefore the castle opening times vary depending on the tides. On open days the castle will open for 5hrs, which will always include 12am–3pm. It will open either 10am–3pm or 12am–5pm. The National Trust flag will fly only when the castle is open. To obtain a copy of the tide tables and detailed opening times send a sae to Lindisfarne Castle stating in which month you wish to visit.

179

Nostell Priory & Parkland

Historic house Garden

Doncaster Road, Nostell, nr
Wakefield, West Yorkshire,
WF4 1QE
01924 863892

OPENING TIMES
House
15 Mar 08–2 Nov 08 1pm–5pm
Wed, Thu, Fri, Sat, Sun
6 Dec 08–14 Dec 08
12am–4pm Mon–Sun
Grounds/shop/tearoom
1 Mar 08–2 Nov 08
11am–5:30pm Wed, Thu, Fri,
Sat, Sun
8 Nov 08–30 Nov 08
11am–4:30pm Sat, Sun
6 Dec 08–14 Dec 08
11am–4:30pm Mon–Sun
Park
All year 9am–5pm Mon–Sun

Notes
Open BH Mons: house
1pm–5pm; gardens, shop and
tearoom 11am–5:30pm, park
closes dusk if earlier. Rose
garden may be closed on
occasions for private functions.
Open local Feb half term.

Plenty for the family to do in the landscaped grounds of this magnificent 18th-century house, built on the site of an original medieval priory in 1733. There are paintings by Lockey and Kauffman, and probably the finest collection of Chippendale furniture in the world – it's like a really good episode of Antiques Roadshow!

A world in miniature

Peek inside the magical 18th-century dolls' house, which is 2m (6ft) high. There's a mini leather dog, an ivory mouse, and a dining table all laid out with tiny cutlery and silver plates. Try and spot the difference in the way the figures of the family and the servants were made.

What to see

- Pets' graves in the rose garden and cows in the park.
- Child-sized Chippendale chairs – sorry, you can't sit on them!
- A clock made by John Harrison, who solved the longitude problem, with workings inside made of wood.

What to do

- In the parkland, find the Obelisk Lodge in the shape of a pyramid.
- Burn off some energy in the adventure playground in the gardens, or watch the kids doing that from the tearoom.
- Walk around the lake and say hello to the ducks, swans and cygnets.

Special events

We have family croquet, a giant chess set and family trails in the house and gardens, special family fun day and boredom-busting days in the school holidays, spooky Halloween evenings, Santa's Grotto and Christmas trails plus other seasonal events.

By the way....

- With advance notice, we can provide touchable objects and surfaces.
- Wheelchairs can be booked; a lift is available to upper floors.
- There are baby-changing and feeding facilities, and we can loan you baby slings and infant carriers (sorry, no pushchairs are allowed in the house).

Nunnington Hall

Historic house Garden

The sheltered walled garden, with spring flowering organic meadows, orchards and the flamboyant peacocks, complement this beautiful Yorkshire house that nestles on the quiet banks of the River Rye. Take the afternoon to enjoy and absorb the atmosphere of this former family home. Explore period rooms while hearing the Hall's many tales and then discover one of the world's finest collections of miniature rooms in the old attic. The Hall also holds a series important art and photography exhibitions across the year. There are family activity packs available across the season with additional trails during school holidays.

Spooky story
People say that the panelled bedroom is haunted by a spooky lady ghost who can fly through the 400-year-old wooden walls.

What to see
- The amazing collection of tiny objects in the Carlisle collection.
- Needlework samplers made by young girls in the 19th century.
- Watch out for the ghost!

What to do
- Find out why the tea caddy in the drawing room has a lock on it.
- Look out for the stuffed animal heads and skins collected on expeditions to India and Africa.
- Watch the peacocks strut their stuff in the riverside walled garden.

Special events
Events all season including children's trails during school holidays.

By the way...
- There are picnic tables in the tea garden, as well as a special children's menu.
- We can loan you infant seats or hip-carrying seats for carrying children and there are baby-changing facilities.
- It's fairly accessible, and we have wheelchairs and can provide assistance. Dogs in the car park only, please, but we have shaded parking where they will be more comfortable.

Nunnington, nr York,
North Yorkshire, YO62 5UY
01439 748283

OPENING TIMES
15 Mar 08–31 May 08
12am–5pm Tue, Wed, Thu, Fri, Sat, Sun
1 Jun 08–31 Aug 08
12am–5:30pm Tue, Wed, Thu, Fri, Sat, Sun
1 Sep 08–2 Nov 08 12am–5pm Tue, Wed, Thu, Fri, Sat, Sun

Notes
Open BH Mons. Hall opens 1pm. Winter weekend opening. See website or tel. for details.

Souter Lighthouse

Coastline Nature reserve Museum Historic building

North East

Coast Road, Whitburn,
Sunderland, Tyne & Wear
SR6 7NH
0191 529 3161

OPENING TIMES
15 Mar 08–2 Nov 08
11am–5pm Mon, Tue, Wed,
Thu, Sat, Sun

Notes
Open Good Fri.

Souter Lighthouse, with its jaunty red and white stripes, is an exciting place to head for if you're in the area. So long as they are accompanied by adults, children can make it up the lighthouse tower's spiral staircase.

All lit up
Souter Lighthouse was opened in 1871 after dozens of ships had foundered on submerged rocks along this dangerous stretch of coast – it was the first lighthouse to be powered by electricity.

What to see
- Huge machines in the engine room, the heart of the lighthouse.
- At the top of the tower you can look out to sea for miles. Don't get too puffed out – there are 76 steps!
- Watch a 9-minute video about the lighthouse.

What to do
- Explore a replica of the cottage where the first keeper, Henry Millet, lived c. 1900 with his family.
- Send a message in Morse code on the signaller, and decode signalling flags using CCTV.
- Have a picnic and a bracing walk along the clifftop footpath above Marsden Bay, where you can look down on the swooping seabirds.

Special events
Annual nature-themed festival in July.

By the way...
- Although access for pushchairs and those with restricted mobility is limited, a camera at the top of the lighthouse tower can be operated from the ground floor, so everyone can enjoy the view from the top.

Treasurer's House

Historic house Garden

Children will be fascinated to spot the fussy habits of the man who lived in this elegant house at the beginning of the 20th century. Can you believe that Frank Green had studs set into the floor to tell servants where to put the furniture? And there are bossy signs all over the place. How many can you find? The house is set in the tranquil Minster Close – great for a rainy day.

Spooky story

A plumber was working in the cellar in the 1950s when he heard a trumpet and saw Roman soldiers coming out of the wall. He was so shocked he fell off his ladder. What's amazing is that the soldiers seemed to have no feet – archaeologists have now found that the Roman road, which went though the house, was 45cm (18in) lower than the new floor. Weird...

What to see

- A model ship made out of bones (left over from meal times).
- Some really clever paint techniques of pretend wood and carving.
- Look out for Frisk, Mr Green's favourite dog.

What to do

- Find out how they stopped mice climbing up the table legs.
- See how fast your eyes can adapt to the darkness in the King's Room, kept that way to preserve the fabrics.

Minster Yard, York, North Yorkshire, YO1 7JL
01904 624247

OPENING TIMES
15 Mar 08–2 Nov 08
11am–4:30pm Mon, Tue, Wed, Thu, Sat, Sun
3 Nov 08–30 Nov 08
11am–3:30pm Mon, Tue, Wed, Thu, Sat, Sun

Notes
Nov opening: access by guided Ghostly Myth tour to selected rooms. Tearoom open.

Wallington

Historic house Garden Park Countryside Lake Wood

Cambo, Morpeth,
Northumberland, NE61 4AR
01670 773967

OPENING TIMES
House
15 Mar 08–30 Sep 08
1pm–5:30pm Mon, Wed, Thu,
Fri, Sat, Sun
1 Oct 08–2 Nov 08
1pm–4:30pm Mon, Wed, Thu,
Fri, Sat, Sun
Walled garden
1 Feb 08–31 Mar 08
10am–4pm Mon–Sun
1 Apr 08–30 Sep 08
10am–7pm Mon–Sun
1 Oct 08–31 Oct 08
10am–6pm Mon–Sun
1 Nov 08–31 Jan 08
10am–4pm Mon–Sun
Shop/restaurant
1 Feb 08–15 Feb 08
10:30am–4:30pm Wed, Thu,
Fri, Sat, Sun
16 Feb 08–25 May 08
10:30am–5:30pm Mon–Sun
26 May 08–30 Sep 08
10:30am–5:30pm Mon–Sun
1 Oct 08–2 Nov 08
10:30am–4:30pm Mon, Wed,
Thu, Fri, Sat, Sun
5 Nov 08–31 Jan 08
10:30am–4:30pm Wed, Thu,
Fri, Sat, Sun

Notes
Last admission to house 1hr
before closing, restaurant
30mins. Shop and restaurant
closed 22 Dec–2 Jan 09 incl.
Farm shop open limited hours
on Christmas Eve and New
Year's Eve, closed 25/26 Dec
and 1/2 Jan 09.

Don't be fooled by the plain exterior of this 17th-century house,
home to many generations of the Blackett and Trevelyan families.
Inside there's oodles of fancy plasterwork, gorgeous paintings and
many fascinating objects. Outside there's a fabulous garden with
sculptures, water features, a wildlife hide and even an exciting
adventure playground.

The mole's revenge

Did you know that King William III died when his horse tripped over a
mole hill? The horse had previously belonged to Sir John Fenwick, who
owned Wallington and whose estates were forfeit to the Crown upon
his execution for treason. Jacobite supporters – enemies of William –
used to drink a toast to the mole, or 'the little black velvet gentleman',
for this poetic justice.

What to see

- A stuffed porcupine fish and other oddities in the Cabinet of
  Curiosities, brought to Wallington by Maria, the wife of the
  5th Baronet.
- A collection of dolls' houses in the servants' quarters. Peep through
  two keyholes and a mouse hole to see the mouse house.
- Some very large stone Griffin heads on the lawn.

184

What to do

- Visit the children's room (no adults allowed!) filled with old-fashioned games and toys.
- Imagine doing loads of washing up in that kitchen without a dishwasher!
- Have a clamber around in the adventure playground.

Special events

We have a range of events for all the family – Easter trails, Mayday celebrations, a Family Fun Day and lots more. Get in touch.

By the way...

- There are lots of small objects within the house, so we do encourage babies to enjoy visiting from the comfort of a front-carrying sling, which we're happy to loan for use around the house.
- The courtyard's a nice place for picnics, and there's a children's menu in the restaurant.

Best of the Rest

Dunstanburgh Castle

A magnificent ruin in an impressive coastal setting, Dunstanburgh castle must be reached on foot along paths following the rocky shore. The castle, managed by English Heritage, was once one of the largest and grandest fortifications in northern England. Vistors to this lonely stretch of beautiful coastline are rewarded with fine cliff-top panoramas.

Contact: Craster, Alnwick, Northumberland, NE66 3TT. Tel. 01665 576231 **Opening times:** 1 Apr–30 Sep 10am–6pm Mon–Sun; 1 Oct–30 Oct 10am–4pm Mon–Sun; 2 Nov–31 Mar 08 10am–4pm Mon, Thu, Fri, Sat, Sun.

George Stephenson's Birthplace

George Stephenson was the inventor of the famous steam-powered locomotive *Rocket* in 1829. He was born into intense poverty in this house in 1781. Hear about his life from the custodian (often dressed in 18th-century mop cap and pinafore) and marvel at just how many members of the family squashed into their one-room home. Children will enjoy the idea of the truckle bed where the Stephenson children slept – it had to be kept under their parents' box bed to save room. You can touch some of the everyday objects in the house and children can even clamber onto the beds to discover what it felt like to be a family asleep in one room. After your visit, take a walk along the river or the old wagonway – the house is in a beautiful setting.

Contact: Wylam, Northumberland, NE41 8BP. Tel. 01661 853457 **Opening times:** 15 Mar 08–2 Nov 08 12am–5pm Thu, Fri, Sat, Sun **Notes:** Open BH Mons.

Ormesby Hall

The large model railway exhibition is a main attraction at this charming 18th-century Palladian mansion. Special layouts include the 'Friends of Thomas the Tank Engine' model railway with lots of buttons to push, and larger layouts, with detailed models of the old Corfe Castle and Pilmoor railway stations and landscapes. There are footstools for shorter enthusiasts to stand on, so that nobody misses the action. Have a go at the children's house quiz, with I-Spy questions for younger visitors. We have a family activity pack too. Take a walk round the gardens and through the Holly Walk, and come back for cake and scones in the tearoom.

Contact: Church Lane, Ormesby, nr Middlesbrough, Redcar & Cleveland, TS7 9AS. Tel. 01642 324188 **Opening times:** 15 Mar 08–2 Nov 08 1:30pm–5pm Sat, Sun **Notes:** Open BH Mons and Good Fri.

Washington Old Hall

Washington Old Hall was home of the ancestors of George Washington (the first President of the United States of America) for 430 years. The great man himself didn't live here – he was born in Virginia in 1732 – but his name came from this village. One of the National Trust's smallest houses, provision for families is fairly limited, although there is a fun children's quiz and you'll find a very warm welcome from staff and volunteers who are always happy to answer children's questions. Independence Day celebrations take place every year when the stars and stripes are flown from the flagpole.

Contact: The Avenue, Washington Village, Washington, Tyne & Wear, NE38 7LE. Tel. 0191 416 6879 **Opening times: House** 16 Mar 08–2 Nov 08 11am–5pm Mon, Tue, Wed, Sun **Garden:** As house 10am–5pm **Tearoom:** As house 11am–4pm **Notes:** Open Good Fri and Easter Sat.

187

Red Squirrel Walk – Wallington

Northumberland

North East

This 3.25km (2 mile) walk meanders through mixed woodland with a wildlife observatory hide, red squirrel feeders and stunning views of the Wansbeck river valley and Shafto Crag escarpment.

Getting there:
Road: A696 north from Newcastle and B6343 from Morpeth.
Car parks: At Wallington (see p.184).
Bus: Bus stop outside Wallington (see p.184).
For public transport information visit www.traveline.org.uk

Distance: 3.25km (2 miles).

Terrain and accessibility: Good walking conditions on gravel footpath. Some gradients.

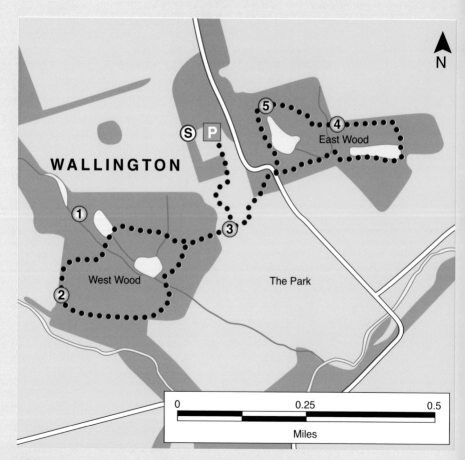

Directions and points of interest:
Start the walk in the car park, as shown on the map opposite. The numbers on the map correspond to the numbers below. Follow the map and look out for the following features:

1 Wildlife observatory hide and red squirrel feeders.
2 Beautiful views of Wansbeck river valley to the east.
3 Spectacular views of Wansbeck river valley and Shafto Crag escarpment to the south.
4 View of the Arches, moved here to make way for the current clock tower gateway in the Wallington courtyard.
5 Look out for further red squirrel feeders here.

Property contact details: 01670 773604

Maps and start grid ref: OS Landranger 81, gr NZ 029 842, Explorer OL29

Facilities available: Parking, restaurant, gift shop, farm shop and toilets.

National Trust properties nearby: Cragside, Hadrian's Wall and Housesteads Fort and Northumberland Coast.

Chirk Castle

Castle Garden Park Fortress

Chirk, Wrexham, LL14 5AF
01691 777701

OPENING TIMES
Castle
2 Feb 08–10 Feb 08 11am–4pm
Sat, Sun
13 Feb 08–17 Feb 08 11am–4pm
Wed, Thu, Fri, Sat, Sun
15 Mar 08–30 Jun 08 11am–5pm
Wed, Thu, Fri, Sat, Sun
1 Jul 08–31 Aug 08 11am–5pm
Tue, Wed, Thu, Fri, Sat, Sun
1 Sep 08–30 Sep 08 11am–5pm
Wed, Thu, Fri, Sat, Sun
1 Oct 08–2 Nov 08 11am–4pm
Wed, Thu, Fri, Sat, Sun
6 Dec 08–14 Dec 08 11am–5pm
Sat, Sun
Garden & estate
As castle* 10am–6pm**
Shop
As castle 10am–5pm***
National Trust shop
As castle 11am–5pm***
Tearoom/restaurant
As castle 10am–5pm***

Notes
Open BH Mons. Last admission
to castle ½hr before closing, Last
admission to garden 1hr before
closing.
*not open during Dec.
**Closes at 5pm in Oct.
***closes at 4pm in Feb and Oct

Chirk Castle was built in the late 13th century and is a rather tough-looking character, with towers and thick brick walls, and a top-of-the-range dungeon on two levels. The castle stands on a hilltop looking over the Ceiriog valley to the south, so nobody can creep up on it unawares. The interior has been refurbished and added to over the years, and it's still home to the Myddelton family, whose ancestor Sir Thomas bought it in 1595 for a mere £5000.

Bloody hand!
Legend has it that the red hand in the family coat of arms comes from a rather macabre running race. Two of the Myddleton lads argued over who should inherit, and agreed to settle the dispute by racing to the castle gates. But the first boy was just reaching out to touch the gates when the other one reached out with his sword and cut off his hand. Now is that called cheating or 'winning on a technicality'?

What to see
- The rather grim dungeons with their very tiny windows. Don't get shut in!
- The 'murder holes' in the stairs in Adam's towers – soldiers threw hot oil and stones down them to hit the enemy below.
- Genuine suits of armour from the Civil War.
- The huge elaborate iron gates – look for the eagles' heads and the Myddelton family crest.

What to do

- Put the kids in the stocks (but please, do remember to take them home afterwards).
- Try on historic costumes and lay seige to the castle in the family activity room.
- Have fun on the hanging ropes, tyres and wooden logs in the children's adventure playground.
- Borrow outdoor tracker packs to explore the countryside.

Special events

We have family activity Thursdays throughout summer school holidays from Costumes and Armour to Plagues and Potions. Special Easter trails and Haunted Happenings, medieval festivals and living-history re-enactments.

By the way...

- There are picnic tables by the play area and a rustic picnic area by the car park.
- Children's quizzes for castle and garden always available.
- There are quite a few steps through the castle and spiral stone staircases in the tower and down to the dungeon.

Dinefwr Park & Castle

Castle Historic house Park Nature reserve

Llandeilo, Carmarthenshire,
SA19 6RT
01558 824512

OPENING TIMES
15 Mar 08–2 Nov 08
11am–5pm Mon–Sun
7 Nov 08–21 Dec 08
11am–5pm Fri, Sat, Sun

Notes
Last admission 45mins before
closing. On Tues and Wed
house is available for booked
conferences. House (1 July–30
Oct) and park (25 March–30
Oct) open daily during school
hols only.

Dinefwr is a beautiful 18th-century park enclosing a medieval deer park. Come into the house too, built in 1660 but now with a Victorian façade and you can experience a glimpse of life in 1912. Our friendly volunteers will be glad to tell you more, and little fingers are allowed to touch many of the objects. There are footpaths in the park leading to the castle, bog wood and some other outstanding views of the Towy Valley.

The Romans woz 'ere

Something for all the family in all weathers. Great new exhibition on the first floor of Newton House, telling the stories of the history and landscape of Dinefwr. Try the White Park Cattle, Dragonfly Walk and others in the stunning park.

What to see

- Shy fallow deer munching away under the trees.
- A herd of rare Dinefwr White Park Cattle.
- A beautiful fancy ceiling in the house.
- The dramatic castle and views for miles over the Towy Valley.

What to do

- Try out the children's trails – we'll help out if you get stuck.
- Take the pushchair along our boardwalk through Bog Wood to the Mill Pond (see how many dragonflies you can spot there).
- If it is wet, help clean coats, boots and hats below stairs.

Special events

We often host family-friendly events. Recently we've had craft activities, carriage driving, The Sealed Knot and even a family fun dog show. Give us a call to see what's on.

By the way...

- Dogs are welcome in the outer park – please keep on a lead. We have baby-changing and feeding facilities and a children's menu in the tearoom (not National Trust). You can also book a wheelchair.

Dolaucothi Gold Mines

Countryside Museum Mines

Come for a guided tour of the unique underground workings, which have great archeological importance. And have a go at gold panning. If you find any, it's yours. There's also an interesting new exhibition on mining history and working trains on the mine floor.

There's gold in them thar hills
... well, not much now, although the mines were in use from Roman times 2000 years ago, right up the 20th century. The Romans built a fort at Pumsaint, so they could keep an eye on things, and brought in slaves and local people to do the digging for them.

What to see
- Tunnels, pits, channels, tanks – if you can dig one, it's probably here.
- A collection of 1930s mining machinery in the main mine yard.
- Pick marks in the rocks made by Roman slaves.

What to do
- Try gold panning, and you'll realise just how frustrating looking for gold can be.
- Go for a walk in the wooded hills, or hire a cycle at the nearby information centre in Pumsaint.
- Experience what mining would have been like on the hour-long tour with only lamps to light your way (younger children allowed only at the discretion of staff – telephone to ask).

Special events
We have an annual living-history weekend when we all go back to Roman times, and have visiting crafts and sometimes Roman cookery. You can come and join in – contact us to find out when it's on this year.

By the way...
- We have a level tour of the mine yard suitable for the less mobile.
- Good idea to wear good shoes for the underground tours; it can be a bit slippy down there.
- There's a caravan site and also fishing available on the estate.

Pumsaint, Llanwrda, Carmarthenshire, SA19 8US
01558 650177

OPENING TIMES
Mines
15 Mar 08–2 Nov 08
10am–5pm Mon–Sun
Shop
15 Mar 08–2 Nov 08
10am–5pm Mon–Sun
Christmas shop
5 Nov 08–21 Dec 08
11am–5pm Wed, Thu, Fri, Sat, Sun
Tearoom
15 Mar 08–2 Nov 08
10am–5pm Mon–Sun

Notes
Groups can be booked at other times. Pumsaint information centre and estate walks open all year. Underground tours last about 1hr and involve hillside walking, so stout footwear is essential; helmets with lights are provided. Smaller children will be allowed on the tours only at the discretion of the property staff. Please tel. for advice.

Erddig

Historic house Garden Park Countryside Wood

Wrexham, LL13 0YT
01978 355314

OPENING TIMES
House
1 Sep 08–30 Sep 08
12am–5pm Mon, Tue, Wed,
Sat, Sun
1 Oct 08–2 Nov 08 12am–4pm
Mon, Tue, Wed, Sat, Sun
8 Nov 08–21 Dec 08
12am–4pm Sat, Sun
Garden/restaurant/shop
9 Feb 08–9 Mar 08 11am–4pm
Mon, Tue, Wed, Sat, Sun
15 Mar 08–31 Mar 08
11am–5pm Mon, Tue, Wed,
Sat, Sun
1 Apr 08–30 Jun 08
10am–6pm Mon, Tue, Wed,
Sat, Sun
1 Jul 08–31 Aug 08 11am–6pm
Mon, Tue, Wed, Thu, Sat, Sun
1 Sep 08–30 Sep 08
11am–6pm Mon, Tue, Wed,
Sat, Sun
1 Oct 08–2 Nov 08 11am–5pm
Mon, Tue, Wed, Sat, Sun
8 Nov 08–21 Dec 08
11am–4pm Sat, Sun

Notes
Restaurant and shop close 1hr
earlier 15 Mar–2 Nov. Open
Good Fri. Last admission 1hr
before closing. Guided tours of
the house are conducted every
Thu in July and Aug.

The original house was finished in 1687 and was added to over the
years as the home of the Yorke family. They were a rather eccentric
bunch and chose not to install electricity, gas or mains water until
well into the 20th century. Don't be fooled by the plain brickwork
exterior: inside, the lavish furnishings are outstanding and the
servants' rooms give an intriguing taste of life 'below stairs'.

Family values
The Yorkes all shared an interest in antiquity and hoarding things, no
matter how trivial. Many of them were vegetarians – in 1749 at age five,
Philip Yorke apparently 'chused chiefly to dine on vegtables'. They were
extremely fond of all their servants, and even commissioned portraits of
them all – complete with little verses penned by the family.

What to see
- A grand kitchen – detached from the house to reduce the risk of fire.
- Many original objects in the stables, forge and more.
- An 18th-century waterfall known as the 'cup and saucer' in the park.
- Very special Chinese wallpaper in the house.

What to do
- Look for the gamekeeper, the housemaid and the blacksmith among
  the portraits of the servants in the servants' hall and basement
  passage.
- Visit the walled garden to spot rare breeds of fruit – did you know
  there was an apple called an Edlesborsdorfer? Neither did we.
- Take a horse-drawn carriage ride.

Special events

We have authentic demonstrations of restored historic equipment, and sometimes you'll meet some 'Victorian' servants in the house. We also have special days, from our increasingly popular Apple Festival to craft making. Call us to find out what holiday activities are planned.

By the way...

- We have wheelchairs and a ramped entrance, but there are stairs in the house.
- Most rooms have no electric light – avoid dull days if you want a really close look at the pictures.
- There are three different walks to follow in the grounds, but please keep your dog on the lead.

Llanerchaeron

Historic house Garden Park Farm

Wales & Northern Ireland

Ciliau Aeron, nr Aberaeron,
Ceredigion, SA48 8DG
01545 570200

OPENING TIMES
15 Mar 08–20 Jul 08
11:30am–4pm Wed, Thu, Fri,
Sat, Sun
22 Jul 08–31 Aug 08
11:30am–4pm Tue, Wed, Thu,
Fri, Sat, Sun
3 Sep 08–2 Nov 08
11:30am–4pm Wed, Thu, Fri,
Sat, Sun

Notes
Open BH Mons. Farm and
garden open at 11 and close
at 5pm. Car park closes at
5:30pm.

Set in the beautiful Dyffryn Aeron, the estate survived virtually
unaltered into the 20th century.

Do it yourself
No trips to the supermarket here, everything consumed or used on the
property was produced here – the house is an great example of self
sufficiency. The workers would have produced all their own cheese and
milk in the dairy, they'd have salted their own meats for preservation
and even brewed their own beer.

What to see
- Visit the dairy, laundry, brewery and salting house and learn how
  they would have made everything themselves.
- The restored walled gardens full of home-grown fruit and vegetables.
- Traditional farming activities: lambing, shearing and hay making.

What to do
- Visit Home Farm, a working organic farm.
- Why not try the Children's Trail available from the visitor building?
- Enjoy one of the many walks around the estate and parkland.
- Learn about the breeds of animals, including Welsh Black Cattle,
  Llanwenog Sheep and rare Welsh pigs.

Special events
Children's craft days and fun days throughout the season. Please call
us for information.

By the way...
- Parents can take part in adult study days.

Penrhyn Castle

Historic house Garden Museum Wood

Penrhyn looks like a fairytale medieval castle, but actually it was built in the 19th century. So, who cares if it's a fake – it's well worth a visit because it's packed with goodies, like the doll's museum and railway museum, and has a wonderful adventure playground too.

Easy as A B C
Richard Pennant, who lived here, made a fortune from the local slate quarry. Every year his workers made 136,000 slates for children to write on in school. Wonder if the children were grateful!

What to see
- An industrial railway museum in the stable block, and a model railway museum.
- A large collection of 19th- and 20th-century dolls.
- Can you spot two chamber pots in the dining room? They were there so the men didn't have to leave to go to the loo after dinner.

What to do
- Visit the Victorian servants' quarters, set up to show the preparations for the banquet put on for the Prince of Wales in 1894. They had pineapple ice cream and foie gras in aspic. Very tasty.
- Look at the one-ton slate bed made for Queen Victoria. Sounds pretty uncomfortable.
- Explore the formal Victorian walled garden and the adventure playground.

Bangor, Gwynedd, LL57 4HN
01248 353084

OPENING TIMES
Castle
19 Mar 08–2 Nov 08
12am–5pm Mon, Wed, Thu, Fri, Sat, Sun
Shop/museum
19 Mar 08–2 Nov 08
11am–5pm Mon, Wed, Thu, Fri, Sat, Sun

Notes
Grounds and tearoom as castle but open 1hr earlier. Victorian kitchen: as castle but last admission 4:45pm. Last audio tour 4pm.

continued...

Special events

We have quite a few family events and activities. Recently we've had Knights and Castles Fun Day, archery and hands-on cooking activities. Call us to find out what's planned.

By the way...

- Baby-changing and feeding facilities, plus sling loan (sorry, no pushchairs are allowed in the house).
- Children's guide and quiz/trail and also a children's menu.
- Touchable objects, including engines in the railway museum.
- We can lend you a wheelchair, and the entrance is ramped. There are stairs to the upper floors.

Powis Castle & Garden

Castle Garden Museum

If you like the idea of a dramatic medieval castle rising over world-famous gardens with statues and even an orangery, Powis is for you. The castle was originally built around 1200, as a fortress for the Welsh Princes of Powys. Over the years the Herbert family have packed it with paintings, sculptures and a fascinating collection of treasures from India, displayed in the Clive Museum.

What's in a name, Clive?
Edward Clive (1785–1848) inherited Powis from his mother's side of the family, but only if he agreed to change his name to Herbert. Things didn't end so well – he was shot and killed by one of his own sons in a tragic accident. This son was apparently known to other members of the family ever after as 'Bag Dad' – not in the best of taste!

What to see
- A solid gold tiger head encrusted with precious stones and 300-year-old giant yew hedges – imagine clipping those without a set of electric clippers.
- The igloo-shaped ice house – used to keep ice cool before fridges came along.

What to do
- Have a go at the children's quiz, available in the castle and garden.
- Find the giant stone foot sculpture in the wilderness garden.

Special events
Behind the scenes tours in the castle and garden, annual Easter-egg hunt, themed summer trail and Halloween activities. Get in touch for more information.

By the way...
- Because of the steep gardens and steps some parts of the property are not very accessible to people in wheelchairs.

Welshpool, Powys, SY21 8RF
01938 551929

OPENING TIMES
Castle/museum
13 Mar 08–30 Jun 08
1pm–5pm Mon, Thu, Fri,
Sat, Sun
2 Jul 08–31 Aug 08 1pm–5pm
Mon, Wed, Thu, Fri, Sat, Sun
1 Sep 08–21 Sep 08 1pm–5pm
Mon, Thu, Fri, Sat, Sun
25 Sep 08–2 Nov 08 1pm–4pm
Mon, Thu, Fri, Sat, Sun
Garden/restaurant/shop
1 Mar 08–9 Mar 08
11am–4:30pm Sat, Sun
13 Mar 08–30 Jun 08
11am–5:30pm Mon, Thu, Fri,
Sat, Sun
2 Jul 08–31 Aug 08
11am–5:30pm Mon, Wed, Thu,
Fri, Sat, Sun
1 Sep 08–21 Sep 08
11am–5:30pm Mon, Thu, Fri,
Sat, Sun
25 Sep 08–2 Nov 08
11am–5pm Mon, Thu, Fri,
Sat, Sun
8 Nov 08–29 Nov 08
10am–3pm Sat, Sun

Notes
Admission by timed ticket on busy days. Last admission to castle 45mins before closing.

Plas Newydd

Historic house Garden Park Coastline Museum Boat trip

Llanfairpwll, Anglesey,
LL61 6DQ
01248 714795

OPENING TIMES
House/garden/walks
1 Mar 08–12 Mar 08
12am–4pm Mon, Tue, Wed,
Sat, Sun
15 Mar 08–29 Oct 08
12am–5pm
Shop/tearoom
1 Mar 08–12 Mar 08
10:30am–5:30pm Mon, Tue,
Wed, Sat, Sun
15 Mar 08–29 Oct 08
11am–4pm Sat, Sun
1 Nov 08–14 Dec 08
11am–4pm Sat, Sun

Notes
Open Good Fri. Gardens and
walks open 11am and close
5:30pm 15 Mar–29 Oct.
Servants hall tearoom and
bookshop open 11:30am.
Rhododendron garden open
early April–early June,
11am–5:30pm.

A very grand ivy-covered mansion, Plas Newydd simply means 'new place' in Welsh. It was built in the 18th century, and is still home to the Marquess of Anglesey. There's a big collection of paintings by Rex Whistler and a military museum with interesting artifacts. It is set in large gardens, with a marine walk along the Menai Straits and spectacular views of Snowdonia.

Little and large

See Rex Whistler's illustrations for *Gulliver's Travels*, costume and stage designs and caricatures. Gaze out over the Menai Strait, with views to Snowdonia and Robert Stephenson's Britannia Bridge.

What to see

- An enormous painting by Rex Whistler – can you find Neptune's footsteps?
- An artificial leg made for the 1st Marquess of Anglesey. He carelessly lost the real one in the Battle of Waterloo.

What to do

- For an additional charge, you can take an historical boat trip that departs from by the house – it takes around 40 minutes.

Special events

We have a fun-packed calendar of special events. Contact us to see what's on.

By the way...

- It's licensed for civil wedding ceremonies, wedding receptions and formal dinners, so if you'd like a nice Plas to get hitched in... Family friendly with baby-changing facilities and baby slings for loan, as well as a children's play area. Lower floors are accessible for manual wheelchairs, and there are wheelchairs available to borrow.

Ardress House

Historic house Garden Farm

64 Ardress Road, Annaghmore,
Portadown, Co. Armagh,
BT62 1SQ
028 8778 4753

OPENING TIMES
15 Mar 08–28 Sep 08
2pm–6pm Sat, Sun

Notes
Admission by guided tour. Open
BH Mons and all other public
hols in N Ireland incl. 17 March.
Grounds ('My Lady's Mile') open
daily all year, dawn to dusk.

Children will love feeding the chickens and wandering among the
peacocks in Ardress's charming cobbled farmyard. They can then let
off steam in the adventure playground. Ardress was originally a 17th-
century farmhouse that was gentrified in the 18th century, with lots
of smart plasterwork. In the outbuildings you can find old farming
equipment, which older generations usually enjoy.

What to see
- Chickens clucking round the place, watch out for their eggs!
- Potato diggers and butter-making gear.

What to do
- Throw seed to the hens.
- Swing your way around the adventure playground.
- Do Trusty's puzzle sheet.

Special events
Most years there are three main events at Ardress: an Apple Blossom
Day in May with Punch and Judy and the like; Country Capers in
August with obstacle races and children's entertainments; Halloween
with ghostly story telling, fancy dress and spooky lanterns.

The Argory

Historic house Garden Countryside

A very imposing house from the 1820s, with lovely garden and woodlands and beautiful riverside walks. It's a real time capsule: not much has changed since 1900, when the Bond family lived here.

Oh do clear up!

The Bond family treasures include a weighing chair, books, portraits, clothing and a rather large working barrel organ, which is still played for our 'musical house tours'. Next time you're told to tidy your room, try explaining that you're starting a museum!

What to see
- Horse carriages, a harness room and a laundry.
- The acetylene gas plant in the stableyard.
- A sundial in the middle of the rose garden.

What to do
- Explore the playground and the environmental sculpture trail.
- Visit the award-winning Lady Ada's tearoom – our cakes are second to none.
- Avoid dull days if you want a really good look – there's no electric light in the house.

Special events

There's an exciting programme of events all year, including our Victorian Christmas Fayre, when you can enjoy music, festive food and a visit from Santa, too.

By the way...
- Try the children's quiz trail.
- There are changing facilities and baby slings for hire.
- The ground floor's accessible, and we have two wheelchairs.

144 Derrycaw Road, Moy, Dungannon, Co. Armagh, BT71 6NA
028 8778 4753

OPENING TIMES
House
3 May 08–29 Jun 08 2pm–5pm Sat, Sun
1 Jul 08–31 Aug 08 2pm–5pm Mon–Sun
6 Sep 08–28 Sep 08 2pm–5pm Sat, Sun
Grounds
1 Feb 08–30 Apr 08
10am–4pm Mon–Sun
1 May 08–30 Sep 08
10am–6pm Mon–Sun
1 Oct 08–31 Jan 08
10am–4pm Mon–Sun
Tearoom/shop
15 Mar–29 Jun* 2pm–5:30pm Sat, Sun
22 Mar 08–30 Mar 08
2pm–5:30pm Mon–Sun
1 Jul 08–31 Aug 08
2pm–5:30pm Mon–Sun
6 Sep 08–28 Sep 08
2pm–5:30pm Sat, Sun

Notes
Admission by guided tour. Open BH Mons and all other public hols in N Ireland incl. 17 March. * Incl. Easter week. Due to conservation work the house will be closed Feb/March 08. Grounds open 2pm–7pm on event days. Last admission 1hr before closing.

Castle Ward

Historic house Mill Garden Park Countryside Coastline Farm
Nature reserve

Strangford, Downpatrick,
Co. Down, BT30 7LS
028 4488 1204

OPENING TIMES
Grounds
1 Feb 08–31 Mar 08
10am–4pm Mon–Sun
1 Apr 08–30 Sep 08
10am–8pm Mon–Sun
1 Oct 08–31 Jan 08
10am–4pm Mon–Sun
House/tearoom
15 Mar 08–17 Mar 08
1pm–6pm Mon, Sat, Sun
22 Mar–30 Mar* 1pm–6pm
Mon–Sun
5 Apr 08–29 Jun 08 1pm–6pm
Sat, Sun
1 Jul 08–31 Aug 08 1pm–6pm
Mon–Sun
6 Sep 08–28 Sep 08 1pm–6pm
Sat, Sun

Notes
Admission by guided tour. Open
BH Mons and all other public
hols in N Ireland incl. 17 March.
Last tour 1hr before closing.
*Easter week. Last house tour
starts at 5pm. Corn mill
operates on Suns during open
season. For Strangford Lough
wildlife centre opening times tel.
028 4488 1411.

Here's a house that can't make up its mind – one façade is classical
and the other side is gothic. In fact, Castle Ward is famous for its
mix of architectural styles, inside and out, as well as the
breathtaking views across Strangford Lough. Worth a visit in spring
especially, for acres of bluebells.

Strangford Lough
From Castle Ward you can watch huge flocks of Pale-bellied Brent
Geese coming south over this huge seawater lake. There's a festival
every autumn to celebrate their arrival. There are also seals and otters.
The name means 'strong fjord', and the current is indeed very strong –
look out for sailboats going backwards, or the ferry struggling against
the current.

What to see

- Farm animals, including some rare Irish moiled cattle (moiled means 'hornless').
- Farm machinery in the farmyard.
- The basement and tunnel inside the house.
- See and touch all the natural objects in the wildlife centre.

What to do

- There's a playground for under 10s as well as a spectacular adventure playground for those with longer legs.
- Dress up or play with period toys in the Victorian Past Times centre.
- Take a picnic or a barbecue, and play ball games on the lawns.

Special events

Shakespeare in the Park, Jazz in the Garden, Murder Mystery Theatre, opera, Pumpkinfest, book fair, Dinner and a Movie, craft fairs, Santa's House.

By the way...

- There are many steps at the front; an alternative entrance has fewer.
- Wheelchairs can be booked.
- Baby-changing facilities and hip-carrying seats for loan. There's a children's menu in the tearoom too.

Crom Estate

Park Countryside Nature reserve Wood Boat trip Wetland

Upper Lough Erne,
Newtownbutler, Co.
Fermanagh, BT92 8AP
028 6773 8118

OPENING TIMES
Grounds
15 Mar 08–30 May 08
10am–6pm Mon–Sun
1 Jun 08–31 Aug 08
10am–7pm Mon–Sun
1 Sep 08–30 Sep 08
10am–6pm Mon–Sun
Visitor centre
15 Mar 08–30 Mar 08
10am–6pm Mon–Sun
5 Apr 08–27 Apr 08 10am–6pm
Sat, Sun
1 May 08–14 Sep 08
10am–6pm Mon–Sun
20 Sep 08–28 Sep 08
10am–6pm Sat, Sun

Notes
Open BH Mons and all other
public hols in N Ireland incl. 17
March. Last admission 1hr
before closing. Please tel. for
tearoom opening arrangements.

If you fancy a spot of fishing, camping or would like to hire a boat to splosh around in a magical maze of water, peninsulas and islands, then Crom's your place. Set on the shores of Upper Lough Erne, this area is rightfully one of the Trust's most important nature reserves.

Wild about life
There are many rare species here, including pine martens, red squirrels and badgers. Put on good shoes and get back to nature. Or put on your best togs and get married – we're licensed for civil weddings too.

What to see
- Wild garlic, violets and rare mosses and lichens.
- The purple hairstreak butterfly – what a name!
- Cormorants and curlews – listen out for the curlew's shrill cry.

What to do
- Arrange to stay overnight in the mammal hide so you can look out for pine martens.
- Wend your way around the islands in a hired boat, or ride through the reserve on the Kingfisher Trail cycle path.
- Explore one of the trails, or take a guided tour.

Special events
We have some summer events like small pet competitions and garden fairs; get in touch for more details. And don't forget – you can stay in our campsite, too.

By the way...
- Dogs are welcome, but on leads only please.
- The 19th-century castle you'll see is not open to the public. But our award-winning visitor centre and tearoom are, so do pop in.
- You can book our wheelchair, if required and the grounds have an accessible route.

Florence Court

Historic house Garden Park

One of Ulster's most important 18th-century houses, which used to be home to the Earls of Enniskillen. The setting is lovely, with the Cuilcagh mountains as a dramatic backdrop to the grounds, and a mill and a walled garden to explore. There's also a playground for smaller people's adventures.

That's a bit fishy...

William Willoughby Cole, 3rd Earl of Enniskillen (1807–1886) was a palaeontologist – he studied ancient rocks and fossils. He was particularly keen on collecting fossil fishes. Now they're in the Natural History Museum in London, although there are lots of other oddities in the house.

What to see

- The famous Florence Court Yew tree, supposed to be the 'parent' of all Irish yew trees.
- A hydraulic ram and water-powered saw mill in the grounds.
- A blacksmith's forge, carpenter's workshop and an eel house. And an ice house, from the days before fridges kept things cool.

What to do

- On Sundays in summer, go on one of our living-history tours to get a taste of life in the house.
- Swing and snack in the playground and picnic area.
- Try out the quiz and trail for younger members.

Special events

Summer weekends are good times to find special family activities like children's fun days, craft shows and even Victorian fashion shows. And we have a spooky Halloween Craft Fayre with face painting – and perhaps ghosts. Give us a call.

By the way...

- We have wheelchairs, and a ramp is available. The 1400m (¾ mile) path around the grounds is mostly very suitable for pushchairs or wheelchairs.
- Baby-changing facilities and baby slings for loan.
- Dogs on the lead, please.

Enniskillen, Co. Fermanagh,
BT92 1DB
028 6634 8249

OPENING TIMES
Grounds
1 Feb 08–31 Mar 08
10am–4pm Mon–Sun
1 Apr 08–30 Sep 08
10am–8pm Mon–Sun
1 Oct 08–31 Jan 08
10am–4pm Mon–Sun
House
15 Mar 08–17 Mar 08
1pm–6pm Mon–Sun
21 Mar 08–30 Mar 08
1pm–6pm Mon–Sun
5 Apr 08–31 May 08 1pm–6pm
Sat, Sun
1 Jun 08–30 Jun 08 1pm–6pm
Mon, Wed, Thu, Fri, Sat, Sun
1 Jul 08–31 Aug 08 12am–6pm
Mon–Sun
6 Sep 08–28 Sep 08 1pm–6pm
Sat, Sun
Tearoom/shop
As house, closes 5:30pm

Notes
Admission by guided tour to house. Open BH Mons and all other public hols in N Ireland incl. 17 March. Last admission 1hr before closing. *Easter week.

Giant's Causeway

Coastline Rock formations

44a Causeway Road,
Bushmills, Co. Antrim,
BT57 8SU
028 2073 1582

OPENING TIMES
All year Mon–Sun

Notes
Tel. shop and tearoom for
opening arrangements. Open
all year, except 25/26 Dec.

These rock formations really do look as if they were made for giants
to stroll along. Discovered by the Bishop of Derry, in the 1600s, they
have amazed visitors ever since. There are lovely paths to follow
along the coastline, and the area is both an Area of Outstanding
Natural Beauty and the only World Heritage Site in Northern Ireland.

Fee foe fie Finn
Legend has it the causeway was built by giant Finn McCool so he
could walk to Scotland and fight Benandonner. Finn fell asleep on the
way, and his clever wife put a blanket over him. When Benandonner
came along she pretended Finn was her baby. Benandonner figured if
that's the baby, his dad must be pretty darned big, and ran off home!
Actually the 40,000-odd basalt columns are the result of volcanic
eruptions, over 60 million years ago. But even that is pretty amazing.

What to see
- Hexagonal (six-sided) stepping stones in the causeway. But can you
  see some that have five, seven or even eight sides?
- A video history of the Causeway.
- Lots of seabirds and other wildlife from the cliffs (but don't get too
  near the edge).

What to do
- Follow the North Antrim coastal path and read the information
  panels. If you walk far enough, you'll get to the Carrick-a-Rede rope
  bridge. Sit in the Wishing Chair Rock and make a wish.

By the way...
- There's a ramped entrance to the visitor centre, and a wheelchair
  available. We can provide a map of an accessible route.
- It's a good idea to wear good shoes if you're going to have a walk.
- Dogs on leads are welcome, as are pushchairs and baby carriers.
  There is a tearoom, children's menu and baby-changing facilities.

Mount Stewart House, Garden & Temple of the Winds

Historic house Garden

The famous gardens here are among the best in the care of the National Trust, laid out in the 1920s by Lady Londonderry in a series of different garden rooms, or 'parterres'. There's something new around every corner, and many dramatic views. The house has world-famous paintings, including a very famous painting of a horse by George Stubbs, almost large as life. The socialite Londonderry family were great party givers, and entertained many well-known politicians, including Winston Churchill. Stories and mementoes abound in the house.

Animal magic

Lady Londonderry made all the politicians who visited members of her elite Ark Club. You can see animal pictures of them in the tearoom – Winston Churchill was 'Winnie the Warlock'. Wonder which animal today's prime minister would be?

What to see

- Dinosaurs in the garden, and a horse with a monkey on its back.
- Find 'Mairi Mairi quite contrary' sitting in the middle of a pond – with her cockle shells and real banana trees.

What to do

- Creep down the underground tunnel by the Temple of the Winds.
- Find the crocodile and the dodo in the gardens.
- Picnic by the main gates and enjoy the view over Strangford Lough.

Special events

We have summer jazz concerts that all the family can enjoy, on the last Sunday of the month from April to September. Activities for smaller visitors include Dinosaur Day and Santa's Grotto. Get in touch to find what's on and book if necessary.

By the way...

- The entrance to the property is level and we have wheelchairs available, though you need to book.
- There's a special sensory trail in the gardens; ask at reception.
- Baby-changing facilities and a children's menu in the restaurant.

Portaferry Road, Newtownards, Co. Down, BT22 2AD
028 4278 8387

OPENING TIMES
Lakeside gardens
1 Feb 08–31 Jan 09
10am–sunset Mon–Sun
Formal gardens
8 Mar 08–30 Mar 08
10am–4pm Sat, Sun
1 Apr 08–30 Apr 08 10am–6pm Mon–Sun
1 May 08–30 Sep 08
10am–8pm Mon–Sun
1 Oct 08–31 Oct 08
10am–6pm Mon–Sun
House
8 Mar 08–17 Mar 08
12am–6pm Sat, Sun
21 Mar 08–30 Mar 08
12am–6pm Mon–Sun
5 Apr 08–20 Apr 08 1pm–6pm Sat, Sun
1 May 08–31 May 08
1pm–6pm Mon, Wed, Thu, Fri, Sat, Sun
1 Jun 08–30 Jun 08 1pm–6pm Mon–Sun
1 Jul 08–31 Aug 08 12am–6pm Mon–Sun

Notes
Admission by guided tour to house. Open BH Mons and all other public hols in N Ireland incl. 17 March. *Easter week. Last admission 1hr before closing. NB: house opens at 12am every weekend. House and formal gardens closed Nov–Jan 09. Lakeside gardens closed 25 Dec. Tel. for shop and restaurant opening times.

Portstewart Strand

Countryside Coastline Nature reserve

Wales & Northern Ireland

Strand Road, Portstewart, Co.
Londonderry, BT55 7PG
028 2073 1582

OPENING TIMES
All year Mon–Sun
Facilities
1 Mar 08–27 Apr 08
10am–6pm Mon–Sun
28 Apr 08–1 Jun 08
10am–8pm Mon–Sun
2 Jun 08–31 Aug 08
10am–9pm Mon–Sun
1 Sep 08–30 Sep 08
10am–8pm Mon–Sun
1 Oct 08–2 Nov 08 10am–6pm
Mon–Sun

The magnificent 3km (2 mile) Strand of glistening golden sand is one of Northern Ireland's finest and most popular Blue Flag Beaches. It is the perfect spot to spend lazy summer days, have fun family picnics and take long walks into the sand dunes that are a haven for wild flowers and butterflies. New environmentally friendly visitor facilities are open at the beach and include toilets, showers, catering and retail and a visitor centre with interpretation.

Oh I do like to be beside the seaside
The magnificent Strand at Portstewart conjures up images of lazy summer days, picnics, sandcastles and long walks. The 3km (2 miles) of yellow sand is one of Northern Ireland's finest beaches, filled with families in the summer and walkers throughout the year.

What to see
- Open sand, dunes and damp hollows provide a wide range of habitats for birds, plants and wildlife – see how many you can spot.

What to do
- The Strand plays host to a wide range of leisure activities, from boating and swimming to horse riding, dog walking and surfing.

Special events
Please contact us for details of our Family Fun days in July and August

By the way...
- Unusually for a National Trust beach, cars can be brought on and parked on the Strand.

Springhill & Wellbrook Beetling Mill

Historic house Garden Museum Mill

Wellbrook offers some lovely walks and picnic places by the Ballinderry River. The mill has its original hammer machinery, and demonstrations of the linen process by costumed guides. Down the road, Springhill is an atmospheric place, known as the prettiest house in Ulster, with an unusual and colourful costume exhibition

No beetles were harmed in the making of this...
Beetling is actually the final stage in the production of linen, a very important industry in 19th-century Ireland. Hammer machinery was used to beat a sheen into the cloth – no beetles involved!

What to see
- At Springhill, Kentuck rifles and blunderbusses. A nursery packed with toys, and the excellent award-winning costume museum. And then there's the resident ghost...
- At Wellbrook, 30 massive noisy hammers working the linen – ear plugs, please!

What to do
- At Springhill, follow woodland walks and test your skill on the Childrens Adventure Trail. Visit the shell house and the play area.
- At Wellbrook, have a go at beetling, and try out the spinning wheel – it's much harder than you think.

Special events
Easter-egg trails plus the Teddy Bears' Picnic in June.

By the way...
- At Springhill and Wellbrook, pushchairs and back carriers are ok, and dogs on leads are welcome in the grounds.
- If steps are a problem, ask to use the alternative entrance at Springhill and look at a photography album for the first floor of the house. We can lend a wheelchair at Springhill.
- There's a handling collection at Wellbrook, and a guide available to talk to visitors. There are some steps involved in the house.

Springhill
20 Springhill Road, Moneymore,
Magherafelt, Co. Londonderry,
BT45 7NQ
028 8674 8210

Wellbrook Beetling Mill
20 Wellbrook Road, Corkhill,
Cookstown, Co. Tyrone,
BT80 9RY
028 8674 8210

OPENING TIMES
Springhill
15 Mar 08–17 Mar 08
1pm–6pm Mon, Sat, Sun
22 Mar–25 Mar* 1pm–6pm
Mon, Tue, Sat, Sun
29 Mar 08–29 Jun 08
1pm–6pm Sat, Sun
1 Jul 08–31 Aug 08 1pm–6pm
Mon–Sun
6 Sep 08–28 Sep 08 1pm–6pm
Sat, Sun
Wellbrook Beetling Mill
15 Mar 08–17 Mar 08
2pm–6pm Mon–Sun
22 Mar 08–25 Mar 08*
2pm–6pm Mon–Sun
29 Mar 08–29 Jun 08
2pm–6pm Sat, Sun and BH/PH
weekends
1 Jul 08–31 Aug 08 2pm–6pm
Mon–Sun (except Fri)
6 Sep 08–28 Sep 08 2pm–6pm
Sat, Sun

Notes
Admission by guided tour to house. Open BH Mons and all other public hols in N Ireland incl. 17 March. Last admission 1hr before closing. Please tel. property for shop and tearoom opening arrangements.
*Easter week.

Best of the Rest

Wales & Northern Ireland

Aberdulais Falls

For over 400 years the Falls provided the energy to drive the wheels of industry. In 1584 a copper smelting furnace was established but today only the remains of a small water-powered tin works can be seen. The site houses a unique hydroelectric scheme developed to harness the waters of the River Dulais – the water wheel is the largest currently used in Europe to generate electricity. The Turbine House houses an interactive computer, fish pass and observation window with excellent views of the Falls.

Contact: Aberdulais, nr Neath, Neath & Port Talbot SA10 8EU. Tel. 01639 636674 **Opening times: Falls** 2 Apr–2 Nov 10am–5pm Mon, Tue, Wed, Thu, Fri; 31 Mar–4 Nov 11am–6pm Sat, Sun; 9 Nov–23 Dec 11am–4pm Fri, Sat, Sun **Christmas shop** 9 Nov–31 Jan 08 11am–4pm Fri, Sat, Sun **Winter opening** 12 Jan 08–31 Jan 08 11am–4pm Sat, Sun **Notes:** Open BH Mons and Good Fri 11am–6pm.

Bodnant Garden

One of the world's most spectacular botanical gardens, Bodnant Garden is situated above the River Conwy, with stunning views across Snowdonia. Begun in 1875, Bodnant Garden is the creation of four generations of Aberconways and features huge Italianate terraces and formal lawns on its upper level, with a wooded valley, stream and wild garden below. There are dramatic colours throughout the season, and plenty of open space for the children to stretch their legs while looking out for the natural wildlife – fish, birds, our resident peacock (George) and his wife, and our elusive family of otters. Our Heliochronometer is accurate to within 15 minutes – can you work out the date and time when you visit?

Contact: Tal-y-Cafn, Colwyn Bay, Conwy, LL28 5RE. Tel. 01492 650460 **Opening times: Garden** 8 Mar 08–2 Nov 08 10am–5pm Mon–Sun **Plant centre** All year 10am–5pm Mon–Sun **Tearoom** As garden 10am–5pm **Notes:** Royal Horticultural Society members free.

Mussenden Temple & Downhill Demesne

Take a stroll around the stunning landscape park of Downhill Demesne with it's beautiful sheltered gardens and magnificent cliff-top walks affording rugged headland views across the awe-inspiring North Coast. Discover the striking 18th-century mansion of the eccentric Earl Bishop that now lies in ruins and explore the romantic Mussenden Temple, precariously perched on the cliff edge. Mid-summer concerts are held here in June – contact us for details.

Contact: Mussenden Road, Castlerock, Co. Londonderry, BT51 4RP. Tel. 028 2073 1582 **Opening times:** **Grounds** All year dawn–dusk Mon–Sun **Facilities** 15 Mar 08–17 Mar 08 10am–5pm Mon–Sun; 22 Mar 08–30 Mar 08 10am–5pm Mon–Sun; 5 Apr 08–29 Jun 08 10am–5pm Sat, Sun; 1 Jul 08–31 Aug 08 10am–5pm Mon–Sun; 6 Sep 08–2 Nov 08 10am–5pm Sat, Sun **Notes:** Open BH Mons and all other public hols in N Ireland incl. 17 March.

Coastal Walk – Penmaen Burrows Gower, Wales

A relatively short walk in the Three Cliff Bay area. This beautiful stretch of the Gower coast is full of history. In spring and early summer, wild flowers are abundant all along the path and in the dunes. Part of the walk can be taken along the beach if the tide is more than half out.

Getting there:
Road: A4118 to Penmaen.
Car parks: Parking sign posted just off main road.
Foot: Part of the coast path.
Bus: Service 118 to Penmaen, Quadrant bus station Swansea.
Rail: Mainline station Swansea.
For public transport information visit www.traveline.org.uk

Distance: 3.2km (2½ miles).

Terrain and accessibility: Moderate walking conditions. Height gain of 80m (262ft) over the walk. The beach is suitable for paddling or swimming at Tor Bay and Nicholston. However, unusual currents exist in Three Cliff Bay and care should be taken if swimming here. Children should be supervised when walking on the cliff paths.

Directions and points of interest:
From the start point shown on the map opposite, cross the road and follow the path down towards Three Cliff Bay. Stay on top of the plateau and continue on this path. At the end of the walk, you can return to this car park by climbing through the woods to the top of the cliffs and then heading back to the village of Penmaen. The road is narrow so beware of traffic, especially in the summer. Follow the map (the numbers on the map correspond to the numbers below), looking out for the following features:

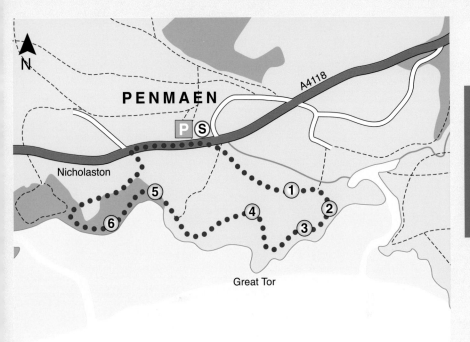

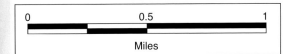

OXWICK BAY

0		0.5		1

Miles

1 Remains of a medieval church overlooking the bay and, to the right a small distance away, the site of a Neolithic burial chamber.

2 Remains of a Norman ring work on the site of a motte (a small fortified building used to guard an area).

3 Pillow mound. These sometimes signify a place where rabbits were kept for food.

4 The small bay of Great Tor.

5 Lime kiln used to make lime for export to Somerset and Devon.

6 Dune slacks, the back of dunes where the sand is more stable and wild flowers grow in profusion.

Property contact details: 01792 390636

Map and start grid ref: OS Landranger 159 gr SS 526 884, Explorer 164

Facilities available: Camp site, toilets, pub at Parkmill.

National Trust properties nearby: Coastal properties at Rhossili, Bishopston and Pennard Cliffs.

215

Red Squirrel Walk – Mount Stewart County Down, Ireland

A 2.3km (1½ mile) walk with exceptional views, beautiful gardens, and beech, mixed and exotic woodland. The mixture of formal and informal gardens provides the perfect sanctuary for one of the few remaining red squirrel populations in the whole of Ireland.

Getting there:
Road: 24km (15 miles) south east of Belfast on Netownards–Portafery Road, A20, 8km (5 miles) south east of Newtownards.
Car parks: From entrance to property, turn left for main car park.
Bus: Ulsterbus 10 Belfast–Portaferry. Bus stop at gates.
Rail: Bangor 16km (10 miles).
For public transport information visit www.travelines.org.uk.

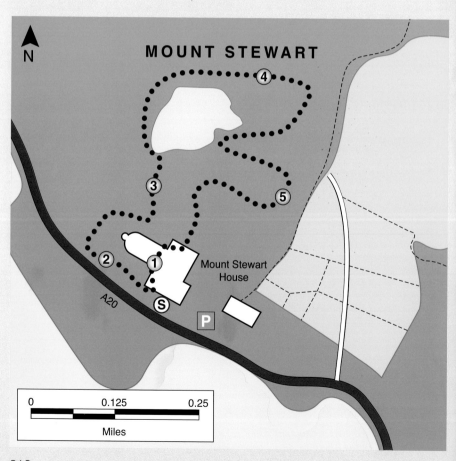

Distance: 2.3km (1½ miles)

Terrain and accessibility: Easy to moderate walking conditions.
All areas accessible.

Directions and points of interest:
Start the walk at point 1, as shown on the map opposite. Follow the
map (the numbers on the map correspond to the numbers below),
looking out for the following features:
1 Exceptionally beautiful formal gardens.
2 Informal gardens including Lilywood and Tir Na'n Og.
3 Dramatic views of Strangford Lough and the Mourne Mountains.
4 Several different paths can be taken from here to extend your walk
  around the lake.
5 There are different paths to take from this point. Walk into the
  Broadleys woodland and along Rhododendron Hill.

Property contact details: 028 4278 8387

Maps and start grid ref: OS 1:50,000 sheet 15, gr J 553 701

Facilities available: Toilet, car park, restaurant, shop, plant sales
and baby-changing facilities.

National Trust properties nearby: Castle Ward, Patterson's
Spade Mill and Rowallane Garden.

Wildlife Walk – Crom Estate

County Fermanagh, Ireland

Discover a tranquil landscape of islands, woodland and historic ruins on the shores of Upper Lough Erne in County Fermanagh. Crom is one of the UK's most important nature reserves, with the largest area of oak woodland in Northern Ireland. Wildlife includes wading birds, bats, pine martens and a thriving otter population.

Getting there:

Bike: 3km (2 miles) of National Cycle Network route 91 (the Kingfisher Trail) runs through the property. See www.sustrans.org.uk.

Boat: Ferry from Derrymore Church (book 24 hours in advance).

Bus: Ulsterbus 95 Enniskillen–Clones (connections from Belfast), alight Newtownbutler, 5km (3 miles) away.

Road: 5km (3 miles) west of Newtownbutler on the Newtownbutler–Crom road or follow signs from Lisnaskea, 11km (7 miles) away. Crom is next to the Shannon–Erne waterway.

Distance: 5.5km (3½ miles). There are other way-marked paths offering shorter walks.

Terrain and accessibility: The grounds are partly accessible to wheelchair users. The grass and woodland pathways are free of slopes with reasonably smooth and level surfaces, but can be muddy.

Directions and points of interest:

Follow the map opposite. The numbers on the map correspond to the numbers below. Start at the visitor centre (shown on the map opposite) to discover more about the wildlife at Crom. It's in an old stone estate yard overlooking Upper Lough Erne. Its barns are a roosting site for bats, with seven different species inhabiting this area. Look at the walls to see the little holes that act as their doorways.

1. Turn left as you leave the yard and walk along the old carriageway towards Crom Castle for a short while before turning left again through a gate into the parkland.
2. Follow the path to the Old Castle. Here you'll encounter one of the oldest yew trees in Ireland. Estimates of its age vary between 400 and 1000 years. Be careful not to stand on its roots as they're really quite delicate.
3. Continue along the loughside, past a pretty boathouse, before crossing the White Bridge onto Inisherk Island.
4. Make a little loop of the island, passing a walled garden.
5. Cross back over the bridge and turn left taking a path through trees with Upper Lough Erne on your left and the grounds of Crom Castle on your right.
6. Reach the castle's main drive and continue walking until a path breaks off to your right near the small inland Lough Naslughoge.
7. Rejoin our first path and turn left, returning to the visitor centre and car park.

Property contact details: 028 67738118;
crom@nationaltrust.org.uk

Map and start grid ref: OS Discoverer 27: H332 2442. Simple
National Trust maps are also available.

Facilities available: Award-winning visitors centre with tearoom
and shop, picnic area, car park, toilets, family-activity packs and
children's play area. School group visits, guided walks, boat hire,
campsite and holiday cottages also available.

National Trust properties nearby: Florence Court, Castle Coole
and Ballymoyer.

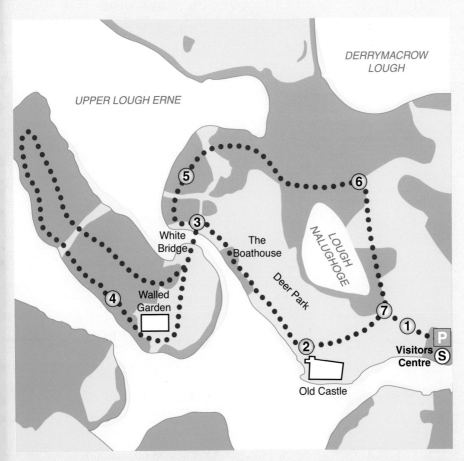

Index of properties

Joining the National Trust

Join the National Trust today and experience unlimited, free days out for all the family. Entertain and educate in some of Britain's most beautiful places, whilst helping to protect them for future generations.

Whether you and your family are interested in gardens, castles, wildlife, or places linked to famous events or people, National Trust family membership offers more than 300 historic houses and gardens, 700 miles of coastline and almost 250,000 hectares of stunning countryside – you'll never be short of exciting family days out.

As members of the National Trust, you'll not only have the benefits of free car parking and entry to our properties, you'll also receive a comprehensive membership pack, complete with our *Members' Handbook* – the complete guide to all our sites – a regional newsletter to keep you informed of all the National Trust events taking place in your area, and a useful Information booklet, which will answer all your membership questions. You'll also receive a copy of our beautifully illustrated *Members' Magazine* three times a year. All this for as little as 16p a day*.

Family Group (2007 rate*: £77.50)
For two adults living at the same address, and their children and grandchildren under 18.

Family one adult (2007 rate*: £58.50)
For one adult and his/her children under 18, living at the same address.

To join, simply visit www.nationaltrust.org.uk or phone 0870 458 4000.

*Rates current to 28th February 2008.

National Trust contacts

National Trust Membership Department, PO Box 39, Warrington WA5 7WD
Tel: 0870 458 4000 (from March 2008 the number will change to: 0844 800 1895); Minicom: 0870 240 3207;
www.nationaltrust.org.uk
Email enquiries@thenationaltrust.org.uk for all general enquiries including membership and requests for
information. Please note that the phones are manned 9:00am–5:30pm Monday to Friday and 9:00am–4:00pm
weekends and public holidays.

Central Office
The National Trust & National Trust (Enterprises) Ltd, Heelis, Kemble Drive, Swindon, Wiltshire SN2 2NA
Tel: 01793 817400; www.nationaltrust.org.uk

National Trust Regional Offices

✉ **Devon & Cornwall**
Cornwall: Lanhydrock, Bodmin PL30 4DE Tel: 01208 74281
Devon: Killerton House, Broadclyst, Exeter EX5 3LE Tel: 01392 881691
✉ **Wessex (Bristol, Bath, Dorset, Gloucestershire, Somerset & Wiltshire)**
Eastleigh Court, Bishopstrow, Warminster, Wiltshire BA12 9HW Tel: 01985 843600
✉ **Thames & Solent (Berkshire, Buckinghamshire, Hampshire, part of Hertfordshire, Isle of Wight, Greater London & Oxfordshire)**
Hughenden Manor, High Wycombe, Buckinghamshire HP14 4LA Tel: 01494 528051
✉ **South East (Sussex, Kent, Surrey)**
Polesden Lacey, Dorking, Surrey RH5 6BD Tel: 01372 453401
✉ **East of England (Bedfordshire, Cambridgeshire, Essex, part of Hertfordshire, Norfolk & Suffolk)**
Westley Bottom, Bury St Edmunds, Suffolk IP33 3WD Tel: 01284 747500
✉ **East Midlands (Derbyshire, Leicestershire, South Lincolnshire, Northamptonshire, Nottinghamshire & Rutland)**
Clumber Park Stableyard, Worksop, Nottinghamshire S80 3BE Tel: 01909 486411
✉ **West Midlands (Birmingham, Herefordshire, Shropshire, Staffordshire, Warwickshire & Worcestershire)**
Attingham Park, Shrewsbury, Shropshire SY4 4TP Tel: 01743 708100
✉ **North West**
Cumbria: The Hollens, Grasmere, Ambleside, Cumbria LA22 9QZ
Tel: 0870 6095391
Cheshire, Greater Manchester, Lancashire & Merseyside: Stamford Estates, 18 Market Street, Altrincham, Cheshire
WA14 1PH Tel: 0161 928 0075
✉ **Yorkshire & North East**
Yorkshire, Teeside, North Lincolnshire: Goddards, 27 Tadcaster Road, Dringhouses, York YO24 1GG
Tel: 01904 702021
County Durham, Newcastle & Tyneside & Northumberland: Scots' Gap, Morpeth, Northumberland NE61 4EG
Tel: 01670 774691

National Trust Office for Wales
Trinity Square, Llandudno LL30 2DE Tel: 01492 860123

National Trust Office for Northern Ireland
Rowallane House, Saintfield, Ballynahinch, County Down BT24 7LH Tel: 028 9751 0721

The National Trust for Scotland (separate organization)
Wemyss House, 28 Charlotte Square, Edinburgh EH2 4ET Tel: 0131 243 9300 www.nts.org.uk

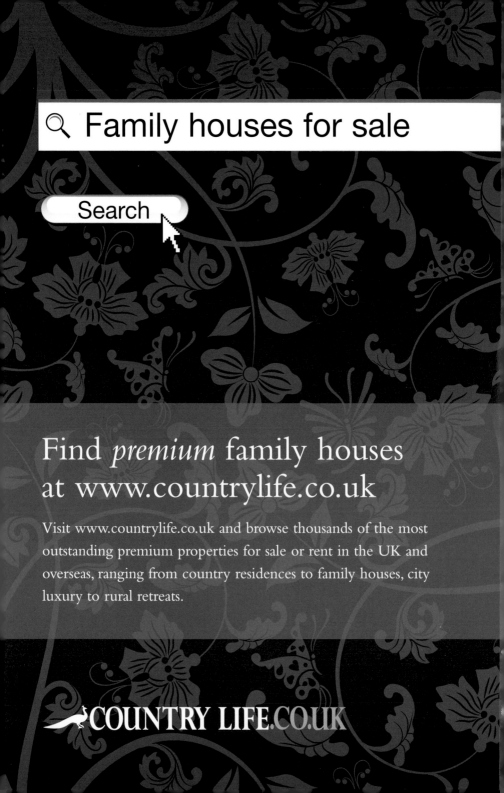

BRING A FRIEND FOR FREE

This coupon entitles one person to free entry (once only) to any one of the participating National Trust properties when accompanied by a paying adult from 21 April 2008 until 16 May 2008. (See terms & conditions for further details)

Standard terms and conditions: Voucher is valid ONLY on completion of name and address details • The person using the 'promotional' voucher must be accompanied on the day of use by a visitor paying the full adult admission charge • This voucher must be surrendered upon admission and is non-transferable against the cost of membership • Photocopies of this voucher will not be accepted • This offer is not valid for coach parties • There is no cash alternative This voucher cannot be used in conjunction with any other offer • Valid at participating properties only during the published opening times. See excluded properties on the reverse of this voucher • Offer valid from 21 April 2008 until 16 May 2008 • Not valid during school holidays, bank holiday or bank holiday weekends • Not valid for events and activities where separate charges apply. For further information telephone 0844 800 1895 or visit www.nationaltrust.org.uk. The National Trust, Heelis, Kemble Drive, Swindon SN2 2NA. Registered charity number 205846.
CODE NT070038V0
SITE CODE _____ (for office use only).

THE NATIONAL TRUST

FREE CHILDREN'S MEAL VOUCHER

Please complete in block capitals. This voucher is ONLY valid on completion of name and address details. This voucher entitles one person to a free children's meal when purchasing any adult main course over £4.95, at any one of the participating National Trust properties (see separate list) during March and April 2008.

Standard terms and conditions: This voucher must be surrendered upon purchase of the meal and is non-transferable against the cost of any other products • Photocopies of this voucher will not be accepted • This offer is not valid for coach parties • There is no cash alternative • This voucher cannot be used in conjunction with any other offer • Valid at participating properties only during the published opening times • Offer valid until 30th April 2008 • Not valid during school holidays or on bank holiday Mondays or bank holiday weekends. For further information telephone 0844 800 1895 or visit www.nationaltrust.org.uk. The National Trust, Heelis, Kemble Drive, Swindon SN2 2NA. Registered charity number 205846.
CODE NT060017V3
SITE CODE _____ (for office use only).

THE NATIONAL TRUST

CHILDREN GO FREE WITH THE NATIONAL TRUST

This coupon entitles up to 2 children (under 16) free entry (once only) to any one of the participating National Trust properties when accompanied by a paying adult from 15 September 2008 until 17 October 2008. (See terms & conditions for further details)

Standard terms and conditions: Voucher is valid ONLY on completion of name and address details • The person using the 'promotional' voucher must be accompanied on the day of use by a visitor paying the full adult admission charge • This voucher must be surrendered upon admission and is non-transferable against the cost of membership • Photocopies of this voucher will not be accepted • This offer is not valid for coach parties • There is no cash alternative • This voucher cannot be used in conjunction with any other offer • Valid at participating properties only during the published opening times. See excluded properties on the reverse of this voucher • Offer valid from 15 September 2008 until 17 October 2008 • Not valid during school holidays, bank holiday or bank holiday weekends • Not valid for events and activities where separate charges apply. For further information telephone 0844 800 1895 or visit www.nationaltrust.org.uk. The National Trust, Heelis, Kemble Drive, Swindon SN2 2NA. Registered charity number 205846.
CODE NT070035V0
SITE CODE _____ (for office use only).

THE NATIONAL TRUST

SPEND £15 OR MORE IN A NATIONAL TRUST SHOP AND SAVE £2

Terms and conditions
Offer available only at National Trust shops on production of this voucher. This excludes NT admission, membership, gift vouchers, mail order and catering purchases. This voucher cannot be used in conjunction with any other offers or exchanged for cash.
Offer ends 31 Dec 2008.

THE NATIONAL TRUST

TITLE _____ FIRST NAME _____
SURNAME _____
ADDRESS_____
_____
POSTCODE _____
EMAIL_____
VISIT DATE _____

🔒 The National Trust collects and processes personal information for the purposes of customer analysis and direct marketing so that we can contact you about our conservation, membership, fundraising and other activities. Please tick this box if you would prefer not to hear from the National Trust in this way ❑

National Trust Enterprises also works with carefully selected organisations and we may contact you with special offers from them that will benefit the National Trust. Please tick this box if you would prefer not to receive these offers ❑

I am happy to be contacted by the National Trust by email and email newsletters about conservation, membership, fundraising and other activities. ❑

National Trust Enterprises also works with carefully selected organisations and we may contact you by email and email newsletter with special offers from them that will benefit the National Trust. Please tick this box if you do want to receive these offers. ❑

Properties excluded from this promotion:
Antony, Ascott, Avebury Manor & Gardens, Buscot Park, Carrick-a-Rede, Chastleton House, Clumber Park, Coleridge Cottage, Coughton Court, Crom, Dinton Park, Dunster Working Water Mill, Eastbury Manor House, 20 Forthlin Road, Gawthorpe Hall, Giant's Causeway, Gondola, Grantham House, Gunby Hall, Hardy's Cottage, The Homewood, Horton Court, Lawrence House, Little Clarendon, Max Gate, Mendips, Murlough NRR, Museum of Childhood, Oakhurst Cottage, Old Soar Manor, Orford Ness, Philipps House, Portstewart Strand, Priest's House, Red House, Shugborough, Stembridge Tower Mill, St Michael's Mount, Tatton Park, Treasurer's House, Waddesdon Manor, Wakehurst Place, West Green House Garden, Westwood Manor, White Mill and **all properties managed by English Heritage and local authorities**

Product Code 37766

5 060075 871740 >

TITLE _____ FIRST NAME _____
SURNAME _____
ADDRESS _____
_____
POSTCODE _____
EMAIL_____
VISIT DATE _____

🔒 The National Trust collects and processes personal information for the purposes of customer analysis and direct marketing so that we can contact you about our conservation, membership, fundraising and other activities. Please tick this box if you would prefer not to hear from the National Trust in this way ❑

National Trust Enterprises also works with carefully selected organisations and we may contact you with special offers from them that will benefit the National Trust. Please tick this box if you would prefer not to receive these offers ❑

I am happy to be contacted by the National Trust by email and email newsletters about conservation, membership, fundraising and other activities. ❑

National Trust Enterprises also works with carefully selected organisations and we may contact you by email and email newsletter with special offers from them that will benefit the National Trust. Please tick this box if you do want to receive these offers. ❑

Properties excluded from this promotion: Antony, Ascott, Avebury Manor & Gardens, Buscot Park, Carrick-a-Rede, Chastleton House, Clumber Park, Coleridge Cottage, Coughton Court, Crom, Dinton Park, Dunster Working Water Mill, Eastbury Manor House, 20 Forthlin Road, Gawthorpe Hall, Giant's Causeway, Gondola, Grantham House, Gunby Hall, Hardy's Cottage, The Homewood, Horton Court, Lawrence House, Little Clarendon, Max Gate, Mendips, Murlough NRR, Museum of Childhood, Oakhurst Cottage, Old Soar Manor, Orford Ness, Philipps House, Portstewart Strand, Priest's House, Red House, Sheffield Park Garden, Shugborough, Stembridge Tower Mill, St Michael's Mount, Tatton Park, Treasurer's House, Waddesdon Manor, Wakehurst Place, West Green House Garden, Westwood Manor, White Mill, Winkworth Arboretum and **all properties managed by English Heritage and local authorities.**

TITLE _____ FIRST NAME _____
SURNAME _____
ADDRESS _____
_____
POSTCODE _____
EMAIL_____
VISIT DATE _____

The National Trust collects and processes personal information for the purposes of customer analysis and direct marketing so that we can contact you about our conservation, membership, fundraising and other activities. Please tick this box if you would prefer not to hear from the National Trust in this way. ❑
National Trust Enterprises also works with carefully selected organisations and we may contact you with special offers from them that will benefit the National Trust. Please tick this box if you would prefer not to receive these offers. ❑

I am happy to be contacted by the National Trust by email and email newsletters about conservation, membership, fundraising and other activities. ❑

National Trust Enterprises also works with carefully selected organisations and we may contact you by email and email newsletter with special offers from them that will benefit the National Trust. Tick the box if you do want to receive these offers. ❑

Properties excluded from offer (correct at time of going to press): Ambleside Fort, Antony Woodland Garden, Avebury (including West Kennet Avenue, Windmill Hill, and the Sanctuary), Avebury Stone Circles, Alex Keiller Museum, Avebury Manor Garden, Bodnant Garden, Bramber Castle, Buscot Park, Castlerigg Stone Circle, Chastleton House, Cilgerran Castle, Dunstanburgh Castle, Eastbury Manor House, Gawthorpe Hall, Gondola, Great Chalfield Manor, Greenway, Gunby Hall, Hadrian's Wall, Hailes Abbey, Hardknott Fort, Hardwick Old Hall, Hardy's Cottage, Housesteads Roman Fort, Lawrence House, Letocetum Roman Baths and Museum, Lundy, Lydford Norman Fort, Max Gate, Mendips (additional), Mount Grace Priory, Mr Straw's House, Oakhurst Cottage, Old Soar Manor, Orford Ness, Red House, Roman Bath', Segontium Roman Fort, Shugborough, Skenfrith Castle, St Catherine's Oratory, St Michael's Mount, Stonehenge, Tatton Park, The Workhouse, Treasurers House & Priest's House, Tyntesfield, Upper Plym Valley, Waddesdon Manor, Wakehurst Place Garden, West Green House Garden, Westwood Manor, White Horse Hill, Uffington Castle & Dragon Hill.